Coaching Skills

Third edition

"This book is a gem for anyone curious about executive coaching – what it is, how it works and how to do it well in practice. As a coaching pioneer and highly accomplished practitioner, Jenny draws upon her extensive experience in coaching, coach training and supervision and brings to life theory and approaches with rich case studies, humour and humility. The third edition benefits from a chapter on the fascinating, emerging field of neuroscience and explores early implications for coaching. As with the rest of the book it is accessible, relevant and well researched. I consider Coaching Skills *to be essential reading for novice and established coaches alike."*

Sandra Grealy, Director of Coaching, Management Futures Ltd

"Jenny Roger's clear writing style, straightforward approach and case examples allow for insight into the coaching process and a glimpse at the learning that occurs for both client and coach. This edition offers even more with enhancements to previous writing and a chapter specifically focused on the brain. Whether you are a coach – new or experienced – a manager or simply interested in learning more about what we do as coaches, this is a must have resource for your library."

Diane Brennan, MBA, MCC, Past President of The International Coach Federation (2008) and co-editor, *The Handbook of Knowledge-based Coaching*

"Jenny Rogers writes with enviable elegance and simplicity about the skills that coaches need. This third edition is a testament to her belief that coaches never stop learning. In this edition she shares the fruits of her recent reading and experiences. There is a good deal of new material, including a chapter on advances in neuroscience, new insights from the recent coaching literature and new models to consider. But Jenny wears her erudition lightly. She takes the reader by the hand through a complex journey, sharing the excitement of her discoveries but not overwhelming with detail. Her strong personal voice comes through in every sentence, understanding, encouraging, pragmatic. I read it from cover to cover in a weekend, and know I will be back to reread before long."

Lis Paice, NHS Mentor of the Year, 2010

*"*Coaching Skills *is much more than just a book containing a wide portfolio of tools, techniques and concepts, brilliantly supported by many case studies. It is a book for practitioners who will find here a profound and friendly presented analysis of the most important models, theories and results of research, with detailed links to coaching as well as guidelines on how to deal with the difficult situations and dilemmas faced by coaches."*

Dorota Porażka, Managing Partner of DORADCA Consultants Ltd

"Among all the coaching books on the market this book stands out for its clarity and wisdom, and for its engaging and unpretentious voice. In designing a coaching course at Fielding Graduate University, I had no hesitation in making it required reading."

Leni Wildflower, PhD, PCC, wildflower-consulting.com

"Coaching Skills: A Handbook *is everything you need in a coaching book. A straightforward approach to the simple art of coaching conversations while offering insight into the complexity and sophistication of coaching for those looking to take their practice to the next level."*

Dr Jonathan Passmore, Independent consultant

Coaching Skills
A Handbook
Third edition

Jenny Rogers

McGraw Hill

Open University Press

Open University Press
McGraw-Hill Education
McGraw-Hill House
Shoppenhangers Road
Maidenhead
Berkshire
England
SL6 2QL

email: enquiries@openup.co.uk
world wide web: www.openup.co.uk

and Two Penn Plaza, New York, NY 10121-2289, USA

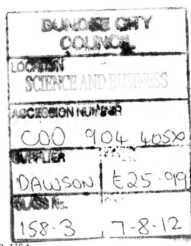

First published 2004
Second edition 2008
First published in this third edition 2012

A catalogue record of this book is available from the British Library

ISBN-13: 978-0-33-524-559-8 (pb)
eISBN: 978-0-33-524560-4

Library of Congress Cataloging-in-Publication Data
CIP data applied for

Typesetting and e-book compilations by
RefineCatch Limited, Bungay, Suffolk
Printed in Great Britain by Bell and Bain Ltd, Glasgow

Fictitious names of companies, products, people, characters and/or data that
may be used herein (in case studies or in examples) are not intended to
represent any real individual, company, product or event.

MIX
Paper from
responsible sources
FSC
www.fsc.org **FSC® C007785**

The *McGraw·Hill* Companies

Contents

Introduction

Like many others who now earn their living as coaches, coaching found me. Twenty-one years ago, I was newly back in the BBC, running its management development programmes. Soon, I began to get tentative phone calls: 'I've done all the courses, but now I'm in a new job and I need to get to grips with this or that issue – can you help?' Or, 'I've got this editor in my team. He's too senior for a course but he urgently needs help with his leadership style. Anything you could do?' Some of these queries had the air of 'Psst! I need help – but don't tell anyone!' Others just assumed that it was only right and proper that tailored and time-effective help was going to be available for some of the most senior people in the organization. Significantly, there was no accepted word then for the process that people were requesting. I believe we referred to it as 'one-to-one sessions', fumbling for a phrase that would accurately describe what would happen.

This book represents the material I wish had been available to me then at a time when there was no training for coaches and I literally knew of no one else who was doing it – though unknown to me many other pioneers and early-adopters were also learning their craft. Knowing then what I know now would have saved so much time and spared clients so many of my well-intentioned but clumsy early attempts at coaching.

I have written the book with a number of different readerships in mind, but they are all united by one thing: a wish to understand what coaching is, how it works and how to do it well. This could mean that you are in a different job or role but are wondering what this coaching stuff is and whether you could make a living at it. You could be working in a professional role, such as training, that looks a little like coaching, and may even think you already do it informally. You could be a trainee coach, resolutely committed to the idea of improving your practice. You might be a therapist or counsellor, considering turning your existing skills to a different kind of clientele and wondering what that would mean for you in practice. You could be a much more seasoned coaching practitioner looking for an affirming benchmark.

Writing this book has emerged from a number of strands of experience. First, I have now had many thousands of hours of coaching with many hundreds of clients from a wide variety of sectors. I have worked as an executive coach – that is, more or less exclusively with senior people from organizations. However, the basic principles I look at here will apply to whatever type of coaching interests you.

All of this has been hugely enriched by over a decade of training other coaches and working as a supervisor with people who are studying for qualifications in coaching. Seeing and hearing at first hand what newer coaches struggle with has been enlightening. It's so easy sitting placidly in your chair, listening to the recording of a coaching session, blithely free of the need to make those split-second decisions that the coach had to make. The wrong turnings are so much more obvious than when you are in that place yourself. It is also humbling – sometimes hearing wonderful coaching from naturally gifted coaches who need little in the way of direction. However, mostly this experience has shown me what the common difficulties are and has given me useful insight into how to guide people towards the approaches that will work.

I am often asked what it takes to be a great coach. There is a quick answer and a slower, more thoughtful one. The quick answer is that as a great coach you have a self-confident fascination with how people achieve their potential and a wish to go with them on that journey; unbounded curiosity about people; intuition into what makes them tick; a high degree of self-knowledge; the self-discipline to keep yourself out of the way; and the ability to resist giving advice or wanting to be right.

The slower answer is that you can't become a great coach by wishing to become a great coach. You will be trying too hard, an understandable and common trap for newer coaches. Coaching well means managing a constant state of ambiguity. You have to have everything I described in the previous paragraph, yet in practice there is so much more. For instance, you have to have curiosity about people, yet know when that curiosity is coming from your agenda and not the client's. You have to have intuition and yet know when to hold it back. You have to be able to resist giving advice and yet know when it is the one time in a hundred when it is not only appropriate but vital to do so. You have to keep yourself out of the way and yet you have to be fully there and a real presence for your client – you are not a coaching cipher, self-restrained to the point of disappearing. You have to like people and yet be able to control much of your need to have them like you because you will often have to challenge and be tough. Coaching is a serious business, and yet, as one of my colleagues once pointed out, you will continually hear boisterous laughter emanating from our coaching rooms.

This is the territory I have covered in this book. I make no assumptions about how many hours of coaching you have done but I do assume your curiosity and commitment. I discuss and describe coaching techniques but I also put forward some ways of transcending the techniques so that your coaching can attain the seamless and flowing quality that the best coaching has. Observing outstanding coaching seems like witnessing the only conversation that could ever have happened on that topic – and yet another equally excellent coach could have had another quite different and equally effective conversation.

Anyone writing this kind of book hits the problem of how to represent clients' stories. I want to bring coaching to life and the best way to do this is through real case studies. Yet, as a coach, I promise my clients confidentiality. I have resolved this problem through a rigorous and wholehearted process of disguise, often blending more than one source while staying true to the real-life themes. When in doubt, I have checked the disguise with the original client.

Many of the influences which have gone into writing this book have probably disappeared into an internalized set of assumptions about human behaviour, going right back to my good fortune as a postgraduate student in encountering thinkers such as Henri Tajfel, Michael Argyle and other social psychologists of the 1960s. The great Kurt Lewin, with his insistence on turning theory into action-centred research, has been a constant source of thought-provoking ideas. My thinking has also been profoundly affected by the work of the early exponents of psychoanalysis such as Sigmund Freud and Carl Jung; by the humanistic-existentialist writers and practitioners such as Viktor Frankl and Irvin Yalom; by the Gestalt school; by Carl Rogers and his Person Centred Therapy; by Transactional Analysis; and by Gerard Egan's Skilled Helper model. All of us in coaching also owe a debt to the Coaches Training Institute in California for beginning the process of synthesizing coaching practice into a workable and elegant model. I have acknowledged these and other specific sources throughout the book wherever I am aware of them, which may not be in every case. My own blend of these and other ideas is eclectic, opinionated and personal. This is not a textbook.

In this third edition I have added new material and updated some of the old. For instance, it is now vital for coaches to know at least a little about neuroscience because it gives a biological explanation for much of what we have guessed to be true from hunch and experience. I have also updated and extended material in other chapters as my own understanding about what constitutes good coaching has gone on developing.

As in the first two editions I have tried to convey the real life flavour of coaching with all its typical ups and downs. Many books on coaching, perhaps unwittingly, give the impression that coaching is a kind of fairytale. The client is puzzled or miserable, the coach waves a magic wand, the client lives happily ever after. Beginner coaches who read these books are often secretly dismayed by the stubborn refusal of their actual clients to behave like the ones in the fairytales. The reality is that however experienced the coach and however willing the client, sometimes there are semi-successes but no discernible happy ending; sometimes there are florid failures, or even worse in some ways, there is no proper ending at all. The same is surely true of every other profession so why should coaching be any different? It is also true that there can be much learning from a flop, as long as you know why it has occurred. I hope this book will help you identify the likely reasons for noble failures as well as for glorious successes.

In the years between the first edition and this one, coaching first grew exponentially as a profession and is now facing the challenges of recession. In the UK, savage cuts in public service employment have created ripples with negative effects that have touched most of the population one way or another. Significantly more of my own coaching now has a career focus – not surprising when so many people have found themselves unemployed or in relentless competition for jobs. I am also acutely conscious that these are hard times for the senior managers who make up the majority of my clients. They can be exposed to extraordinary levels of anger and dismay. For instance, there was the boss who was barricaded inside his own office for three hours, another who received silent phone calls at home and the sorts of death threats which justified 24-hour police protection. I have many clients who routinely face the disloyalty and tantrums of senior colleagues, the unbridled rudeness of disappointed shareholders or brutally direct public probing about whether they deserve their salaries.

It would be foolish to imagine that somehow we coaches are immune from what's going on. We need to be able to preserve our own stability when faced with such vivid distress. Many coaches are struggling to keep a viable practice going because whole swathes of potential clients have disappeared or else clients fear that it could seem an unjustifiable expense to have a coach, even though coaching is needed now more than ever. That this fear is well warranted can be seen in the universally hostile reporting in 2011 of how one local authority chief executive was ousted, where part of the accusations against her was that she had spent public money on what was described as 'personal coaching', implying that this was some kind of bizarre self-indulgence.

Our own sense of optimism may be damaged by the general climate of anxiety. Many of the people I train are also facing the temptation to take on clients with issues that are too big for the coach's experience. Coaching in periods of optimism and growth now looks relatively easy. Coaching in times of austerity takes every bit of skill and courage that we can muster.

However, it is still the case that to be a coach is to have a wonderfully privileged job. It is never less than demanding and never dull. Clients ask you to walk with them at key moments in their lives and careers, sharing their triumphs and disappointments, their vulnerabilities, their hopes, their dreams. The discussions have an openness, candour and directness that few other conversations are likely to have. The Chinese sage who pronounced that 'What we teach is what we most want to learn' was completely correct. As a self-development process *for the coach*, you can't beat coaching, and yet you will never get to the end of it. There will never be a point where you can stand back and say, 'Well, I made it – I'm now the complete and perfect coach.' That is one of many factors which will make your likely learning lifelong.

I invite you through this book to learn how utterly stretching, fascinating and enjoyable this process is.

1   What is coaching?

This question can puzzle both coaches and clients. There seem to be a number of reasons for this puzzlement, many of them arising because the word *coach* is so loosely used.

'Coach' may suggest a teacher earning extra money by helping your reluctant children through a loathed maths or French exam. Or it may suggest the pushy parent figure in tennis who also acts as coach and manager to a prodigiously talented child. More attractive images may be from other kinds of sports coaching. Here a coach may be a clever, sophisticated and highly paid guru figure whose tantalizing and competitively sought coaching secrets are eventually revealed in books and newspaper articles. This idea is still clearly alive and well, as I discovered to my dismay when I rang one client's office to hear his colleague shout, 'John! It's your guru on the phone!'

If not guru, there are also associations with management consulting which may not help. For instance, I often heard it alleged as a proven fact (needless to say it was no such thing) that one former director-general of the BBC was merely the puppet of the McKinsey consultants who had a permanent office a few doors down the corridor. 'X [one McKinsey man] works his arms and legs and another works his mouth' was how it was described. I admit to having wondered if there was truth in this scurrilous rumour when, the only time I appeared before the great man and his board, I was surprised to find X sitting smugly at his right hand.

In some organizations, even now, having a coach is still unusual and is reserved for very senior people with performance problems, where the intention can therefore be frank corrective training and to need coaching is then understandably seen as being a sign of shameful failure. 'Is this outplacement in advance?' one client asked me suspiciously. This was at a time some years ago when I was relatively new to the field. Alas, I came to see that in her case it probably was outplacement in advance, and that her company was seeking to show that it had done everything it reasonably could before sacking her. In this case I had been manipulated by the organization as much as she.

While these are recurrent concerns and confusions, it is probably much more common to be troubled by an underlying comparison with psychotherapy and counselling. Many potential and actual clients ask worriedly about this. When coaching is described to them, they may say, with visible suspicion, 'This sounds like counselling!', implying that if coaching is just counselling in disguise, then it's not for them, thank you. In spite of much more enlightenment in the way we view mental health, there are still many hugely unhelpful clusters of associations with needing help in this area of our lives. The thrum of underlying belief is that we 'should' be able to deal with difficult issues on our own. These are not rational concerns. They have to do with fear of the power of our own emotions, of losing control, of the veneer of grownup-ness being ripped away.

The themes that unite all of these concerns are basic to understanding what coaching is. Take it as axiomatic that all clients, whoever they are and however grand, successful and important, fear two things: vulnerability and loss of control. They are right in these fears because coaching is about change and to change you do make yourself vulnerable and you may indeed not appear to have the degree of control you want over your life while the changes are happening.

The role of theory

This is a potentially confusing field. Psychology emerged as a branch of philosophy. Psychotherapy was originated by doctors who were psychiatrists. It was presented originally as a science. These early beginnings are still telling. Essentially psychotherapy and counselling are part of the health sector, whereas executive coaching is a branch of management development, and life coaching an approach to personal development closely paralleled by the popularity of the many thousands of self-help books.

Coaching, by and large, is a pragmatic trade drawing on borrowed theory. At the moment, theory therefore tends to play a much smaller role in the training of coaches. The best current summary is in the book edited by Leni Wildflower and Diane Brennan (2011), *The Handbook of Knowledge-Based Coaching*, where it is clear that our theoretical base comes from an extremely eclectic range of ideas. Currently, practice leads theory and I have heard coaching described as *a-theoretical*. Depending on your point of view, you can see this either as a strength or as a weakness which needs addressing. Perhaps it is both.

It makes me smile when I read the assertions of former athletes and other fleetingly famous British sportspeople – who came to coaching through sport and sports coaching in the late 1980s – that they are in some way the true originators of the profession. In fact, the growth of coaching as a discrete activity in the last two decades of the twentieth century had much to do with the so-called Human Potential or New Age Movement of the early 1970s, where Erhard Seminars Training (EST), founded by Werner Erhard, involved many of those who became pioneers of what we now call coaching. New Age writers such as Eckhart Tolle and Deepak Chopra are among the popular philosophers of coaching. EST became Landmark Education in 1991 and still trains many thousands of people a year, but the actual origins of coaching have tangled roots in all of the following: psychology, psychiatry, medicine, physics, systems theory, linguistics, therapy, hypnosis, management development, anthropology, organization development, training, selling, religion and philosophy among many others. Coaching, whether dignified by the label or not, must be as old as human society. There is, for instance, a case for pointing out that Socrates was doing a form of coaching 2400 years ago in Greece when, according to Plato, he seems to have claimed that his only knowledge was of his own ignorance and that his role as a philosopher was analogous to that of a midwife: you do not give birth yourself but you play a vital role in enabling the mother to do so. The Socratic Method involved solving a problem through forming a question. In doing so you would be forced to look at your own beliefs, questioning their validity. As an encapsulation of coaching in the twenty-first century, that seems spot on to me.

A definition of coaching: choice in action

My definition is a simple one that conceals complexity.

> Coaching is a partnership of equals whose aim is to achieve speedy, increased and sustainable effectiveness through focused learning in every aspect of the client's life. Coaching raises self-awareness and identifies choices. Working to the client's agenda, the coach and client have the sole aim of closing the gaps between potential and performance.

Behind this definition there is one overriding principle. This is the principle of choice. The assumption is that we can always choose how we respond to any of life's challenges. We may not always be able to choose what happens to us, though to a large extent we choose this as well, but we can always choose how we respond.

Here are six foundation principles which elaborate on this and help differentiate coaching from some other apparently similar disciplines.

Principle 1: the client is resourceful

The client has the resources to resolve his or her problems. The client has not come to be *fixed*, though there may be others in the client's world (e.g. a more senior manager paying the bill) who believe that this is the purpose of the coaching. Clients may share this belief sometimes: 'If you were me, what would you do?' Only the client can really know what to do because only the client knows the full story and only the client can actually implement the action and live with the results.

This does not preclude the coach from offering useful information, but it is the client's choice whether or not to use it.

Principle 2: the coach's role is to develop the client's resourcefulness through skilful questioning, challenge and support

It follows from the first principle that the role of the coach is not advice-giving. When you give advice you imply that you know best and that the client is a lesser person. When you do this you will most probably get sucked into the 'Why don't you?' . . . 'Yes, but' game:

> Why don't you lose a bit of weight?
>
> Yes, I agree I should but I can't do it yet . . .

Advice-giving also leads to dependency – the opposite of what you are trying to achieve as a coach. There is more about this in Chapter 3. The coach's role is to ask the penetrating questions which take clients into territory they have never previously considered. In doing this, clients will build their own resourcefulness.

Principle 3: coaching addresses the whole person – past, present and future; work and private lives

Coaches working in the corporate field sometimes see their role as strictly being about work. I believe that this is a mistake. Difficulties in the professional lives of clients are usually paralleled by difficulties in their personal lives. Also, relationship patterns formed in early life always have a bearing. Coaching is not psychoanalysis, but unless you know a little about a client's early life and issues they are experiencing in their current life beyond their jobs, you are unlikely to be able to work with the client as fully as is possible when you and the client take a more rounded view.

Principle 4: the client sets the agenda

This is where there is a difference with teaching. There is no set agenda with coaching. The coach may indeed have a mental model of, for instance, effective leadership, but if this is not a concern for the client, then it should not appear on the agenda of the sessions. The agenda is set by the client. When the client agenda is exhausted, then the coaching must stop, even if only temporarily. I have occasionally had enquiries from potential clients who have heard that coaching is 'interesting' and want to try it, but when they learn that they have to provide the agenda, their interest wanes.

Principle 5: the coach and the client are equals

The coach and the client work together as a partnership of equals. The model is colleague–colleague, adult–adult, because it is based on total respect. Suspending judgement is essential. Where you cannot respect a client for some reason, or where the client does not respect you, it is unlikely that your coaching can be effective and you must end or not start it.

Principle 6: coaching is about change and action

Clients come to coaching because they want something to change. Essentially they want to be more effective and the core purpose of coaching is to increase self-awareness, to make choices explicit and to close the gap between what they are capable of doing and what they are currently doing. The role of the coach is to help them achieve this increased effectiveness. It follows therefore that you cannot coach a client who does not want to change – so third-party referrals should always be regarded with initial caution. Equally, if a client says they want to change, but seem to be unable or unwilling to do so in practice, then the coaching may have to stop – or you could consider referring the client to another coach.

My assumption is that as coaches we are dealing with both the *being self* and the *doing self*. In my practice, I represent this whole approach to coaching in diagrammatic form, as in Figure 1.1.

The being self is the inner personality and the sum total of the experiences, attitudes and roles that we play or have played in our lives. It is about core values and beliefs – who we are rather than what we do.

The doing self is the externally focused person with tasks to accomplish and skills with which to do them. It is usually the doing self which initially presents for coaching. For instance, 'Please help me become more effective in my work'; 'Show me how to run a meeting better'; 'Help me write a proper CV', and so on.

The request for coaching is always triggered by change. If there is no change then it is unlikely that you have a genuine client. The change could be internally triggered – a being self area. Birthdays with a nought or a five on the end may well be cause for reappraisal of life and direction. So may a serious illness or a major change in personal status such as marriage, having children, the death of a parent or a divorce. Alternatively, or often in addition, there is externally imposed change. The organization may be losing or gaining staff, the client's role may have changed through promotion or restructuring. Skills that seemed perfectly adequate before may not look so impressive now. There may be a new boss who demands a different kind of performance with consequent pressure for change in individuals. The client may have actually lost their job or be threatened with doing so. The crossover area in the middle creates the agenda for coaching.

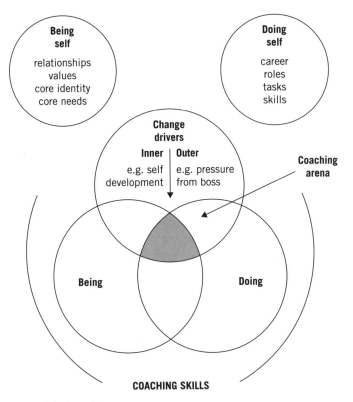

Figure 1.1 A model of coaching

This is why it is essential to take a whole-life perspective and to accept the client's initial agenda as merely the starting point for the coaching. The inexperienced coach often fails to act on the instinct which tells him or her that this is the correct way to go. As a new coach myself I was sometimes far too overawed by the seniority of my clients to ask them what felt then like impertinent questions about their backgrounds and childhoods. I quickly discovered what a mistake this was and now ask routinely about early life experience.

What happens in a coaching session: an overview

Typically coach and client will meet on the coach's premises for a series of hour-and-a-half or two-hour sessions over a period of a few months. The coach prepares the client for the first session with some introductory paperwork and 'exercises', including the client's draft of their goals for the whole coaching programme. Typically goals take two forms:

- *Dilemmas*: which of two or three paths should I follow?
- *Puzzles*: how can I make something or someone more comfortable, work better, be more focused, get past a block?

Examples might be:

- improve an important relationship;
- manage my time better;
- make more money;
- find a way of sorting out my debts;
- decide what I want to do as the next step in my career;
- tackle performance problems in my team;
- plan my entry into a new job;
- restructure my organization;
- learn how to make more convincing presentations;
- acquire the skills I need in a new role;
- launch myself into a freelance career or start a business;
- tackle the stress in my life;
- get a better balance between work and home;
- leave full-time work and decide whether a portfolio career or retirement is something I want.

Normally there will be two or three topics in each session. The client will leave with a plan of action around each of their goals. The first part of the next session reviews how the 'homework' has gone. This is an obvious point, but easy to miss: *the changes themselves happen outside and between sessions.*

A typical framework for a coaching session might be like this:

5 minutes	What has happened between the time we last met and now?
10–15 minutes	How did you get on with the action points we agreed last time? What have you tried? What have you learnt?
5 minutes	What items do you have for our agenda this time? • What priority do those items have in terms of their potential for impact on your life? • How much time would you like to devote to each during this session? • How does each of these items link to the overall goals we set for the coaching?
90 minutes	Coaching on the agenda items
5 minutes	What 'homework' will you be doing between this session and our next?
5 minutes	What feedback do you have for me on this session?

As coaching grows in popularity and familiarity, it is developing a number of distinct branches.

Life coaches concentrate on whole-life dilemmas: personal relationships, life balance, planning for the future. It is also the case that people who offer all kinds of familiar advisory services are now describing what they do as 'coaching', so debt counsellors are now *debt coaches*, acting tutors offer *audition coaching* and marriage guidance has been repackaged as *relationship coaching*. *Sports coaches* increasingly work from the core coaching principles I describe in this book. *Executive coaches'* work is generally concentrated on the most senior executives in large or medium-sized organizations. Clients expect a familiarity with and a track record in management. Potential topics for coaching include everything in the life-coaching agenda plus any and every aspect of running organizations. As with life coaching, executive coaching is also developing its own niches – new leaders, managing the first 100 days in a new job, retirement planning for older leaders, stress and burnout, finance, careers, finding a new job after redundancy, interview preparation, presentation skills, voice, image, strategy, and many others. Executive coaches may also work as *team coaches*, where they apply the same principles to whole teams. Fees for executive coaching are generally many times higher than fees for life coaching.

Differences between coaching and other disciplines

Coaching and psychiatry

A psychiatrist is a doctor trained in treating severe mental illnesses. Entry to the profession is strictly controlled by licensing after lengthy training, and practice is monitored and audited. If your licence is withdrawn, you cannot practise. Continuous updating is mandatory.

You might see a psychiatrist if your GP believes you could benefit from stabilizing medication prescribed by a specialist or if for some reason you feel you have temporarily lost your way in some form that feels serious. Psychiatrists also deal with disabling forms of mental illness such as schizophrenia, severe post-natal depression, drug and alcohol dependency or chronic depression. Forensic psychiatrists specialize in people whose illnesses or personality disorders involve danger to themselves or others.

Successful therapy often involves drugs as well as a 'talking cure' where the patient would typically be referred to a psychotherapist. However respectfully psychiatrists treat their patients, and the best ones do, there is little doubt about who has the power. Even when psychiatrists refer to their patients as *clients*, and increasingly they do, the model is overtly medical. The patient – a telling word – is sick and the helper is a doctor whose role is to cure sickness. The doctor has the power of superior knowledge, the power to make a diagnosis, the power to prescribe drugs and, in some cases, the legal power to restrain and lock up the patient.

As a distantly related discipline, psychiatry is about as far from coaching as it is possible to be.

Coaching and psychotherapy

How coaching differs from psychotherapy is probably the difference that worries coaches most. In Colin Feltham and Ian Horton's excellent *Handbook of Counselling and Psychotherapy* (2000: 2), psychotherapy is defined as:

> addressing psychological and psychosomatic problems and change, including deep and prolonged human suffering, situational dilemmas and crises and developmental needs, and aspirations towards the realization of human potential.

There is a huge spectrum of approaches to psychotherapy and a number of rival 'schools' using different models. Some people claim that there are as many as 400 different schools and approaches. This probably accounts for the widely varying effectiveness reported.

My own experience reflects this in a small way. A few years ago a personal crisis left me needing psychotherapeutic help. I could not shake off the feelings of overwhelming anxiety which haunted me for months afterwards. My world seemed to be dissolving. In seeking psychotherapeutic help, I experienced first a very poor and then a profoundly helpful experience of therapy.

My doctor referred me first to 'Dr X' who operated out of an elegant private medical practice. I probably alienated him from the start by asking if his doctorate was a medical one. This was a bit naughty as I already knew it wasn't, but I was by now annoyed by the grandiosity of the way I had been kept waiting and treated as a petitioner. He sat at a world domination desk, sideways on, while I sat on a very much lower sofa on what felt like the very far side of the large room. It was a smart, black leather sofa, but in sitting so much lower I couldn't help but feel that I was meant to be literally sitting at his feet. He asked me about my 'symptoms', dispensed a good deal of platitudinous advice, all of which I had heard before, and ended the session ten minutes early. I paid for an hour but received 40 minutes. I did not go back.

Instead, I sought help from Sue, a fellow coach who also operates as a therapist. Her steady, calm exploration of feelings and mutual exploration of practical strategies for dealing with them were just what I needed. If proof were needed that a high price is no guarantee of high quality, her charges were a quarter of those demanded by 'Dr X'.

Where is the boundary with psychotherapy?

In some of my recent work as an executive coach I have encountered these situations with clients: a finance director wanting to re-enter work after recovering from a severe episode of bipolar disorder; a chief executive whose most pressing issue was her marital problems; a banker whose misery at work meant that he was visibly upset through a great deal of the session.

The less experienced you are as a coach, my guess is that the more likely you are to read of these clients with a shudder of dread: surely these are just the sorts of situations where a coach should keep well out of the way and refer the client to a therapist? If so, I disagree. I believe that the squeamishness of so many coaches is unjustified and unnecessary. Their fears are reflected in much of the literature on coaching, sometimes suggesting for instance that any deep exploration of feelings is inappropriate, that any topics connected with personal life should be avoided in executive coaching, or that somehow 'everyone knows' where therapy is needed. In the first edition of this book I dutifully went along with this even while I was privately wondering if it were true. My belief now is that the boundaries with therapy are extremely shadowy and that I am content that this should be so.

Many coaches fear 'getting in too deep', or 'doing harm'. Discussing their concerns usually reveals many common misconceptions about therapy – for instance that it is a monolithic discipline, always about the past, that it involves the therapist as interpreter, that it goes on for years and is somehow mysterious and unfathomable and therefore 'dangerous'. These stereotypes fail to represent the reality of vigorous and mutually antagonistic squabbling between different types of therapy, as well as the thinness of the line between many kinds of therapy and coaching and also the additional reality of 'brief therapy' – a short programme, often as little as six hours (less than many coaching programmes), and arising because funding and therefore access to therapy is rationed. The naïve view of therapy is heavily influenced by film and TV, where the therapeutic model implied is most often psychoanalytical, the earliest form of therapy, still being practised, where it is common for therapist and client to meet several times a week. You should note that this form of therapy seems to be in sharp decline with many psychoanalysts struggling to recruit clients.

Some clients are suspicious that coaching is just 'therapy-lite', though I privately believe that it is 'therapy-plus'. However, there is a common view that therapy is something that is for gullible wimps, so as coaches we do indeed need reassuring and honest answers to such challenges. The debate has also been stoked by attacks from therapists asserting their own version of the stereotype, this time that coaching is superficial, short term, ridiculously expensive, unregulated and conducted by charlatans or by people who have failed in other careers. For a view of this sort, see Steven Berglas's article (2002) in the *Harvard Business Review* where good psychotherapy is melodramatically compared with bad coaching to (unintended) comical effect.

The truth is that without therapy there would be no coaching, though I find that many coaches seem to be unaware of this debt. Most strands of theory and all of our techniques have descended from therapy one way or another. I am shamelessly eclectic in my own choices here, lifting ideas and approaches from many traditions. If it works, I will use it.

Much of the muddle about therapy and coaching starts from the false assumption that human beings are rational. So, allegedly, coaching deals in rationality and therapy deals in emotion. In fact, as so much recent research in neuroscience (see Chapter 2) makes abundantly clear, the limbic system of the human brain, its emotional centre, is far more powerful than the prefrontal cortex – the seat of thinking and reason. Decision-making is emotionally, not rationally, led. How can it therefore make any sense to exclude emotion from our work with clients? However, conscientious coaches do worry about whether they might 'harm' a client through unskilled dabbling in therapy, and I say more about this on page 274.

It's true that much executive coaching starts with work issues because these are safe to declare and the organization is paying. But problems in work life are always affected by what is going on in a person's private life, and vice versa. Banning the discussion of personal issues results in thin, lopsided coaching and no problem worth looking at in coaching is without an emotional dimension.

Concentrating exclusively on work issues and on so-called 'performance coaching' results in an overemphasis on the behavioural approaches which have dominated our first 30 or so years as a profession. These may be useful as far as they go, but their impact is often limited and superficial.

Some differences between psychotherapy and coaching

In general when you compare psychotherapy and counselling with coaching you will tend to see a number of differences. The most important is the probable mental state of the client. A client for psychotherapy or counselling is far more likely to be in a persistently distressed and disabling state than a client for coaching. Feltham and Horton's definition, quoted above, refers to 'deep and prolonged human suffering'. Many psychotherapists still refer to their clients as *patients*. Where this is the case, the underlying model is clearly the medical one of doctor–patient and not the adult–adult partnership of equals that I describe above as Principle 5.

By contrast, I, in common with all the other coaches I know, assume that my clients have robust mental health unless proved otherwise. I am looking to work with my clients on functional rather than on severe psychological problems. All schools of psychotherapy stress that therapy is a partnership. I believe that in practice this critical difference in assumed mental state will almost inevitably lead to a profound imbalance in power which makes a genuine relationship of equals a lot less likely in a therapist–client relationship than in a coach–client relationship. For instance, psychotherapists may be motivated by a sincere and profound wish to *help*, and by feeling pity for the suffering of their clients. They will describe their work as a *helping* discipline. The helper, almost by definition, feels as if they are in a stronger place than the helpee. Coaches are more likely to describe what they do as *working with* a client.

With executive coaching there are some further tweaks to the power relationship which are significantly different from therapy. These coaching clients are generally both well paid and powerful people and they – or their employers – are paying premium fees for their coaching. By contrast, therapy and counselling may sometimes be provided free or very cheaply to the user (for instance, through the NHS, a voluntary agency or an employer via an Employee Assistance Scheme) and are potentially therefore subject to the peculiarly corrosive tendency to see such users as petitioners, lucky to get their rationed treatment.

Not all, but much psychotherapy looks to the past to explain the present, and the therapist is interested in answering the question 'Why?' Insight into cause and effect and the origins of emotions is a strong feature of some (though not all) schools of therapy. The coach may look briefly to the past but is more interested in the client's present and future and is probably more concerned with the question 'What?', as in 'What to do?' than in the question 'Why?'

There are also some differences in practicalities and mechanics. Coaches will see clients for an average of six two-hour sessions, probably spread over a period of months. Therapists will tend to suggest seeing their clients for a 'fifty-minute hour' every week. This gives a distinctly different timbre to the experience – for both therapist and client.

My colleagues and I have trained many therapists in how to become coaches. We find that large numbers of the skills overlap. We also find that therapists may bring as many prejudices and assumptions about coaching as coaches may hold about therapists. While therapists may assume that coaching is 'superficial' compared with therapy (it's not), coaches may allege that therapists glory in the distress of their clients, or enjoy 'wallowing' in the past. None of these stereotypes is true. What we have also noticed is that our therapist trainees comment on how much more overtly goal-focused coaching is compared with therapy and that it does move at a much faster pace with more future focus. I describe this, again as anecdotal evidence, with no assumptions that lack of goal focus makes therapy inferior or that a faster pace is necessarily 'better'.

Coaching and counselling

Counselling is sometimes described as the 'shallow end' of psychotherapy, though it is also sometimes used as a synonym for psychotherapy itself. As with psychotherapy, heroic efforts have been made since the mid-1960s to control the quality of counselling through better training and accreditation. The Samaritans wisely call such people 'befrienders' and devote considerable effort in training them, emphasizing the limits of the role.

Counselling and psychotherapy are often used as interchangeable terms, but by custom and practice the word 'counselling' seems now more likely to mean a short-term engagement around a particular crisis. Often, the client will have been managing perfectly well until the onset of this crisis.

Typical examples would be trauma counsellors who work with survivors of a major accident; relationship counsellors who work with couples (the 'marriage guidance' area); spiritual counselling offered by religious groups; police officers who counsel rape survivors or the families of missing children; specialist nurses who counsel people newly diagnosed with life-threatening illness; and priests who counsel the bereaved.

More than any of the other approaches described in this chapter, counselling has come to carry with it an emphasis on the powerful comfort of non-judgemental listening in the moment. This means talking it through extensively, without either counsellor or client feeling any of the obligation to *action* which both coaching and psychotherapy may imply.

Coaching and mentoring

This is an easier one.

The word *mentor* comes from the Greek myth of the king who asked Mentor, an older, wiser man, to look after his son during the king's absence. Pure mentoring still has this implication and is how the word is most often used.

In practice there are two distinctly different forms of mentoring. One is best described as *sponsorship mentoring*. This means being a career friend, someone who knows the ropes in an organization, is extremely senior and influential and can act as patron. The implication is that the mentor takes a keen interest in the career of the mentee, passes on useful hints and tips and, when the time comes, may influence promotion decisions on behalf of the mentee. The other form of mentoring is *development mentoring*. Here, the mentor may or may not be in the same organization, though probably is in the same sector, and may only be a little older or more senior. The aim is different: to develop the mentee's confidence and skill.

In practice, mentoring does have the overtones of implying that the older and wiser person will be passing on their advice. Where this is so, mentoring is a different activity from coaching. Where coaching principles apply, mentoring and coaching are synonyms for the same process. In practice, *mentoring* is coming to seem like an older-fashioned word for *coaching*.

Coaching and training

If coaching is about learning, and it is, then how is it different from training? There are some major and some subtle differences.

A trainer has a set curriculum and rightly presents as an expert in his or her subject. Some trainers behave more like lecturers than coaches, doing a lot more of the talking than any coach would consider appropriate. There may be externally agreed standards involving accreditation or assessment which the trainee is expected to reach and on which by implication the trainer is assessed. So for instance, in schools, Standard Assessment Tests (SATs) *grade* the pupil but *assess* the school and its teachers against nationally agreed norms. On many training courses, the participants have been enrolled against their will whereas coaching has to be entered into voluntarily.

A coach definitely has no set curriculum and would rarely talk for more than a few minutes at a time, but may be an expert in his or her subject – for instance, negotiating, leadership, life-planning or human relationships generally. There is no equivalent of SATs in coaching. As with mentoring, training is far more effective as a learning process when it proceeds from coaching principles.

Line manager coaches

Interest in coaching as an alternative to command and control is growing. This is because in a non-authoritarian society people reject command and control. Developing a 'coaching culture' has become a desirable aim for many organizations. Here coaching is an approach to performance management which emphasizes the manager's role as *developer* rather than as *controller*. Line managers use a *coaching approach*, encouraging team members to develop self-confidence, resourcefulness, skills, belief in the value of their own decision-making and so on through a process of accelerated learning. However, the line management responsibility puts a significantly different slant on how the line manager coach can work. As a boss, it is entirely probable that you are part of whatever problems your coachee has and this can be difficult to see let alone to acknowledge. Also, it is always more difficult to promise confidentiality, encourage or expect complete disclosure, set aside your own considerations or remain detached from the possible outcomes. As a boss you have a stake in the outcome, whereas when you are purely a coach you do not.

'Situational' coaching or mentoring

Every now and then a particularly useful idea comes along which has the power to help us see an old question in a new way. Anne Brockbank and Ian McGill's book, *Facilitating Reflective Learning through Mentoring & Coaching* (2006), is one such and one of the first genuinely new attempts for a decade to define coaching and mentoring. The book takes sociological perspective, written by a husband and wife team with backgrounds in psychotherapy, sociology and action learning. It asks: *Whose view of 'reality' prevails here? Who owns the purpose?* Is it subjective, that is, the individual's own view, as opposed to some assumed-to-be-objective view? Second, it asks '*What is the* (often unspoken) *purpose?* Is it to preserve the status quo, or is it transformation? If you follow this matrix (see Figure 1.2) it makes no difference whether you call the activity *coaching, training* or *mentoring,* or whether you are talking about line management coaching or life coaching.

The four quadrants in Figure 1.2 are now explored in more detail.

Quadrant 1: improvement coaching

The unspoken aim here is to maintain the status quo and get people to fit in.

This is the traditional apprenticeship model and is what people often mean by the word *mentoring,* but it can apply to coaching just as readily – for example, if you are asked to take on a client whose performance is about to derail (and in effect be doing the work that should be done by the line

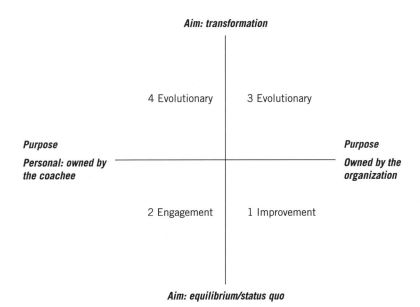

Figure 1.2 The Brockbank-McGill matrix (adapted from Brockbank and McGill 2006)

manager). The assumption is that there is an objective reality out there – for instance, a competency framework or a set of professional standards – and that these are fixed benchmarks. It is useful for demonstrating 'the way we do things around here'. It reinforces the existing power relationships and what Brockbank and McGill call the 'power horizon' remains invisible; 'taken for granteds' (TFGs) are never challenged. This is often the purpose of training – for example, management development, where organizations have their own 'leadership model'. The individual's view is not considered to be important. Many social mentoring projects have this as their aim – for example, projects which aim to reduce social exclusion. Coaching as a line management activity often has this flavour because coachee and manager are assumed to share the organization-set agenda.

Quadrant 2: engagement coaching

The unspoken aim here is to minimize opposition to change.

In this type of coaching the individual's subjective view is taken into account, but essentially the aim is to maintain the status quo. It is useful when an organization needs to train people in acquiring an unpopular skill such as appraising people, or giving feedback, or to persuade them to accept unpopular changes. The power relationships are unchanged and still largely invisible. When coaching is undertaken here it is to 'correct' the 'mistaken' ideas of the individual, but to do it nicely. As external coaches, we may be asked to undertake coaching as a way of developing a 'high-flier' but again, ultimately, what is expected is behaviour change and conformity to the organization's norms. With both improvement and engagement coaching, the focus is on work and work skills – in my model it is entirely about the *doing self*. Personal life is not on the agenda and organizational clients may be surprised by or even opposed to the idea that it could be. Coaching may have this flavour where the emphasis is on skill development and where it therefore has more of the feel of one-to-one training.

Quadrant 3: evolutionary coaching

The aim here is explicit transformation. The coachee is expected to take responsibility for their own learning and life. Their agenda is what matters.

This is the model I endorse: my being/doing model is another way of expressing the same beliefs. The coachee's goals are the foundation of the work, although in executive coaching the line manager's/organization's goals are also fed into the agenda; values are explicitly explored. Evolutionary coaching encourages questioning and challenging, including taking a cool look at 'the power horizon' – how decisions are actually taken as well as the things that are TFGs. The work is holistic: both work and private life are explicitly on the agenda. The rock-bottom assumption is that people are infinitely resourceful. It is always possible that the coachee may leave the organization as a result of the work. Questions relating to life purpose, the quality of relationships (work and home), feelings, career and health may all be explored legitimately. Techniques used here have a more obvious debt to psychotherapy and are linked in a clear line to humanistic psychotherapy, for instance to the work of Carl Rogers.

Quadrant 4: revolutionary coaching

The aim here is the transformation of society or the organization.

Where the aim is social (e.g. Marxism, some forms of radical Islam, some kinds of fundamentalist or dogmatic Christianity as well as many cults), the coachee's views are unimportant. The coaching takes the form of instruction. In organizational terms, this would involve a radical revamping of the organization, perhaps in the wake of a take-over or financial crisis.

I find the quadrant model very useful indeed, not least as a way of reminding myself what kind of coaching I am engaged in at any one time. So, for instance, when I am doing career coaching I am somewhere on the crossing point between Quadrants 1, 2 and 3. I have information about how to handle a job interview which assumes that there are useful rules about interview behaviour which I need to pass on to the client. My purpose is transformation, and the client is setting the agenda ('help me get that job'), but to help the client get there I need to offer information and advice which comes from my view of the world and from principles I have found that interviewers expect, rather than the client's view of the world. When an organization asks me to coach a problem performer, I am aware that they are asking me to operate out of Quadrant 1 or 2 – in other words, to get the client to fit into organizational norms and to deal with their potentially disruptive or difficult behaviour. My whole-person approach may therefore not be the right fit and I need to raise this explicitly at the outset.

Where organizations offer coaches, mentors or 'buddies' to newly-hired staff, the intention is almost always to offer the helpful support that falls squarely into Quadrant 1 because it is entirely about how to fit in – for instance, how to learn the hidden rules of the culture quickly. Line manager coaches are virtually always operating out of Quadrant 2 because their role is essentially to accustom their teams to inevitable change.

The Brockbank-McGill matrix has been refreshing to me because it draws attention to the importance of understanding what it is we are doing and why, rather than obsessing about what we call it or how, exactly, to define it – and also makes it plain that there is a legitimate place for all four kinds of activity.

When does a client need specialist help?

Clients may benefit from all kinds of specialist help, for all kinds of reasons, either in tandem with your coaching or serially.

CASE STUDY

Lynne

Lynne was a manager newly appointed into a senior role. Our agenda was to work on her first 100 days in her new role, but feedback indicated that she also had a problem with what her organization called 'personal impact'. Lynne's confidence issues stemmed from a childhood where she had felt socially disadvantaged as one of the few free-place children in a famous public school. She had a reputation for mumbling and swallowing her words, rushing at them, apparently to get them out of the way. She and I were able to work effectively on a strategy for her first 100 days, but I referred her to a specialist colleague on the speech issues. My colleague, trained as an actor and voice specialist, was able to see that, along with the psychological issues, Lynne had a complex set of problems, some of them physical, with tongue and breath control. She prescribed a series of exercises which, when rigorously implemented, were able to make a significant impact on Lynne's performance at meetings and when giving presentations.

Developmental disorders

Over my two decades as a coach I have probably worked with at least eight clients who were somewhere on the autistic spectrum. None was labelled as such and my 'diagnosis' is a speculative one made with hindsight. However, these clients, all men, typically presented with similar issues and all had been referred by someone else, usually in the context of organizational change.

Any one of these 'symptoms' could be benign on its own, but it is when many or most of them are present that you may begin to suspect some form of mild autism such as Asperger's syndrome:

- difficulty with eye contact;
- over-formal speech patterns: I remember several such clients who never used an elision but always, for instance, would say *should not*

rather than *shouldn't* or spoke using the passive tense and in convoluted sentences;

- repetitive body movements such as mild finger-flapping or foot-tapping which the client finds it hard to control;
- reported problems in creating rapport and making emotional contact with colleagues;
- a reputation for eccentricity;
- physical clumsiness: I remember one such client repeatedly stumbling as he came into the room and later managing to bang his head against our front door as he left; another spilt his coffee in all but one of his sessions;
- inflexibility about time-management – for instance, insisting on particular routines;
- skills concentrated on a restricted spectrum;
- intense resistance to change;
- extreme and obsessive interest in hobbies which involve counting and collecting; I also remember one such client whose commitment to a football club came a long way before the needs of his job, his health, his wife or his children.

All these clients were intelligent and articulate men at middle-senior levels in their organizations. Most were in what seemed to be viable partner relationships and had children. Often they had been able to sustain their jobs, typically specialist roles in information technology or finance, in a protected pocket of the organization until a change had dislodged them. The coaching probably had limited success. Mostly it was about closely offered feedback and in some cases frank teaching about social interaction – for instance, learning the importance of eye contact or of asking social questions of others and how to sustain this effectively.

A suspicion that your client has some kind of developmental disorder of this kind is not a reason for refusing to coach the client, but it may be a reason for understanding that the coaching will need to have a different flavour and pace. It will also be important to be realistic, both with the client and the organization, about what the coaching might achieve. Now that conditions such as Asperger's syndrome are better recognized and the associated stigmas less intense than they were, we might increasingly expect clients and their organizations to let us know that this is what we are jointly up against.

Psychotherapeutic help

There may be occasional clients who can benefit from therapy and others where you may notice a need for therapy but decide not to raise it with the client.

CASE STUDY

Kamila

Kamila was a client who had a perfectly conventional list of performance-related work problems, many of them to do with her perfectionism and lack of self-confidence. At the outset of her coaching programme she had said that having a major tidying up of her flat was one of her goals. When we had worked with moderate success through most of her list, I commented mildly that the tidier flat had been consistently avoided as a topic. Kamila tentatively said a little more about her home, describing hoarding thousands of newspapers and feeling unable to invite anyone into her home as a result. This did a lot to explain the social isolation of which she had complained. Knowing that such excessive hoarding was a classic symptom of obsessive-compulsive disorder (OCD), that it often accompanied just the perfectionism and lack of confidence that Kamila had described, and that hoarders with OCD are often reluctant to seek treatment, I left it at that, feeling that I did not have permission to go further.

Understanding common psychotherapeutic or psychiatric conditions

As a coach you do need a working knowledge of common psychological and psychiatric problems. For instance, as well as the kind of encounter I describe with Kamila, above, I have had several clients whose extreme fluctuations in mood might possibly have been mild versions of bipolar disorder. One such senior client was eventually removed from her post. There was an official reason given which was to do with 'reorganization', but I wondered privately whether the actual reason was that her grandiose plans for her organization, her casual lack of interest in their practicality and her sudden, unpredictable plummets in energy and optimism came to be seen as far too risky.

It is not at all uncommon to find that some clients have partners with serious mental health problems – for instance, delusional states of one kind or another. One such client was secretly followed into work by her husband, convinced that she was merely pretending to be a manager in her organization and was actually working for MI5. Another client's wife believed that their TV had personal messages for her and that the water supply to their flat was being poisoned. Problems of dementia in ageing parents, and the bizarre behaviour associated with some forms of it, are extremely common. The distress all of this causes to loved ones is beyond agonizing, and I observe that it is often too painful for discussion anywhere but in the privacy of the coaching room. Your role here is to allow the client to explore their feelings and also to consider what action, if any, they need to take. Again, you may be able to suggest specialist sources of advice. So with one client whose husband was very ill, in the grip of a long-running psychotic episode, but refusing treatment, I was able to suggest she book herself a conversation with a fellow coach who is also a consultant psychiatrist. This coach accepted the brief on the understanding that he could not prescribe treatment for the husband without seeing him as a patient, but that he could and did work with my client on ways to manage interactions with her husband.

Be ultra careful in how you enter this arena because it is fraught with tripping points. Classifying and labelling psychiatric disorders is controversial even among the professionals dealing with mentally ill people. Richard P. Bentall, a professor of clinical psychology, has written a cheerfully iconoclastic book, *Doctoring the Mind: Why Psychiatric Treatments Fail* (2010), about the way the pharmaceutical industry has taken over treatments based on what he says is the myth that mental illness has a physical basis. He writes:

> My own view is that most psychiatric diagnoses are about as scientifically meaningful as star signs, a diagnostic system which is similarly employed to describe people and predict what will happen to them, and which enjoys a wide following despite compelling scientific evidence that it is useless.
>
> (2010: 110)

So we should consider ourselves warned.

When might a client need psychotherapy?

There is no universal way to pinpoint when a coaching client needs psychotherapy, but these are some rules of thumb that I find useful.

- The client cries: frequently, intensely and uncontrollably.
- The client describes suicidal feelings or actual suicide attempts.
- There are threats of harm to others.
- The client returns over and over again to one relationship, typically with a parent, parent-figure or sibling.
- One major fear appears to dominate the client's life – e.g. abandonment, ever-present dread of complete catastrophe, rejection, loss of control.
- When the client tells their life story it features a major trauma. Examples from my own practice include: living through a major house fire; being the apparent cause of the death of a sibling; childhood as a refugee; a mother leaving children behind after moving into a new relationship; being the survivor of child abuse; an entirely unanticipated divorce after a long marriage; the theft and destruction of a PhD thesis by a trusted colleague.

- The client is unable to move on from one incident: everything seems to be seen through the prism of that event. Typically the event will involve loss of some kind.
- The client frequently resorts to 'if only . . .':
  - he/she/they would change;
  - that hadn't happened;
  - I hadn't done that;
  - I wasn't the way I am;
  - I didn't look the way I do.
- A bereavement has never been acknowledged and worked through.
- There is an inability to accept personal responsibility: victim-thinking has become a way of life.
- The client describes symptoms of frequent mental dysfunction which intrude significantly into everyday life – e.g. depression, anxiety, panic attacks, agoraphobia, OCD, hypochondria.
- There is a denial of 'reality': the client lives in a fantasy world.
- The client engages in substance misuse: drink, eating problems, drugs.
- The client has other kinds of addictive behaviour – e.g. gambling, compulsive risk-taking, sexual promiscuity.
- The client behaves in troubling ways with you – e.g. heavy flirting, displays of anger, constantly failing to turn up for appointments.

Note that all of this behaviour could have other, more innocent explanations, and many of us might consider ourselves perfectly mentally healthy while subject to a few of such symptoms occasionally. But the more of such behaviour that is present in a client, and the more persistent it is, the more likely it is that you are in therapeutic territory. Overall, probably the most important single indicator is your own feeling that *you are out of your depth* or that *something is wrong*. Trust that feeling and listen to your worries, but don't panic too soon. I believe we should stop searching for a non-existent boundary with therapy. It is, and always will be, grey, and as you gain experience, confidence and skill it will most probably become greyer. As well as trusting your own feelings and judgement, trust your clients. If they believe you can help them, they are probably right.

Handling the conversation about referral

As coaches we probably need to accept that few clients are likely to take up the therapy option, even it is clear to you, and possibly also to them, that they could benefit from it. The difficulties of finding a suitable therapist, the feelings of shame still associated with needing therapy, the hope that the distress may go away all on its own, the fear of change, the cost and the poor reputation that some therapy has, may all deter a client from pursuing it. None of this should prevent you from making the suggestion when you feel it is right. GPs are always the first and best point of contact for mental health issues. Here, the coaching is about how the client can find specialist help rather than working directly on the issues.

- Tell the client that you feel you are at the limits of your skills. Beware of appearing to blame the client for their problem.
- Stress your respect for the client and your desire to support them.
- Explain the differences between psychotherapy and coaching; describe how psychotherapy might help.
- Ask for the client's reactions.
- Encourage the client to contact their GP and to suggest a therapist.
- Clarify the boundaries of the future coaching relationship.
- If you both agree that the coaching should stop, offer to contact the client at an appropriate future date for feedback on their progress.

When done well, all the approaches I have described in this chapter have a great deal in common. When done badly all also fall into similar mistakes. So there are mentors who act indistinguishably from the best coaches and coaches who can fall into the traps of the worst mentors. There are coaches who do psychotherapy without labelling it as therapy and therapists who might as well be coaches. To be successful, all depend on unforced respect for the client – the foundation stone of which is what Carl Rogers, one of the most significant thinkers of the twentieth century in this area, called 'unconditional positive regard'. All require the practitioner to create and sustain an extraordinary degree of rapport and to act from the highest ethical standards. All need an extraordinary degree of self-awareness and self-management. All demand extraordinary levels of listening and questioning ability plus the capability to challenge appropriately – and an infinite curiosity about and interest in people.

2   Brain-wise

As a keen filmgoer, I have noticed the way sci-fi films have changed. Gone are the spaceships, ray guns and green-faced aliens with funny-shaped heads. Instead we have movies where the focus is the human brain. The plots involve creating multiple perspectives, the blurring of dream with apparent reality, the suggestion that thought alone can alter events – and much more. At one level, films like *The Matrix, Inception* or *Source Code* may appear to be mimicking video games. At another, they reflect the rapidly expanding field of neuroscience. Being able to look into a living brain with functional magnetic resonance imaging (fMRI) scanners has overturned so many of our previous assumptions about how our brains work. Just like the actual themes of these more recent sci-fi films, the questions raised are profound: what does individual identity mean? What is 'reality'? What is human consciousness? How is the mind different from the brain? How far can one human being permanently change the thought processes of another, whether for good or evil?

Why coaches need to know about neuroscience

All coaches need to have at least some understanding of this material because it is overwhelmingly the most important single recent development in our field. Overall, the message is that there is a biological basis to human psychology. Our role as coaches is to work with people on the changes that will make a difference to their lives. What the neuroscientific research shows without any shadow of doubt is that it is emotions that drive human behaviour. If we don't understand this, we will work on the assumption that choices are rational – so getting agreement intellectually – and no profound change will happen. The research also demonstrates that it is safer for the human brain to do what it has always done: 'This has worked so far, so why change anything?' Clarifying and working on the intention to change is an *emotional* not a rational process. The work of the brain is to rationalize, not to be rational, as so many people believe. Good coaching grounds itself in the limbic system, the emotional centre of the brain. This means that everything, and I mean everything, in coaching involves emotions, including the relationship with the coach. This is why creating a vivid relationship of mutual warmth, acceptance and liking is so very important because without it both we and our clients will be role-playing change rather than truly working on it. Warmth, acceptance and liking create trust. Without trust, coaching is impossible, so trust is the essential precondition for a healthy coaching relationship.

Our predictable irrationality

Professor Dan Ariely has written entertainingly on our hopelessly irrational behaviour in his book *Predictably Irrational* (2008). As Professor Ariely is an ingenious designer of experiments to test how rational our behaviour actually is, the book is full of wryly recounted results, showing for instance that if we believe a pain-relieving pill costs $2.50 per dose, we will attribute more pain-relieving power to it than if we believe it costs a mere 10 cents, even though in both cases the 'pain reliever' is actually plain old vitamin C. In various other experiments, Ariely establishes that the more removed we are from actual cash, the more likely we are to cheat with money. So, for instance, would our disgraced MPs of 2010 have been likely to acquire duck houses or pornographic movies if they had been required to pay for them by actually asking for and handling the money in cash from some benevolent parliamentary authority? Of course not. Writing it down on an expenses sheet made it easy for brazen flexing of the system to take place. The internet has also added to our opportunities for irrational behaviour – for instance, it can now be grounds for divorce if you prove that your spouse has been 'unfaithful' to you with an avatar on the internet game *Second Life*. How irrational is that? No actual infidelity has taken place or ever could, yet believing it to be 'true' is enough to end a marriage.

Links with coaching

Such emotionally-based behaviour has powerful links with coaching and can be explained at least to some extent by the findings of neuroscience. So, for instance, resistance to change has a biological as well as a psychological component. Learning involves creating new neural pathways. Imaginary experiences are treated by our brains entirely as if they are real, and all of this has stunning implications for how we work with clients. It begins to prove much that coaches have previously asserted based on experience and intuition – but experience and intuition do not amount to data that would convince a scientist, or indeed a sceptical client. The same principles will save us from wasting our own and our clients' time with techniques and approaches that are unlikely to work, as well as suggesting many that possibly we underuse or fail to use at all. The fundamental purpose of any coaching is learning, and to learn you have to manage all the intrusive emotion that gets in the way. These struggles are not optional – they are biological and psychological necessities if there is to be growth. In effect, we are working with clients to increase their self-awareness and their tolerance of discomfort. Bear in mind, too, that we need to know about these principles because of course they apply every bit as much to ourselves. In this chapter I summarize some of the most important current themes and ideas about the human brain, but this is now a huge and expanding field and all of the books I reference here are worth reading for the much more detailed treatment they give.

The emotional brain

We have self-flatteringly named our own species *Homo sapiens* (*thinking*/wise man), but *emotion* has far more impact on our lives and in our decision-making. Emotion precedes thought. All our important decisions (whether to marry, have a child, change jobs etc.) are made on a feelings basis and later justified with rationality. We can try to suppress emotion but it will resurface one way or another. The explanation lies in how the human brain evolved. Like other animals, the brain stem (also called the 'snake-brain' because even reptiles have it) came first in evolutionary terms. This controls breathing and heartbeat. Then came the limbic system, the emotional centre of the brain. It is responsible for two powerful tools: learning and memory. These allowed all mammals to start forming relationships and so to be able to care for their young as well as refining their responses to danger, thus increasing their capacity for survival. So for human beings the capacity to learn would also mean avoiding danger another time – for instance, if you ate a food that led to illness. About a million years ago, the brains of mammals, including early humans, added an extra layer of brain cells: the prefrontal cortex, a thick layer of cells wrapped around the outer edge of the brain. In *Homo sapiens*, emerging around 150,000 years ago, the prefrontal cortex is many times larger than in any other land-dwelling species. This is what makes us so distinctly human. What is happening inside the limbic system is out of conscious awareness, but the prefrontal cortex is the centre of thinking and allows us to synthesize our ideas. It enables us to do long-term planning and strategizing, and to weigh up one path against another. It has also enabled us to nuance our emotional responses. As you go up the evolutionary scale, the sheer mass of the prefrontal cortex increases and so does the mass of connections to other parts of the brain. There is more prefrontal cortex connection to the limbic system in humans than in any other species, which is why we are able to display so many more emotions, and do so much more subtly than other mammals. The emotional brain is around 100 million years old but cognition is a youngster by comparison. Contrary to what we like to assume, cognition is the servant of emotion, not its master.

Every single human being interprets the world from an internal perspective. There is no such thing as 'objective reality'. External circumstances are far less important than how we interpret them. Some researchers believe that external events are responsible for as little as 10 per cent of our feelings of well-being. It is our internal – and emotional – 'map of the world' which influences us. This is why *re-framing* is so important in coaching: the stories we tell ourselves are what influence our mood and behaviour.

The importance of the amygdala

The amygdala (pronounced am-*ig*-dalla) consists of two small almond-shaped parts of the limbic system. It is the brain's alarm system, controlling the fight, flight or freeze response. It also stores memories of previous situations which have aroused strongly negative emotion. When faced with anything that we perceive to be dangerous or difficult, the amygdala sends the stress hormone cortisol to close down the higher brain functions of the prefrontal area and diverts all available energy to the back of the brain: the part that prepares us for action in an emergency. So brain functions unnecessary for fighting or fleeing are shut down, reducing the amounts of glucose and oxygen that are available for intellectual processing, including memory.

The tendency in such instances is to generalize, to make more sweeping assertions and to revert to linear rather than to creative ideas. The amygdala is also responsible for phobic reactions which typically resist rational analysis, and for our inability to think properly when under stress. The amygdala stores *all* our negative memories, which is why childhood experiences have such a powerful impact, even if we have forgotten the specific circumstances. The 'away-from' approach – i.e. resisting change because it is seen as 'dangerous' – is more powerful than the 'going-to', reward response. The perceived risk that the new may be horrible is often overwhelming, therefore we may prefer the familiar discomfort of the present. Knowing how deep-rooted our commitment to the present is, even when it is painful, is a sobering reminder for any coach of the importance of being realistic in our ambitions for coaching our clients.

Anyone who has felt panic in a job interview will recognize the impact of amygdala activity: even the simplest question cannot be answered, words disappear, you have an overwhelming wish to run away and hide, and later on, memory of the event is blurred. So *danger* can mean symbolic danger such as giving a presentation, sitting an exam or meeting new people. It can also include hearing an opinion we perceive as an attack, so *amygdala attack* or *hijack* can easily happen in a coaching session – for instance, being given advice clumsily or being confronted aggressively will mean that the client is not able to bring the prefrontal area of the brain into play. This explains why advice-giving is normally so counterproductive in coaching. The client can no longer think rationally because all his or her energy is absorbed in the indignation of feeling patronized, misunderstood and generally not heard. Clients may also arrive for coaching in an emotional state which tells you that the same processes are at work – for instance, angry about their bosses or upset at their failure to find a new job.

The prefrontal cortex

This part of the brain controls activities such as planning, reasoning, speech, empathic communication, insight and moral awareness. It can integrate emotions and experience, responding to signals from the mid-brain. It can generate positive, optimistic mood. Activity in this region of the brain can mean we are able to reassess emotional responses, reconsidering the nature of whatever the danger is and therefore controlling aggression or other impulsive behaviour by meeting such emotion with positive rational argument. This part of the brain make us capable of identifying the split second between emotional stimulus and response. The right prefrontal area seems to be the seat of negative emotions such as fear and aggression. In studies of stroke patients with lesions in the left prefrontal cortex, the patients were much more prone to catastrophic worries about their futures.

I have found that just explaining these simple facts of brain function to clients can have considerable impact. Human beings can often be puzzled, shamed and alarmed by the behaviour which the limbic system triggers, let alone having any clue about how to change it.

CASE STUDY

Gil

Gil was a chief executive client who fizzed with energy, intelligence and optimism. The job was stressful but he had coped with it well for the first two years. Appointing a director of operations altered the dynamic of his senior team and, at the time he asked me to work with him, he felt it had changed dramatically for the worse. 'This man is stubborn and won't listen and I no longer trust his judgement,' he said. There had been three events where a professional disagreement had become an argument and had then quickly deteriorated into a shouting match, though as Gil admitted he had done most of the shouting. 'A blinding rage came down on me and I was dimly aware that I was pounding the table.' On one such occasion, two secretaries had come running in from their office outside to check that Gil was not actually physically attacking his colleague (he wasn't). Gil's amygdala had 'fired' and he had given way to frustration and then anger. These feelings had engulfed him, something he admitted had happened far too often in his life in other situations. Cortisol would have flooded his prefrontal brain, disabling his usual rational decision-making processes. He did not need me to tell him that such behaviour was highly inappropriate, laying him open to accusations of bullying as well as being extremely unlikely to produce the change of mind he had hoped for in his colleague – and in fact the whole relationship had deteriorated yet more as a result. Like many other clients, Gil sought help on how to change someone else (the colleague) but soon realized that to have any chance of doing this, he had to change himself first.

The ultimate aim of coaching is learning, and in order to learn we have to become acutely self-aware, approaching problems rather than running away from them. Teaching a client like Gil how the amygdala, and the limbic system generally, works can be a first step to controlling it. I often draw this diagram for clients:

Stimulus $\Longrightarrow$ Response

This is how we describe our emotional reactions in situations where we have behaved impulsively. The response feels as if it has a life of its own. Thought has apparently not come into it – and indeed it has not. A better way of functioning is this, all of which can happen in a few micro-seconds:

Stimulus $\Longrightarrow$ Thinking $\Longrightarrow$ Decision $\Longrightarrow$ Response

The more aware you are of how your limbic system works, even though, paradoxically, it is out of conscious awareness, the more likely it is that there will be at least a fleeting moment of thinking between the stress stimulus and your response. In fact, even the traditional *counting to 10* will work. Saying to yourself, 'I am not physically under attack here and I can keep my prefrontal brain working' can transform your chances of this happening. I asked Gil to monitor his emotional reactions on a daily basis for a week, using a tiny notebook to jot down any insights he had into which types of challenge created what types of reaction in him. Here is part of an email he sent me some months later when our coaching programme was nearing its end:

> As you know I soon saw the pattern. The problems were always with men who are peers. If they challenged me in a particular way I saw it as a threat to my status and sense of myself as powerful and

competent. After a week of keeping that miniature diary I began to be able to forecast exactly what I needed to watch out for. After that, practising a new kind of response with you made all the difference.

What is happening here is that consciously bringing the prefrontal brain into play means that part of our middle prefrontal circuits, the 'uncinate fasciculus', releases neurotransmitters that calm down the amygdala. The cortical area can also release a peptide known as GABA – short for gamma-aminobutyric acid – which, it seems, can override the activity of the limbic region.

These tactics will also work with clients who describe many other types of situation where the amygdala is doing its work. Examples given to me on a weekly basis by my clients include: high levels of generalized anxiety about work, especially in a climate of unpredictable change; worries about facing a difficult meeting; giving tough feedback to a subordinate; and giving a presentation at a conference. Gil's story also shows that simply *naming* an emotion can help release its grip on us. This is because the process of naming comes, again, from the prefrontal areas of the brain and will help the prefrontal brain do its work of acting as a brake on the activity of the limbic system. So being able to say, 'I am frightened here because I feel I might make a fool of myself', or 'I am angry because this colleague is threatening my self-esteem' is in itself a way of short-circuiting the emotion.

'Journaling'

Writing down your feelings and thoughts about troubling events has also been shown to be effective in creating improvements at a physiological as well as a subjective level, as it was with Gil. In writing your feelings down and naming them you are acting as a reporter on your own life. This creates some beneficial *dissociation*. One research project demonstrated that this remained true even when the writer never re-read what they had written nor showed their jottings to anyone else.

CASE STUDY

Natalia

Natalia was a senior solicitor working for a high-profile City law firm. She came to coaching to work on a possible change of career. At 42 she told me she was 'bored with the law' and was ready to consider doing something else. In our first session it emerged that a year previously Natalia had made a serious error of judgement for which she had been reprimanded by her professional body, the Law Society. She had defended herself feistily, had been supported by her firm and was allowed to continue to practise. At the time I worked with her, the whole incident still haunted her, intruding into her dreams and creating irrational anxiety about inadvertently repeating the error. Telling herself that this was 'silly' was not helping. I explained how beneficial it could be to actually name whatever emotion she was experiencing. She had already told me that what troubled her was the knowledge that she had damaged the emotional wellbeing and finances of her client. I asked her what name she would give to the feelings that were bothering her. There was a long pause during which, as she told me later, she was weighing up whether she could bring herself to utter the words. These were, 'I am deeply ashamed of what I did. Even though there was nothing criminal in it, it was just a lapse of judgement, but yes, the emotions are shame and guilt.' As she said these words, I noticed a few tears in her eyes. In public Natalia had had to remain self-confident and composed. She had never been properly able to express remorse. Her comment to me later was, 'I know you're not a priest but it felt like going to confession and getting absolution because you did not judge or express horror and from that point on I was able to look at the whole incident more calmly and to learn from it.' I encouraged Natalia to write a private account of the whole episode, including her feelings and reflections on her learning, and to add to it whenever she felt there was something further to consider. Without any additional input from me, she named it her 'self forgiveness diary', a document I never saw. Natalia's eventual decision was to continue her legal career but to set up her own firm, something she has done with success.

The SCARF model

One of the themes in neuroscience is how much of our energy is concerned with basic survival needs that are as much emotionally as physically based. Human beings are social animals. We need to belong, we need approval. These needs to avoid social threat and to seek social reward appear to involve the same brain networks as those involved in physical survival. So, for instance, you are attacked by a mugger and you fear for your life. You are attacked by a colleague in a meeting and told you are incompetent. The brain responds to the physical or the psychological attack in the same way. It also seems that our brains are more finely tuned to see threat than to seek reward and that our needs to protect ourselves from threat are never far from our minds, though perhaps not always at a conscious level. This may explain why newspapers sell on bad news rather than good; it may also explain racial and religious prejudice, why politicians lie so readily, why so many coaching clients are so self-critical and why their sense of self-esteem is so fragile. The research is summarized by the writer David Rock (2008) and he also describes his useful model based on the acronym SCARF, which stands for status, certainty, autonomy, relatedness and fairness.

Status

We need to feel as good as or better than others. We need to know where we stand in any of the hierarchies, formal or informal, in which we operate, and the smallest threat to status can trigger uncontrollable emotional responses. So for instance, I have lost count of the number of times clients have described disproportionately heated wranglings over 'box-ratings' in performance appraisals: 'I marked myself at four but my boss marked me at two! He can go xxxx himself if he thinks I'll ever put myself out for him again!'

Being offered feedback of any sort can also create a threat to status, which is why when we do it in the coaching room we need to do so very skilfully (see page 251). Promotion is a status reward and the need for it can explain why clients will often fight to get a job where the monetary reward is insignificant, but the job title apparently bestows increased status.

Possible differences in status are at work in any coaching conversation. *Is this client more or less senior than me? Can I really challenge a client who is older than I am?* It can work the other way around too: a client may worry that a coach is either too inexperienced or too young (lower status), or too experienced (higher status), than they are. Some coaches have confessed that they are 'status snobs': they *like* the feeling of borrowed power that comes from working with a well-known or very senior person.

Certainty

We like certainty. Familiarity is comforting. If we have to weigh up every situation on the basis of ambiguity, we will have to engage the precious resources of the prefrontal brain areas. This is exhausting, so we try to avoid it. In situations of uncertainty we become preoccupied until we can create certainty again. Unfortunately, uncertainty is a pervading feature of organizational life: *will there be a take-over? Will work be outsourced to India? How many job cuts will there be? Is my own future at risk?* As a coach, remember how often this will intrude into your work – for instance, that a new client will most probably be worried about what it will be like working with you when they have not yet met you. You can reduce this uncertainty by spelling out in advance how you will run the first session or by suggesting that a new client talks to an existing client to get some honest feedback on your coaching style.

This need for certainty may also reinforce the importance of clear goal-setting in every session, because the process of setting a goal reduces uncertainty.

Autonomy

Many years of organizational research have shown correlations between physical and mental health and the degree of autonomy people have in their work. This is why an inability to delegate, essentially an exercise in giving others autonomy, can mean that a managerial client gets mediocre results from their team members and why it is therefore worth working with such clients to help them learn how to delegate more effectively. Autonomy is also the driver behind so many requests for career coaching: 'I need more freedom than I have'. This is especially true in public sector organizations where constant intrusion from regulators so often drills away at people's beliefs that they can make their own decisions. Needing more autonomy is virtually always the drive behind the wish to leave corporate life for the greater risk of running your own business, because however stressful this turns out to be at least you no longer have to respond in the same way to other people's needs for control.

Autonomy needs to be respected in coaching relationships and is yet another reason why advice-giving is so perilous. Even when giving a client some of the vital information they need in order to come to a decision, emphasize that you know it is the client who has to make the decision and live with the result: 'Here's the information – but it's up to you how you use it. What do you think?'

Relatedness

We are herd animals and cannot live alone. Survival in our earliest years of existence as a species depended critically on knowing instantly who was a stranger and might therefore be a threat to the life of the tribe. *Am I in or am I out?* To be banished is the worst possible punishment for human beings, short of death. It frequently lies behind the tragedy of teenage suicide and also behind the rapid descent into ill health and depression of people who describe themselves as chronically lonely. The need to belong rubs directly against our need for autonomy, as any member of a team will know, and the majority of us will barter at least some autonomy for the sake of feeling accepted by others.

In coaching, everything we do is about relatedness. If we do not feel a bond with the client, we cannot work with them. It is the essence of why coaching works. *Does this client accept and like me? Do I accept and like him or her?* If the answer to these questions is *no* on either side, then the coaching will come to a rapid close. I say more about this in Chapter 10.

Fairness

Perceived *unfairness* creates resentment and anger: a threat response. Unfortunately, organizational life abounds with obvious unfairnesses. For instance, low morale in an organization can often be traced directly to the enormous gap between the salaries of extremely well-rewarded senior managers and the meagre wages of their workforce. Managers who devise 'value statements' and then demonstrate contempt for them in their own behaviour, a boss who has favourites or who resources one department more favourably than another, a foreign owner who abruptly closes down an entire factory – all of these will generate a similar response.

In practice, all the emotional responses that are triggered by SCARF needs may be present *at once*, something that can explain the extremity of reaction in clients. Elizabeth's case study, below, is a good example of this.

CASE STUDY
Elizabeth

Elizabeth had worked successfully for the same organization for 30 years. A reorganization was announced and she had to compete for a job in the new structure. The job went to a younger rival with considerably less experience and Elizabeth was made redundant on terms that she found ungenerous and disappointing. The decision had been made by a colleague whom she had regarded as a friend, so the betrayal of trust felt overwhelming. She was full of vigour and energy and needed to earn a living, but knew that at 58 it could be difficult to fight age prejudice and find a new job. At her first coaching session she was trembling with anger at how she had been treated. She kept returning worriedly to how she was going to pay her mortgage and voiced her shock at the loss of a friendship. Sleepless nights had become the norm. Would she have to sell her house? How would she talk about her departure to people who had been her peers and juniors? Would her marriage survive all the changes? Would her health hold up?

In Elizabeth's case, her sense of herself as a senior and respected person was threatened – she felt she had lost status in her own and others' eyes. She faced an uncertain future in the job market and did not know if she would be able to pay her mortgage and keep her house. The decision infringed her autonomy because it had been made by someone else. Her need for relatedness was compromised – she would no longer be part of the team and she felt the 'betrayal' by the former friend keenly. The decision felt unfair because a person with significantly less experience had been appointed, leading Elizabeth to conclude that the whole selection process had been a set-up. Explaining the SCARF model to Elizabeth was immediately helpful. It turned what had felt like a hurtful and shaming personal experience into something that made sense as a biological as well as a social phenomenon. Her view was that it significantly shortened the adjustment time.

You can also, as I did with Elizabeth, use the SCARF model with clients when it comes to making new decisions. When she was playing with ideas of establishing a portfolio career, I drew a blank grid on a flipchart, like this:[1]

Category	Status	Certainty	Autonomy	Relatedness	Fairness
Pluses? (rewards)					
Minuses? (threats)					

As I asked Elizabeth questions around each, she filled in the boxes. I have found this far better than simply making a freestyle list of pluses and minuses, not least because it acknowledges that it is powerful emotions and the strong needs and drivers that lie beneath them that make up our minds, not lists based on logic.

The power of the imagination

The power of human imagination is awesome. This can be a plus or a minus. The brain does not seem to make much distinction between a remembered or imagined experience and an actual experience. On the positive side, this is why visualization of a peaceful scene can calm the amygdala down, or why recalling a success can precondition us to repeat it. One intriguing experiment demonstrates that this is no trivial feat. In his book *The Brain that Changes Itself* (2007), Norman Doidge describes an experiment where mental rehearsal was shown to be virtually as effective as the real thing. Two matched groups of total beginners were taught to play the piano. One group practised on a real keyboard. The other group sat in front of a keyboard but *imagined* playing the pieces, including hearing the sounds and moving their fingers. Both groups devoted two hours a day to this activity. The group that did the actual practice were slightly but only slightly ahead of the other group when both were assessed, but when given one session of actual practice, the mental rehearsal group did just as well. The success of the British cycling team in the Olympics and other international competitions is attributed by them and others to the coaching they had from the medical doctor and sports psychologist, Steve Peters, who describes these and other techniques in his book *The Chimp Paradox* (2012).

Neuroplasticity

It used to be thought that our brains had a fixed number of cells which declined in number over the years, making new learning difficult. This turns out to be misleading. The brain is 'plastic' and is able to make new connections at any time, a concept that is described as *neuroplasticity*. Focusing energy and intention can change the brain. Its physical shape will evolve in response to how it is used. So, for instance, violinists often have a hugely expanded cortical region in the area of the brain that governs the use of the left hand (involved in fingering). A friend who studied for three gruelling years to become a London cab driver would certainly endorse the enormity of the task involved in 'The Knowledge', the exam that London taxi drivers have to pass to be licensed, and would not be surprised to learn that the hippocampi (memory centres) of professional taxi drivers can be enlarged because they have had to work so hard to remember a vast mass of spatial detail. In both these examples *intention* is important: the changes have happened as a result of practice, commitment and hard work.

The best way to change behaviour is not to work on what is 'wrong' but to develop new behaviours, creating new neural pathways which can, over a period of time, become dominant. So, for instance, for people who suffer from OCD, rather than teaching them to confront the behaviours which trouble them (e.g. for people who obsess about hygiene, forcing them to have dirty hands), it has proved far more successful to teach them how to *interrupt the thought*. (For more on this see *Brain Lock*, by Jeffrey Schwartz, 1996.) It is likely that you can increase plasticity and readiness to change simply by paying attention to the need for mindfulness and the emotional triggering that this involves.

Relaxation and mindfulness

As a coach you can build on the plasticity of the brain by combining it with the power of imagination in a number of ways. Your aim is to create awareness of awareness. So first, don't be shy about showing clients how relaxation techniques work. These have been familiar to the human species for at least 2500 years and probably longer. They have been a feature of all Eastern philosophies and essentially work by focusing on bodily state: how do I feel now, this minute? What is happening to my limbs, gut, torso, heart, face, breathing? Often what is happening is a tense set of muscles, raised shoulders, a compressed chest cavity which squashes the lungs, and the shallow breathing that comes from gulping in air from the upper part of the chest. Try one of the simplest techniques now – as you are reading this.

> *Settle quietly into your chair. Uncross any crossed arms or legs and keep your feet firmly planted on the ground. Release any tension in your body, starting with your feet and working slowly upwards to your face. Notice your breathing. Put your arms on the sides of your body at your waist, hands pointing to the middle. As you breathe in you should feel your hands being pushed outwards. Imagine drawing breath from below your waist as if you are inflating a balloon. Picture your breath. Breathe in through your nose and blow the breath out as if you are gently blowing out a candle. Now, count steadily and slowly: seven for the in-breath and eleven for the out-breath. Concentrate on this, closing your eyes, repeating it at least 20 times.*

What typically happens when you do this? First, you are distracting yourself by focusing on your body and on the mechanics of breathing. By becoming *mindful*, you are entering an intentionally-created light trance state – something that we all do on an involuntary basis most days, for instance when driving along a familiar route or listening to music. Such positive states seem to discharge a number of hormones in the brain – for instance, the dopamine released by listening to music is similar in quantity to the amount that is created by taking cocaine. A trance state most probably creates receptivity in our brains. By slowing your breathing down you steady yourself and if you were yoked to an EEG machine you would see that the electrical impulses in your brain would be producing the alpha waves that are associated with calmness and shutting down the visual cortex, rather than the beta waves associated with alertness, busyness and stress. Like any other discipline, relaxation needs to be practised until you can produce it at will. There is a complete script for a visualization to use with clients on page 200.

Now let's suppose that you want to learn a new way of overcoming an old habit, something that is getting in the way for you. Typical examples given to me by clients include reaching too readily for that evening glass of wine, worrying about how to deal with a particular colleague at a meeting, being unable to delegate a task, and staying late at the office despite being too tired to work.

Yes, the human brain is plastic: it can go on making new connections indefinitely. But as the reverse side of this strength, the more we reinforce a habit, the harder it is to change. One of the best ways to do this is through *mental rehearsal*. Constant rehearsal of the imagined better way can make it much easier to change behaviour. Technically what is happening is that you are growing new connections (synapses) between the neurons in your brain, including strengthening the myelin sheaths that reinforce the pathways. Follow these steps first.

1 The goal
What is it you want to change? This should be stated in the positive and in the present tense – i.e. as if it is already happening – and should be as specific as possible.

So don't say: *I want to avoid staying at the office late every day* (a vague statement and a negative, so the brain will just remember the words *stay* and *office*, thus reinforcing the very thing you want not to do).

Do say: *I leave the office every day at 6pm with a light heart.*

2 Triggers
What triggers the problem? Think about how you want to respond differently, e.g. *I see the last emails coming in and I know I can deal with them tomorrow.*

3 Thoughts and feelings
Think about what thoughts and feelings you will have in your mind when faced with the problem-stimulus. *I am calm and accept that it is fine for the emails to wait.*

4 Imagining your actions
Think about what you will be doing – imagine it in detail. *I get my things together, say goodnight to colleagues and walk out calmly to the car park, looking forward to a pleasant evening.*

5 The benefits
Think about the benefits doing all of this will bring you. *I am proud of myself, calm and energized, enjoying my feelings of freedom.*

Now rehearse all this in your mind, making it a smooth sequence. Visualize yourself doing the actions, hear any sounds, experience any feelings.

Now rehearse it again and again. Do at least 10 mental rehearsals a day.

Here is an account of how one client got on with this technique.

CASE STUDY

Vanessa

My problem was my overwhelming sense of duty about my to-do list. It was creating problems with my husband who saw me continually putting my professional and domestic tasks over my relationship with him. I was also constantly tired, harassed and irritable. I talked it through with my coach first and agreed that my goal was to release at least an hour of relaxation a day just for me. I learnt relaxation and breathing techniques and then set aside time to do mental rehearsals of the new routine. Of course, this in itself became a 'task' on my to-do list but that was OK. I quickly got to enjoy my rehearsals and realized that just doing them was something I was looking forward to. The remarkable thing was that within a few days of practising I found that I was going home at 6 instead of 7.30, that I was not switching on my laptop at home, that I kept Saturday totally free and that somehow I was already doing the very thing I had wanted for such a long time.

In reading Vanessa's account, you should note that I combined showing her the mental rehearsal protocol with using the Kegan-Lahey Immunity to Change approach (see page 182), where we identified her fears about change, which in her case were about associating tasks and duties with being a 'good person' and her 'big assumption' was that neglecting them would show that she was an 'uncaring person'. Practising alternative behaviours was part of her set of experimental tests of the assumption.

Empathy and mirror neurons

Meta-research into therapy (see page 249) shows that warmth and empathy are the most critical factors in the success of any therapeutic intervention and there is no reason to suppose that coaching is any different. Brain-based science shows that there is most probably a physical explanation. When we are closely attuned to another person, the same areas of the brain will 'light up' in each individual. These are known as *mirror neurons*. So the feeling of empathy is a physical and biological phenomenon as well as a social one. The inner state of the other person directly affects us, but how far this is true seems to depend on self-awareness of our own bodily state. Thus, as a coach, the more you are seamlessly able to monitor your own responses while remaining able to listen deeply to your client, the better the coaching you will be able to provide. You will be responding to the client – and the client is going to be responding to you, because neurons will be signalling to neurons. Being fully there for your client frees them to respond fully to you. Anyone writing about this phenomenon struggles with how to describe it, though perhaps we all know it when we experience it. It is the basis of 'Level 3 listening' (see page 68) – that transformative sensation of 'feeling felt', 'being contained', 'being attuned' or 'being deeply connected'.

Attachment patterns

Fifty years of research has shown how critical our need for love is if we are to flourish physically. So, for instance, like other primates, if you deprive human infants of being touched and cuddled, they fail to thrive. In their book *A General Theory of Love* (2001) Lewis *et al.* describe the work of the psychoanalyst René Spitz, showing that children reared in foundling homes under such regimes invariably became withdrawn, lost weight and often died. Death rates in some such orphanages were routinely 75 per cent – a staggering figure. Another impressive and well-known study was called 'The Infant Strange Situation' and is described in Daniel Siegel's readable and influential book *Mindsight* (2010). First, observers were trained in a methodology for classifying the interactions of a baby and its mother during the first year of life. Then the babies were faced with an experimental situation where their mother left the room for a short time. The study made direct correlations between the babies' behaviour and the patterns the observers had seen. These children were followed up in adult life.

Securely attached children, 60 per cent of the sample, cried bitterly and greeted the mother with ecstasy and relief when she reappeared, physically clinging to her. These were the children of mothers who had shown immediate responsiveness to the babies' needs in the earlier observations. As adults, these people were able to build secure relationships and had a good chance of combining confidence with self-awareness. When they appear in the coaching room, these clients are the ones every coach likes to work with: often high-flyers, open to new ideas, eager to learn and prepared to take responsibility for themselves. In neuropsychological terms their attachment circuits are in good order.

Twenty per cent of the babies were described as demonstrating *avoidant attachment*. The children made no fuss when the mother disappeared and showed little interest in her return. These mothers had shown indifference or coldness to their babies, often ignoring their cries and minimizing physical contact. In adult life such babies grew to be cool in their relationships and were often seen by others as controlling and difficult to like. All coaches will meet and work with a large number of clients of this sort. In my own practice I have observed how often this pattern appears in the people whose father was cold and demanding, dominating his wife as much as he dominated his children so that she became as remote as he as far as the children were concerned. Such children learn to live with being ignored and criticized in equal measure. They acquire a prickly independence. They have learnt that emotion is dangerous so it must be suppressed. As clients I notice they often have a striking lack of emotional vocabulary. I remember one such client telling me in all seriousness that he really had no idea what people meant by 'feelings'. Most probably the left prefrontal cortex is overdeveloped in such people: this area of the brain is literal, likes lists, facts and logic. It is digital in its approach – yes/no, right/wrong, on/off. The right hemisphere, on the other hand, mediates social behaviour. It is more holistic and non-verbal, controlling visual and spatial perception, empathy, concern for others and autobiographical memory. It is the part of the brain which enables us to imagine what must be going on in someone else's mind. In people shaped by avoidant attachment the right hemisphere is likely to be underdeveloped: they are severely rational in their thought processes, are impatient for others to fall in with their ideas and have little awareness of or interest in how others see them, or ability to empathize. They turn up frequently in the coaching room because their careers can progress smoothly until the point where task intelligence is no longer enough and they are expected to interact skilfully with peers through rapport and subtle influencing rather than through cool power. One give-away is that when you ask them for autobiographical detail they look blank and will tell you that they remember little of their childhoods except that 'everything was OK'. I notice that such clients are as tough and uncompromising on themselves as they are on others. Even if you do not ask for autobiographical detail from your clients, your assumption should be that when you see extreme rigidity in a client's thinking, you are mostly probably working with the product of this kind of childhood. It is not at all uncommon for coaches to receive demands from organizations to transform such people: 'Please make him emotionally intelligent.' Be realistic about the chances of this happening. Emotional intelligence is not a software program that can be installed with a few clicks into the human brain.

In his dense and scholarly book, *The Master and his Emissary* (2009), Ian McGilchrist argues convincingly that in western society we have generally glorified the left hemisphere at the expense of the right, resulting in a mechanistic overemphasis on structure, logic and materialism, at great cost to ourselves. Most people reading his book would have to agree – and as coaches, would probably conclude that this is at least part of what makes coaching so necessary and so helpful.

Ten per cent of the babies in the study demonstrated *ambivalent attachment*. Their mothers had been inconsistent. Sometimes they were attentive, sometimes they were dismissive. In the experiment, when the mothers left, the baby had often already shown jumpiness and uncertainty. Their behaviour was clingy and agitated. Even when picked up it was difficult to pacify them. As adults their typical behaviour was anxious and sometimes over-emotional. We meet these people as coaches when they say they lack 'assertiveness' or ask us to help them with over-arching difficulties such as 'confidence'. Feedback will usually reveal that colleagues view them with suspicion because their behaviour is needy, inconsistent and capricious, and you may find that colleagues avoid them because they talk obsessively and abuse the boundaries of other people's time and energy.

The researchers described the final 10 per cent of the sample as *disorganized*. These were the children of chaotic and troubled households – for instance, where one or both parents was abusing drugs or alcohol. The babies' response was predominantly one of fear, often cringing from the mother, alternately crying and trying to avoid contact. These babies typically grow up unable to attach or relate to others. In effect their ability to create emotional connections with others has collapsed. Such people are unlikely to have successful careers and are more likely than those with any of the other types of pattern to end up in prison or with serious mental health problems. They have been severely damaged, often responding impulsively and unwisely to others, overly dependent as teenagers on peers who are products of the same type of upbringing. Every once in a while you might meet someone like this as a client, usually because they have been able to see the damage done to them by their childhood and have been able to re-invent themselves, maybe with the help of a therapist.

The nature versus nurture debate is still alive and well and you may be wondering what part genetics plays in all of this. Clearly it plays an important part, but many of the writers and researchers in this area comment that such attachment prototypes seem to be universal and happen independently of genetic links.

All of this research and its links with patterns laid down in the brain demonstrates how important it is in coaching to accept that we have the whole person in the room with us. It also indicates that wherever feasible we should ask clients for an autobiographical account (see page 107 for some suggested questions), even though we know that the hippocampus, the seat of memory, does not develop properly until we are 7 or 8 years old, so we will have implicit rather than explicit memories of life before that time. Following this path will show us – and the client – not only what happened in the client's early life, but also how the client is interpreting these events. The hopeful feature of all of this is that it is the story you tell yourself that governs how you respond. A client who told me a doleful tale of her life in a succession of foster families was able to reframe this in coaching as surviving the emotional wasteland in which she had grown up. She had been able to make a happy marriage and to form strong attachments with her own children. Another, a gifted paediatrician, had experienced several traumas in childhood.

His mother had left the family home when he was 6, his father had then married a woman who was hostile to the existing children and this client had also had successive surgeries for an orthopaedic problem. He said that he had become a paediatrician precisely because he knew how it felt to be lonely and frightened as a child.

Summary of implications for coaches

Neuroscience is young and all of its current conclusions must be seen as tentative: hints, beginnings, shadows, suggestions, hypotheses. New material is emerging all the time. Little is known for sure, but it is not a field we can ignore.

- The stimulus to engage in coaching is rational: it involves the left prefrontal cortex. In coaching we need to keep this part of the brain engaged for as much as possible of the coaching session while also accepting the supreme importance of emotions. It makes no sense whatsoever to avoid emotion – for instance, by being too embarrassed to ask how a client feels. It is feelings that will get in the way of change and feelings that will liberate the energy for change.
- The role of the amygdala and its long memory justifies why it is important to enquire into the client's childhood.
- Giving advice will alert the amygdala to 'danger' as will setting a goal that is too big and therefore overwhelming. A 'small steps' approach to goals is more likely to enable the client to manage their emotional responses more rationally.
- A playful, optimistic tone in at least some parts of the coaching will engage the right hemisphere, the seat of creativity.
- Far from dreading the 'dependency' of our clients we need to build emotional connection with them. It is through dependency on someone dependable that we become centred and whole in childhood and we can mirror this process in coaching. Empathy is a biological as well as a social phenomenon.
- We need to be aware that the main reason change is far more difficult than it seems is that the whole brain is heavily involved in preventing change (e.g. if the change involves confronting negative emotional patterns learnt from the past).
- The threat response of the brain to social challenges uses the same circuits as threats to physical survival and this is why the emotions involved are so intense.
- We may often be working with clients who over-rely on the left hemisphere, the centre of logic and objectivity, at the expense of the

right hemisphere, the part of the brain which manages empathy and self-awareness.

- A distressed client cannot engage either the left or the right prefrontal cortex and may benefit from learning dissociation techniques as well as self-calming approaches.
- Visualization is powerful – all coaches should learn how to do it with and for clients, and for themselves.
- Since there is no such thing as 'objective reality', exploring limiting beliefs and assumptions is vital to making permanent positive changes; therefore all coaches need to have a suite of approaches for doing this.
- Introducing the idea of stimulus and response and the 'nanosecond of choice' enables the client to stop assuming that they 'can't help' their emotional reactions. Unless they have brain damage, they *can* control their responses. All of us can learn how to bring the prefrontal cortex into play more deliberately and earlier.
- The SCARF model shows how fragile our sense of wellbeing can be and to me it suggests once more the importance of creating trust with clients. Trust will be breached if we do anything that threatens the status, sense of certainty, autonomy, need for relatedness and sense of fairness between ourselves and our clients. It is why it is so fundamental to act on the belief in partnership and the assumption that clients are resourceful people who can make their own decisions.
- We are as much affected by all of the above as our clients, so our first task is to manage this stuff in ourselves.

Note

1   I was given this idea by Professor Paul Brown. It will appear in its full glory in his forthcoming book.

3 Creating trust: foundation values and practices for coaches

A coaching conversation is unlike most other discussions. It involves a high level of trust and candour on both sides. Creating and sustaining this unusual environment is what gives coaching its power. To do it as a coach involves abandoning some of the normal conventions of conversation in our society and replacing them with high-level, alternative skills, all of them about communicating acceptance and respect. In this chapter I look at some foundation principles that are necessary to create trust, returning to the topic in more detail in Chapter 10.

The concept of choice in coaching

One of the ground precepts of coaching that I described in Chapter 1 (page 7) is a belief that the client is resourceful, can make choices and is responsible for him or herself. Underneath this belief are the fundamental principles of choice and self-responsibility. Making these principles explicit has been the great gift of mainstream twentieth-century psychology to the world. They are the foundation, for instance, of the Transactional Analysis (TA) school: that whatever misery and dysfunction there is in your life, you can transform yourself through conscious choice. Its underlying assumption is similar to many in other schools of psychological thinking: human beings, uniquely among animals, are able to look to the future, therefore we are not the prisoners of our past.

The American psychologist Will Schutz, developer of the personality questionnaire FIRO-B™, also skilfully articulated these principles, though from a different perspective. Schutz took the concept of choice to its ultimate in his book *The Truth Option* (1984: 18): 'I choose my whole life and I always have. I choose my behaviour, my feelings, my thoughts, my illnesses, my body, my reactions, and my spontaneity.'

Schutz's philosophy was that choice is not a moral concept, only one which has consequences. If you assume that you can make choices then you take responsibility for your life. You bring areas that are unconscious into the areas of consciousness. For instance, you may feel afraid of your own violent or sexual feelings but your overtly expressed values do not allow you to admit this to yourself. You conceal your fears in hearty condemnation of people who do indulge their violence or sexuality.

Similarly, if you express fear of your boss or a colleague, there may be no objective reason at all for the fear; your real fear is of being unable to cope. If you see others as the cause of your fear then you will spend a lot of time and energy criticizing, trying to change others or avoiding them. Equally, your life may be filled by anticipation of being humiliated, ignored or rejected, regardless of whether this is actually likely or not. Once you see that the fear is in you, you can work on your ability to cope: a very different strategy, and one that is at the heart of coaching. Essentially, coaching is about the client becoming aware of, staying aware of, and being in control of, their own power.

Avoiding the principle of choice always involves a pay-off. For instance, if I take a lofty line on people who abuse their power, then my pay-off is that I hope to be seen as morally superior. If I claim that the organization is causing me hideous stress by overworking me, my pay-off is that I am a victim and will attract sympathy, attention and possibly financial compensation as well. If I claim to be confused then people may excuse my inability to make a decision. Schutz stressed that accepting the principle of choice does not involve blame, either of yourself or others. At its heart it involves taking responsibility for yourself.

Similarly, you cannot take responsibility for others. I sometimes challenge clients to show me how they could actually *make* someone else happy or unhappy. No client has yet been able to show me how this could happen. We all choose how we respond to any stimulus, often at an unconscious level, but we choose nonetheless. When you take inappropriate responsibility for others, you will quickly get to burnout – something familiar to all experienced coaches whose clients describe the stress that accompanies believing that you have to do everything yourself. This idea also explains the importance of avoiding asking clients 'How did that *make* you feel?' No one can *make* you feel anything and asking the question that way implies that others are responsible for the client's emotional wellbeing. A better question is 'How did that feel?'

If you really accept that people are resourceful then you have to believe in the concept of choice. It follows that you can't be a victim, or be brainwashed or manipulated. As Schutz commented, 'Nothing is stressful to me unless I interpret it as stressful.'

This concept has never been more powerfully illustrated than by the Austrian psychiatrist and neurologist Viktor Frankl in his moving book *Man's Search for Meaning* (1959). Frankl was imprisoned in Auschwitz and other camps during the Holocaust in conditions that were at the most extreme edge of anything human beings can be asked to bear. He did not know whether his wife and family had survived (his wife, mother, father and brother in fact all died in the camps). He had been imprisoned purely on grounds of his Jewishness and stripped of his professional identity, his clothes and even the hair on his head by his Nazi captors. He was ill, cold, malnourished, surrounded by desperate and dying people, forced to do brutally hard physical work and in constant fear of being murdered. Yet in his book he describes feeling that although his captors had physical liberty, he had more freedom:

> . . . there were always choices to make. Every day, every hour, offered the opportunity to make a decision, a decision which determined whether you would or would not submit to those powers which threatened to rob you of your very self, your inner freedom; which determined whether or not you would become the plaything of circumstance.
>
> (Frankl 1959: 87)

Frankl chose to separate himself mentally from his surroundings. At one stage he had a vision of himself after the war, giving lectures and writing about his experiences. This sustained him and saved him from the 'give-up-itis' described by the Allied soldiers who eventually liberated the camps. They observed that many former prisoners simply lost their will to live. In Schutz's terms, they chose to die. Viktor Frankl chose to live. After the war he founded a still-thriving Institute devoted to his own version of psychotherapy, 'Logo-therapy', wrote many more books and died full of honours in 1997 at the age of 92.

One way of defining coaching is that it is about raising self-awareness as a precursor to exposing the nature of the choices we are making. Realizing that we have choices is in itself powerfully motivating, rather than assuming that the default choice (do nothing), of which we are often unaware, is all that is possible. At the same time, never underestimate how frightening this idea can be when you have hidden inside a belief that somehow others are responsible for your happiness. Most of us secretly or overtly want to have at least a little or a lot of dependency on others and simultaneously want at least a little or a lot of autonomy. If you feel you have cracked this conundrum you are lucky indeed because few of us have.

You insist, I resist

Coaching is about drawing out intrinsic human resourcefulness. It follows, then, that if you do genuinely believe in the resourcefulness of your clients, you will have to find alternatives to giving advice. So the first step to establishing trust is to abandon advice-giving as a coaching tactic.

This is easy to say and to write, but it is probably the single most difficult task for a coach. Many people who become coaches have had earlier jobs where they have been paid to give advice. Their professional training has positioned them as specialists and a great deal of their professional identity is invested in being an expert.

For instance, human resource specialists are trained to tell managers what the employment law is and to help them avoid making catastrophic mistakes when hiring and firing staff. Doctors are trained to know more than their patients about the human body. Accountants are trained to interpret balance sheets and to give clients the benefit of their advice on personal finance. So when confronted with the messy and sprawling issues that clients bring to coaching, inside, the coach may be thinking:

> It's my job to find the solution for this client – I'll have failed if I don't.

> I can't bear this client's pain and confusion. I need to help her by telling her what I think she should do.

> It's so obvious – he needs to do x or y.

If advice worked as a helping tactic, it might be possible to make a case for it as a prime approach to coaching. However, it doesn't.

Think for a moment about something you do which is generally acknowledged to be unwise. This might be something like smoking, drinking more than the recommended number of units of alcohol a week, driving too fast on the motorway, eating unwisely, being over- or underweight for your height, not taking advantage of health-screening services or getting too little rest. Now imagine a good friend is giving you advice on the topic.

This is what typically happens:

You:	I'd really like to give up smoking, but it's so hard!
Helpful friend:	Yes, you should you know, it's the one way we can reduce the risks of heart disease – and think of the money you're wasting!
You:	Yes, I know, but it's so hard to do.
Helpful friend:	The best way to do it is to go cold turkey.
You:	Mmm, I tried that four years ago and it didn't work so I don't think I can do that.
Helpful friend:	You could! My friend Emma went to a wonderful hypnotherapist and she stopped straight away. Has never had a fag since.
You:	Yes, but that's Emma. It may have worked for her but I don't think I could do it just like that.
Helpful friend:	Yes you could.
You:	Well I'm not ready yet.
Helpful friend:	(gives up in exasperation).

In this example, you and the helpful friend are playing the 'Yes, but' game. The friend makes a suggestion and you say, 'Good idea – but . . .' The chances that you will give up smoking on the basis of this conversation are nil.

The reasons are that, first, however well meant the advice may be, being the recipient of it is probably creating feelings of anger and guilt. No one enjoys being told to change something they already know they should change, so all your energy is going into repelling the advice. When you feel you are being told what to do, your first response is virtually always to defend your existing position. In neurobiological terms, your amygdala is alerted and is ready to resist (see Chapter 2). It becomes impossible to listen carefully to what the other person is saying, however sensible it is.

Second, it is most unlikely that you will not have heard this advice before, as the reasons that people continue to smoke have little to do with ignorance of its long-term effects. Third, the tone of the conversation precludes any real honesty on your part. It will guarantee that you withhold the most important aspects of the issue for you. It neither gets to the reasons why you smoke nor taps into any of the reasons that you might want to stop. Most seriously, the conversation implies that your friend is a well-adjusted human being whereas you are a bit of a sad addict, so, however well meant, the conversation could undermine your confidence.

Furthermore, you have to live with the results of the advice, not your friend. If you do take your friend's advice and it all goes horribly wrong – for instance, days of cold-turkey-hell where your relationships temporarily collapse under the searing anger and misery of withdrawing so suddenly from tobacco, the friend is a handy scapegoat: 'He/she made me do it'. If the advice turns out well, then it reinforces the notion that other people have more willpower, are cleverer, more able and more decisive.

Even at its most apparently straightforward, advice-giving actually runs a significant risk of being ignored. Doctors are respected professionals who complete a long training before being let loose on us, their patients. Their advice carries genuine authority. Yet research has shown that between a quarter and a third of all prescriptions are either never taken to the pharmacy or remain in the patient's bathroom cabinet.

Some advice-giving is about control. Think about the most recent time when you passed on a piece of advice and ask yourself how far it was really an attempt to control the other person through the apparently benign process of giving advice. If you are the parent of a teenager, for instance, this is a particular trap. The wish to save our children from the distressing consequences of their inexperience often leads to a deluge of do-it-my-way counsel. This can be interpreted by its recipient, quite accurately, as an attempt to maintain parental control and can have two sorts of undesirable consequence: meek, under-confident adults who lack robust assertiveness or, at the other extreme, compulsive rebels, still psychologically fighting their parents even in middle age.

Advice-giving can feel generous. It can come from a warm heart. When a client expresses misery, it can be tempting to take refuge in expressing fellow feeling through describing something similar that happened to you. Reading your own biography into a client's concerns is dangerous for any number of good reasons. Most obviously, you are not the client. However similar your situations may appear, the client's history, personality and circumstances are totally different so his or her responses and choices will also be different. In addition, the client may very well have held back the most important aspect of his or her situation. Here is an example.

CASE STUDY
Penny (coach) and Michael (client)

Penny was coaching Michael, a middle-manager client inside her organization. He came for help on how to move his career on. By the end of their second session, Penny was becoming increasingly puzzled: Michael said he wanted another job, yet he seemed reluctant to think broadly about the possibilities. Penny knew the organization and the whole sector well. She could see that Michael had considerable ability and was outgrowing his current role. She told him that she sympathized. In her own career she said she had hit a similar plateau, saying that in her case she had made a sideways move. This involved taking a job in the same company but in a different city. This had worked for her, so surely it would work for him?

The coaching ended after its scheduled three sessions with Michael politely thanking her for her help and Penny acutely puzzled. She was aware that the coaching had not been effective. A year later Penny discovered that Michael's wife, also a manager in the organization, was seriously ill with motor neurone disease. At the time of the coaching the illness had been diagnosed but Michael's wife had asked him not to tell colleagues. Staying put geographically was important because they both felt it guaranteed the continuation of the excellent medical care she was receiving.

In reviewing this work with her supervisor, Penny realized that the turning point in the coaching, guaranteeing its failure, was this apparently bland piece of advice-giving, wrapped up as help. She had not been able to establish sufficient trust with Michael to enable him to tell her of his wife's illness. And at the point where this might have been possible she, in her own words, 'blew it'.

Saying 'Something just like that happened to me' can seem like a good idea. It is a disclosure and may therefore seem as if it will create trust. Just occasionally it might. But far more often it seems to be saying, 'This worked for me so it will work for you. Do it my way.' It suggests that you are not really listening because you are queuing to speak – telling your story is more important than listening to the client's. My friend and colleague Phil Hayes enjoys recounting an achingly bizarre example of this tendency:

Friend 1:   How are you – haven't seen you for a long time?
Friend 2:   No, I've just recovered from meningitis. It was awful and I've only just come out of hospital. In fact I nearly died.
Non-listening Friend: Oh – I nearly died once.

Less extreme examples of the same behaviour run the risk of appearing to trivialize the client's concerns by not exploring them. Common responses to other people's distress or worry include clichés such as:

Don't worry, time will heal.

There, there . . .

Buck up – it's not that bad!

You'll get other chances.

Plenty more pebbles on the beach/fish in the sea.

Least said, soonest mended

. . . and so on.

Coaching as rescuing

The human impulse to care for the vulnerable has obviously been essential to our survival as a species. Human infants with their prolonged period of defencelessness need the kind and skilled care of adults. Adults are programmed to respond to overt dependency with tenderness.

I still remember the overwhelming emotion of looking at my tiny firstborn, seriously ill at 10 days old in what looked like a huge cot at University College Hospital in London. His survival was the only thing that could possibly matter, then or ever. Less traumatically, I still remember the fierceness of my response when faced with a tearful 8-year-old saying, 'Mum, Stephen says he'll break my arm if I don't do what he says.' Charities ruthlessly exploit these innate feelings with explicit bids which tap into our urge to rescue. 'Ten pounds will provide clean water/a week's schooling for this appealing child.' 'Twenty pounds will save this donkey/dog/cat from starvation.' Appealing to this instinct is necessary for successful parenting and probably for charity fundraising, but it is a false trail in coaching.

If you step in as rescuer with clients, you deny them their ownership of the issue. By rescuing, you actively or by implication behave as if you feel they are too frail to solve the problem themselves. This can happen when clients are overwhelmed by their anxiety. They pour out their hearts, telling you how unbearable it is to be burdened by such problems. The pressure to help by finding a solution for them can feel monumental. There are two equally unhelpful ways to respond:

- The client spills out his or her anxiety and the coach simply listens and empathizes, without asking the questions which move the client on. This hand-me-down love results in the client skipping away feeling temporarily lighter, though without having increased his or her capacity to solve such problems in the future. The coach, by contrast, feels unbearably stressed: the client has successfully transferred all the anxiety.
- The client asks the coach to find a solution. The client implements the suggested solution and looks to the coach for answers to similar questions in the future. The coach quickly gets to be seen as *managing* the client and the client is subtly demeaned in their own and others' eyes.

Sometimes the client will make an overt request for rescuing. Here is an example.

CASE STUDY
Maria (coach) and Richard (client)

Maria was coaching Richard, a client who was in dispute with his organization. He had applied for a number of jobs unsuccessfully and was now on its *At Risk* list, meaning that unless he found another job within an agreed length of time, a redundancy process would be triggered. Richard had also registered a grievance about his boss's behaviour, alleging bullying.

Maria was finding it hard going with Richard. He frequently broke down in their sessions. When asked to name his goals for the coaching sessions, Maria described him as giving vague answers which essentially amounted to 'I need a shoulder to cry on.' Richard also lavished Maria with compliments, for instance about how easy she was to talk to and about how well she understood the organization.

At their third session, Richard made a specific request. He wanted someone to accompany him to the informal meeting which would start the grievance process. 'You understand me so well,' he said, 'and I don't trust myself to give a good account of all this stuff at the meeting. Will you come with me?'

Maria is in coaching because she likes people and wants to help. She understood Richard's vulnerability because she had been in an apparently similar situation herself. However, she knew that she had to resist because by accepting she would have been colluding with Richard's belief that he was powerless. Agreeing would have implied 'You really are in a bad way'; 'I can step in and look after you'.

Maria wisely refused Richard's invitation, seeing that her true role as Richard's coach was to tackle his lack of self-belief. One of the ways she was able to do this was to help him prepare so that he could represent himself at the meeting with skill and confidence. If she had fallen into the trap he had laid for her, she would also have been stepping spectacularly outside her coaching role. Appearing as an *advocate* for Richard would have made it impossible in subsequent coaching sessions for her to have given him the robust feedback, challenge and confrontation that he needed, in addition to the empathetic support that she was already providing.

You are at risk of rescuing when you find yourself thinking or doing any of the following:

What would they do without me?

I'm not looking forward to this session; it'll be round and round the same loop.

I don't think they are going to get this right – their old pattern is going to assert itself yet again.

Impatience: why can't they just do what I say?

Making harsh judgements about the client's capacity.

Believing that if you were in their shoes you'd do the job better.

Toying with the idea of actively intervening in the client's system on their behalf.

Rescuing implies that the client is a victim and if you act on the impulse to do it, it will for certain undermine the client. If you do rescue, you may also find that the 'victim' turns on you: 'You didn't rescue me cleverly enough!'

In general, when you lose faith in the ability of clients to solve their own problems, you are losing faith in the coaching process, thus ensuring that it fails. That is why it is so important to avoid all the many ways in which we can subtly dishearten our clients through giving advice.

What if clients ask for advice?

Every now and then a client will ask for advice outright:

> What do you think?
>
> If you were me, what would you do?

Where you are holding back your advice with extreme difficulty, this can be a seductive invitation. What you do depends on the circumstances because nothing in coaching is an absolute rule.

An experienced client will even challenge you on your home territory:

> Come on, I know coaching isn't about advice, but I'm actually begging you to tell me what to do!

There are any number of possible ways you can avoid the advice-giving trap when invited to fall into it by a client.

- Ask the client, respectfully what it would do for them to know what you would do. This challenges a client's belief that the answer is 'out there' rather than in themselves.
- Say, 'I could tell you what I would do, but you and I are very different people, so I'm not sure that would help. The answer you come up with yourself is the one that will work for you.'
- Say, 'I will tell you, but let's explore what ideas you have first,' by which time the client has usually lost interest in hearing the advice.
- Avoid a direct answer and go straight to a dilemma-solving technique such as identifying all the options and then rating them all for pluses and minuses.

Conditions that need to be in place to give advice

There are occasions when it is appropriate to give advice. Here are some of the conditions that need to be in place before offering it:

- There are clear right/wrong answers to a question the client is asking – e.g. on the legal, medical or financial position.
- It is a crisis and needs rapid action.
- The client's physical, financial or mental wellbeing will be in danger without having the piece of advice.
- The client is not in a position to make their own decisions – for instance, may be temporarily overwhelmed by the impact of some crisis.
- You are offering facts, not opinions.
- The client has specifically asked for information and has made it clear that they will make up their own mind on how to use it.
- The subject is genuinely bewildering and needs expert guidance for the client to be able to understand it. You have unquestionable expertise, rather than just another personal opinion, in the area on which the client is seeking advice.
- Giving the advice is unlikely to create dependency, to humiliate or to encourage unwise optimism.
- Your own motivation does not include any of the following:
  - a wish to impress and show off
  - wanting to control
  - being too lazy to use coaching techniques
  - feeling a need to pay the client back for some slight.

Even here you need to be careful. It is always better to offer what you say as *information*, making it clear that the client has to make up their mind about using it to make a decision and positively inviting the client to comment: 'These are the facts as I see them, but what do you think?' Or, 'This is the law on this point but what's your reaction to hearing that?' It may also be helpful to suggest that the client might like a second opinion, checking out your advice with another expert.

In practice, these guidelines can seem fuzzy. Here is an example.

CASE STUDY

Liz (client) and John (coach)

Liz had lost her local authority chief officer job because of a merger. As her coach, John had helped her come to terms with the initial shock. She had a strong commitment to public sector work and thought initially that she wanted to stay inside local government. John and Liz revamped her CV and also did some interview coaching. She soon landed an offer for an interesting-sounding change-management job in a profit-making organization allied to her old specialism. This did wonders for her battered self-esteem but she still felt her heart was in the public sector and that perhaps she wanted to be a chief officer again after all. But did she want it or not? At an emergency coaching session she and John looked at the upsides and downsides of accepting or rejecting the job, including the possibility that in a tight jobs market this was likely to be the best offer she would get. She was still no clearer about whether to accept or not.

The next day she was on the phone for perhaps an hour of agonizing. 'I want you to tell me what to do,' she begged. True to the principles described above, John said that he could not do that. The core of John's dilemma was that privately he strongly felt that she should accept as it was probably the best offer she was likely to get in her current market.

She turned the job down.

Three months later she still did not have a permanent job and was miserably doing a series of temporary projects. She bitterly regretted having rejected the private sector job.

So should John have 'told' Liz to accept? Of course he, too, agonized about this, but came to the conclusion that he was right to stick to his principles. First, there was no knowing whether she would have taken any notice of his advice. There was a strong chance that if she had accepted the job she would have been as unhappy and regretful about leaving the public sector as about her eventual decision to try and stay in it. As part of the coaching, she and John had examined all the options, including how realistic it was that she would be offered another local government job that she really wanted. It was her gamble, her life, and she made her choice.

In this case, as in all good coaching, John was clear that he was responsible *to* but not *for* the client.

Authentic listening

Genuine listening is about acceptance. Genuine listening is also rare. Mostly what we experience is pretend listening. One of the worst offenders I have known here was a former client of mine, in most other respects an excellent fellow, but who had a phenomenally low tolerance for boredom. He anticipated boredom in most conversations, so his coping tactics included roaming restlessly around his magnificent office, opening his fridge to take out a drink or a bar of chocolate, looking out of the window or adjusting the volume on the speakers of his iPod while all the time protesting, 'Go on, I'm listening . . .!', often while he had his back to his guest. As a way of ensuring that his visitors never stayed long, it was successful. As a way of communicating acceptance it was disastrous.

Rapport and congruence

Just as there are urban myths that sound plausible the first time you hear them, there are what I think of as *management trainer myths*. One of the most popular is that 'research' has demonstrated that X per cent (think of an extremely big number somewhere near 100) of all human communication is non-verbal. I have many times seen trainers proudly show PowerPoint pie charts demonstrating the alleged breakdown of percentages. The trouble is that there is no such research. If it were true then no one would ever need to learn a foreign language – we could just smile, scowl and gesticulate away. Despite this, the myth persists because it is so plausible. Like all other animals, we do indeed communicate non-verbally, though not on the scale suggested by naïve trainers whose myths have been treasured through several generations of predecessors. Teaching so-called 'body language' has become a cliché of management training courses, often reduced on these events to a trivialized exercise in mimicry of body posture.

I was reminded of this recently when I had an introductory gym session with a personal trainer. This young man leaked boredom. He said the right things and asked the right questions (though only when, it seemed, he had mentally jerked himself awake enough to remember them). His eye contact constantly wandered away from me and over my shoulder. His smile looked false. I knew with absolute certainty that his 'interest' in me was faked and my indignation at his discourtesy intruded unpleasantly into my ability to learn from what he was telling me. I daresay he had been on a course where he had been taught the 'techniques of rapport'. But rapport, congruence and empathy are not 'techniques'. They are *ways of being* with a client.

Real rapport is more than copying body posture, though two people who are actually in rapport will indeed mirror each other in how they are sitting or standing. When you are in rapport, you will be matching the other person: body, voice volume, breathing, gesture, space, language, pace and energy. You are entering that person's world. 'Mirror neurons' (see page 43) will be doing their work. To an observer it will look like an elegant dance, first one leading and then the other. In an ideal world this would happen naturally. The coach's world is often not ideal because all kinds of intrusions make it difficult to sustain rapport.

Real rapport comes from unconditional acceptance of the client. This is not the same as liking the client, though in practice you will probably come to like the majority of your clients. When you unconditionally accept a client you will be congruent and when you are congruent you will be in rapport.

Unconditional acceptance means that you are curious about the client. You want to know what it is like to inhabit their emotional world. You accept not just the nice bits – that is, the admirable parts, the behaviours that spring from values just like your own – but the parts that are less admirable and about which the client may feel ashamed or worried. Most of us grow up learning that acceptance is conditional. Some examples might be that love and acceptance depend on being nice to people all the time and putting their needs first; being quietly spoken and modest or alternatively lively and entertaining, always smiling; being 100 per cent successful 100 per cent of the time. An important part of the coaching process is to uncover what these conditional assumptions are – I describe some approaches to this in Chapter 7.

Coaching works when it offers clients the opportunity to discover that they can be valued as a whole – moving past the conditional assumptions that have cramped their growth. The coach will not judge. This is so rare in our society that clients may doubt at first whether they can trust it; hence the cautious feel that many first and second sessions have. It does mean, of course, that as a coach you have to know, deal with and move beyond your own assumptions about what is 'worthy' and what is not. If you cannot, you will find yourself *simulating* congruence instead of *being* congruent – a distinction immediately obvious to any client.

Ten traps: when rapport and congruence break down

These are the 10 most common reasons for loss of congruence.

Fear
The coach fears not being good enough and fear floods the internal system. Extreme self-consciousness then prevents the coach from managing the rapport at a conscious or unconscious level. There may be some congruence and rapport but unfortunately it will consist of the client leading the coach most of the time, rather than the graceful *pas de deux* that happens when there is genuine rapport.

Overwhelming need for the client to like you
We all need to like and be liked, but if the wish to be liked gets out of hand it will prevent you challenging appropriately. This feeling again arises from fear and lack of self-confidence. 'If I challenge, this client won't like me.' In ordinary conversation with friends we may have cheerful disputes, but in general we keep profound disagreements to ourselves – and most probably select our friends because they share our opinions and prejudices. A coach often has to disagree, but the disagreement comes from the security of knowing that when it is done respectfully it will be totally acceptable to the client and you will maintain rapport and congruence.

Believing you already know

The client starts their account and the coach immediately jumps to the conclusion that they already know the answer. 'I've heard all this before', or 'I know what he/she should do'. As soon as this thought kicks in, you stop listening.

Judgement

The coach cannot suspend judgement about some perceived aspect of the client – maybe their profession ('I never did like journalists/bankers/estate agents'), their values, their clothing, their nationality, race, religion or their personality. This sort of disapproval, that originates in prejudice, will leak out in all kinds of ways and is usually perfectly apparent to the client.

Imposing actual or implied values onto the client

The coach dominates the process with values that overwhelm because they are projected so strongly through their behaviour, normally through showing enhanced or withdrawn attention. This imposes new restrictive conditions on the client so that the client feels, 'I am only valued when I talk about my successes', or 'This coach likes it best when I cry', or 'I feel I have to over-dramatize my problems – that's what he/she seems to respond to'. Forcing the client into incongruity in order to please the coach is one sure way to damage the coaching process.

Psychologizing and interpreting

The coach attributes simple behaviours to some past trauma ('I can see that this reminds you of your abusive father') or to heavy underlying significance, when in fact they are just simple behaviours.

Compulsive explaining

The coach loves to offer the client little box and arrow diagrams which encapsulate his or her pet theories; interrupts the client in order to offer endless potted versions of favourite management or psychology textbooks.

The wish to reform the client

The coach sees that the client has certain unhealthy or undesirable habits such as smoking, over-eating, working too hard, not exercising enough and cannot refrain from offering suggestions about people who might help – or new wonder-methods of controlling the pesky habit.

Preoccupation on the coach's part

The coach has so many issues going on in their own life that it is impossible to concentrate on the client.

Unawareness on the coach's part

The coach does not know that they are fixed in particular ways of talking and communicating. For instance, when training coaches, one of the most common ways that I notice an inexperienced coach gets this subtly or dramatically wrong is in mismatching the client's pace. The client is languid in style but the coach is energetic – or vice versa. Another example would be that the client has an unusually quiet voice, but the coach remains loud. Yet another might be that the client's language shows a liking for a particular sort of metaphor but the coach does not spot it and uses his or her own version of the same words instead.

All of the above are bigger and more common traps than you might suppose. Success as a coach always involves high levels of self-awareness and ruthlessly exposing yourself to your own prejudices and assumptions. In just the last few weeks I have worked as supervisor and trainer to three relatively experienced coaches who ruefully discovered that their coaching had been less effective than they had hoped:

> The coach had had a highly successful career in banking as one of the few women to make it to the top. Working with a much younger woman client also in banking, she found herself responding disapprovingly to the client's decision to prioritize a personal relationship with a man rather than ruthlessly pursuing her career.

> An American coach confessed to being lured into arguing with a British client about healthcare systems in the two countries.

> A doctor coach with strongly-held feminist principles was coaching a more junior fellow doctor for the first time and realized she had felt instant prejudice on the basis that her Muslim client was wearing the *hijab*.

Real congruence starts with a buoyant and sincere wish to understand the other person – to see the world as they see it. At the same time you have to be self-aware and self-accepting, letting your own barriers down, free of the need to defend yourself. When you no longer fear others you will not feel the need to protect yourself from difference and when you are able to do this you will probably find that everything else follows. You may also have to accept that there will indeed be times when your own values and the values of the client are at odds in ways that make it impossible to work on the issue they present. You can respect the client's right to hold such values, work on understanding the values, and also reserve the right to say 'no' (see page 220).

Mismatches

When you mismatch someone, you break rapport. Sometimes it is possible to mismatch without there being any malign intention, but the client may easily misinterpret what they see. For instance:

- fiddling with your watch, pen or ring may suggest impatience;
- looking at a clock or watch may seem to imply that you want to move on to something else;
- staring unblinkingly at the other person can seem aggressive;
- waggling your foot may suggest nervousness or impatience;
- sitting with crossed arms can look as if you are defending yourself against the other person's ideas;
- sitting with crossed legs; sitting hunched may look as if you are trying to make yourself smaller and therefore as if you lack confidence;
- turning your chair slightly away from the other person may seem to indicate a lack of interest or (depending on other body language) lack of confidence;
- sitting back in your chair when the other person is sitting forward may suggest lack of involvement;
- touching your face while talking can imply timidity, especially if the hand is actually in front of the mouth;
- rubbing your nose, looking away – some people feel this indicates lying;
- scowling or frowning may look like disapproval though for many people this is just a habit they have got into when concentrating;
- avoiding eye contact can look like lack of interest or of confidence.

Constant mismatching will distract and dismay your client. But occasionally a deliberate piece of mismatching is very useful. Here is an example from a colleague.

CASE STUDY
Jane

I had been asked to coach Jane, a senior television producer whose boss reported that she could not manage her team. Allegedly, Jane's influencing tactics could be reduced to one style: tell people what to do and if they don't do it, bawl at them. Jane appeared for an introductory discussion looking distinctly hostile with 'What's all this about?' and 'I don't want to be here' conveyed in every aspect of her appearance.

Throughout the meeting, Jane huddled in her chair with her shoulders pointing away from me, avoiding eye contact and radiating anger with an abrupt and loud voice. Feeling uncomfortable, I made a conscious attempt to match her posture and voice volume. After 10 minutes I deliberately broke whatever rapport there was, sat up energetically in my chair, then immediately softened my voice and slowed it down, asking her to tell me about the feelings that this apparent organizational assault on her confidence was creating for her. It was hard to keep doing this conscious mismatching in the face of such resolute resistance. However, after a few minutes, she slowly swivelled around to face me for the first time and her own voice dropped. We were then in genuine rapport for the first time, and the real conversation could begin.

Mismatching is also useful when you want to punctuate a coaching session by moving from one agenda topic to another, or where the client appears to have got stuck in a mood that does not seem helpful. Sometimes this break can be something as obvious as 'Why don't we get up and have another cup of coffee?', or just a more subtle change in your own posture and energy level.

Is this manipulation? No, because to work it depends on your thoroughgoing commitment to 100 per cent respect for and curiosity about your client.

The three levels of listening

It would be rare to confess to being a poor listener – about as rare as owning up to being a bad driver or to having no sense of humour. However, coaches can't afford the luxury of self-delusion. A high standard of hard-nosed honesty is the only possible tactic.

I like the framework proposed by the Coaches Training Institute because it allows for a hierarchy of listening effectiveness, all of which depends on the self-awareness of the coach. It is described in an excellent book by Laura Whitworth, Henry Kimsey-House and Phil Sandahl, *Co-active Coaching* (1998) and like many other coaching concepts it has its origins in psychotherapy.

Level 1

This is the client's level. As the client you are self-absorbed. You don't have to worry about anything except getting your story out. As a client this level is fine. As a coach it is disastrous. You will be thinking about yourself, not the client. Signs that you are at Level 1 include:

- finding yourself asking the client for more facts: 'how many; when; who; what's the structure; what's the history', when the client hasn't mentioned them;
- noticing that you are getting flustered, that your inner dialogue is about your own anxiety:
  - What can I ask next?
  - Was that a good enough question?
  - Will this last for the whole session?
  - Does the client like me?
- wanting to give advice;
- talking about yourself: lots of I and me.

Sample Level 1 conversation

Client: I need to get better at delegating. I'm working 70 hours a week at the moment.

Coach: Yes, that's really not a good idea; you'll wear yourself out.

Client: But I can't really see what else I can do, we're so busy.

Coach: You'll probably find the whole way you're doing it is a bit wrong. I've got a really good handout I can show you. It's worked for lots of clients so it should work for you.

Client: Mmm, well . . .

Coach: It starts from an analysis of how you typically spend your day. I've got a sample here. Shall we work on it now?

In this example, the coach is over-concerned to position herself as the expert. She wants to be helpful, but she is not listening because her own agenda is getting in the way and she has resorted to giving advice before she has established what the client wants.

Level 2

At Level 2, coach and client are seamlessly locked into an absorbing and intensely concentrated conversation. They are most definitely in rapport, their body posture, voices and energy levels subtly matched. The conversation will flow but the client will be doing most of the talking. The coach's questions are skilful, picking up on the language the client has used, working exclusively from the client's agenda and never giving advice. The questions explore, clarify, summarize and probe, always extending the client's thinking and willingness to learn something new. As the coach you hear what is not being said as well as what is. You are listening for the underlying meanings and are aware of your own impact on the client.

If you can remain at Level 2 for most of a coaching session you are doing well: it is the level at which the majority of effective coaching takes place.

Sample Level 2 conversation

Client: I need to get better at delegating. I'm working 70 hours a week at the moment.

Coach: That sounds tough. How should we work on this?

Client: Well, I think I'm doing it OK, but my staff tell me I'm not. I don't know what they mean really. I find myself getting anxious about it.

Coach: What exactly do they say to you?

Client: An example would be that my assistant tells me I'm constantly checking up on her, but how else am I supposed to find out how things are going?

Coach: Checking up . . . So that's her feedback. 'Finding out what's going on . . .' And you say you're getting anxious about it. Do you want to stay with this one as a useful example?

Client: Yes, OK.

Coach: So what's this anxiety about, exactly?

Here the coach is following the client's agenda scrupulously, using his words, deepening the conversation and generating useful data for the conversation that follows.

Level 3

At Level 3 you are doing what has been described as 'radio-field listening', aware not just of everything that is happening at Level 2, but also of the emotion, of the risks it might be possible to take in the conversation, of the underlying choices and of what could be at stake for the client. You trust your intuition. You feel connected with the client at an emotional as well as an intellectual level, even if no emotion has been named. You see the whole coaching relationship stretching out behind and in front of you and it feels special. These are moments of real connection – of a kind that few of us ever reach in a 'normal' conversation with a friend.

Sample Level 3 conversation

Client: I need to get better at delegating. I'm working 70 hours a week at the moment.

Coach: That sounds tough. How should we work on this?

Client: (small silence and a laugh)

Coach: (gently) So? (another pause) That laugh sounds strained.

Client: (long hesitation) It is. I can't take this pace. My staff tell me I'm 'interfering', but I don't know how else to keep everything under control. It's ruining my personal life and if I don't watch it my health as well. My wife complains she never sees me and I don't know when I last put our daughter to bed because I'm home so late. I'm awake

every morning from 4.00 a.m. and then I can't get back to sleep worrying about work. It's an enormous strain.
(another silence)

Coach: So this is an enormous strain and it feels as if there's a huge amount at stake for you, job and home.

Client: Enormous. It's a burden I don't want.

Coach: Burden is a heavy-sounding word! What does that mean for you?

Client: Unbearable – literally, like a load I'm carrying and that I'd like to put down because I can't control it.

Coach: So this is about a burden you don't want and would like to put down. Shall we explore how you might do just that?

Through working at Level 3, the coach has established a whole-life perspective and has focused the client's mind on what is at stake through continuing to work so many hours. She has done this through listening for the silences and hesitations, by listening for the metaphor and for the emotion behind the words. She has left spaces inside the conversation which the client can fill if he wishes. By doing this she makes it clear that she neither condones nor condemns the long working week, but is simply accepting and respecting the position the client finds himself in. She has spotted the underlying need that the behaviour serves. By noticing the negative energy that his stress is creating she has also harnessed a willingness to begin the change process.

The therapist Fritz Perls had a phrase that I like when he talked about this level of listening. 'A good therapist doesn't listen to the content of the bullshit of what the patient produces, but to the sound, to the music, to the hesitations' (1969: 57).

Working from the client's agenda

Implicit in all of this is the assumption that it is the client's agenda that matters, not the coach's. The minute you stray into Level 1, you will be working from your agenda, not the client's. Coaching starts and finishes with the client's agenda. This is because coaching is about change. Clients come to coaching because they want to change their lives and get results which show that change has happened. Clients know their lives in a way that the coach never can, so only the client can say what the agenda for change is.

The coach's role is to ask the questions which uncover the client's agenda and make it explicit, turning this agenda into the goals which the client can work on and safeguarding it as the only agenda for the coaching. The coach links the agenda with the client's core values and beliefs and works with the client to identify and then move past the blocks and fears which are holding them back.

Being worthy of trust: a two-way process

As a coach, I ask my clients to trust me. I am always aware of what a huge assumption this is. Why should they trust me? What can I do to accelerate that trust? Equally, my starting place in the relationship is that I will trust them. Where trust is broken, it can of course be repaired, but as with a piece of shattered china, the repair will always be there, even if apparently invisible, and it will never be so strong as it was when unbroken.

Trust may grow slowly, depending on the skill of the coach and the willingness of the client to be open. This is hard for many clients. They have become accustomed to defensiveness and sometimes to performance. Realizing that they do not have to perform for you is often the turning point in the effectiveness of the coaching: realizing they really can trust you with their failures and uncertainties and that you will not condemn or judge. Equally, they realize that you will acknowledge their achievements and their efforts to change.

As with so many other issues in coaching, this is a two-way process. What does trust really involve? The answers must be honesty, predictability, commitment and reliability.

The client's side in creating trust

First, the client is consistent in what he or she says. When the client describes a particular set-up, they will describe it in roughly the same way each time. If I get to see the client in action with their team, I will see the situation they have described – plus a great deal more, but the client's tale will still ring true.

When clients commit to the process of coaching, this means treating the coach as respectfully as they expect to be treated themselves. In a healthy coaching relationship, what the client says and what the client does are one and the same. The commitment to the coaching is more than just words. If we agree 'homework' it is done and, even if it is not done, there will be learning in why it has been put to one side for the moment. When clients say that they will continue to ponder some theme we have discussed, they do. When they say they will give me candid feedback, they do. One of the specialist services I offer is weight loss coaching and the programme starts with the client getting a full assessment from their GP, including blood pressure and blood lipids. One client broke this trust when he assured me that he had been to his doctor and had emailed me the results. A few moments of discussion made it obvious that none of this had happened – and that was the swift end of the relationship.

What the client says outside the sessions is also important. What is said inside the sessions should be consistent with what is said outside. Where this is not the case, trust will be destroyed. An example of this happened to one of my colleagues who had coached an angry senior manager made redundant by his organization and still smarting from the hurt and rejection. My colleague had asked for feedback at the end of each session and the client said that he had found the sessions 'very useful' and spelt out the usefulness in some detail. Yet two weeks later my colleague heard that the client had described the coaching to a third party known to both of them as 'pointless navel-gazing'. When respectfully challenged about this at their next session, the client blustered and equivocated. Not surprisingly, that was their last session.

Clients gain my trust and respect where they are willing to give the coaching process a go. Signs that they are willing to do this would be, for instance, if they are ready to explore previously forbidden emotional areas or hear tough feedback and to sit out the resulting discomfort without attacking me as the bearer of bad news. Coaching demands an unusual degree of openness from both client and coach. Clients who are prepared to make themselves vulnerable through honest disclosure will earn my confidence.

Lack of commitment is betrayed in many large and small ways. For instance, a client who consistently cancels the date at the last moment for what seem like implausible reasons is indicating for sure that they do not give a high priority to the coaching. A client who arrives for sessions late, ill-prepared and bemused about the agenda tells you that their mind is on other things. Such clients could be showing that their interest in learning with you is fragile and may be waning.

The coach's side in creating trust

All of these conditions need to be equally present in the coach. The first step is to look at your own assumptions about how far you can trust the client. You don't need to like every client in the way that you would like a close friend – in fact it is impossible to do so. You will respect the many aspects of the client which are admirable, but will also be curious and interested in the many self-protective barriers which the client has skilfully erected around him- or herself.

Many clients may present initially as disagreeable people. For instance, a client who bullies or manipulates represents a style of management that I particularly dislike. However, I have worked successfully with many such clients, though I would not have lasted a week with them if they had been my boss. At the other end of the spectrum are the clients who lack assertiveness. They may be condemned by their colleagues as 'weak', or, more kindly, as 'lacking toughness'. With these clients, too, I can usually work well, yet if I worked with them as colleagues they might exasperate me.

What is the difference? As clients I am intrigued by their dilemmas and difficulties. I want to know what self-imposed barriers they have created to success. I accept their plusses, their quirks and failings unconditionally. My role is to encourage well-grounded belief in their own talents and resourcefulness. I don't have to like them in the way I need to like a close friend.

As a coach what you say and what you do have to be consistent. At the simplest level, you must deliver on your promises. If you say you will email an interesting article, you must do it. If you declare enthusiasm for coaching, you must be enthusiastic. You will give the client 100 per cent of your attention in every session, just as you expect 100 per cent attention back. It will be immediately obvious if you are drifting off or coaching on autopilot.

You will refer to clients respectfully outside the sessions, never belittling them with other coaches or saying anything that could identify them as a client, unless you have their specific permission to do so. Where you feel you cannot work respectfully, then the coaching must end. As you expect from your client, you will never cancel or arrive late for a session on spurious or trivial grounds.

You do not need clients to be just like you to be able to work with them successfully. My own assumption is that I will be able to work with more or less any client until circumstances prove otherwise.

You will strictly adhere to your promise of confidentiality. Any betrayal here will find its way back to your client in very short order. A colleague of mine describes the most common approach to confidentiality as 'only telling one other person'. As coaches we need to do better than that. If there are limits to confidentiality, tell the client what they are. Clients need to trust that we will not gossip or betray any of the many secrets we hear in the coaching room. This may range from early knowledge of a company takeover, with its potential to buy shares cheap and sell them dear later, to other kinds of insider knowledge about adulteries or people's sexuality.

The openness you expect from a client needs to be matched by openness on your side. This might mean *very occasionally* trusting the client with your own vulnerability, but this will always risk the possibility of you and your client changing places (these themes are explored in more detail in Chapter 10). It does mean staying open to the client's views, listening without judging, *walking a mile in the other person's moccasins*, helping the client to voice views that it might otherwise be difficult for him or her to express.

It also means that you are open to any request or challenge from a client. So, for instance, in one session the subject of a client's difficult marriage was on the agenda, and she suddenly stopped in mid-flow to say, abruptly, 'I need to know that your marriage wasn't always perfect.' There was no way we could continue the conversation until the feeling behind this request had been candidly explored. This turned out to be not so much a request for intimate confessions from me to her, as a sudden feeling on her part that somehow I was judging her. Exploring honestly what that feeling was and staying open to her feedback was essential to re-establishing trust.

Finally, as a coach you will demonstrate willingness to learn from your clients. This is something that is taken for granted by the best coaches in other fields – for instance, singing and sport. An outstanding opera singer will usually have a singing coach. The best theatre companies employ voice coaches, even for distinguished actors. These coaches will tell you how much they learn from their coachees. Similarly, as life or executive coaches, when we stay open to influence from our clients in the same way that we expect them to be open to influence from us, the coaching relationship will be infinitely the richer.

4 Simple but not easy: the skilled language of coaching

Asking the right questions, phrasing your comments judiciously . . . this is a prime coaching skill. When done well, it looks effortlessly easy. When not done well, it gets in the way. If you can learn how to do it well, you will have cracked one of the most challenging barriers to effectiveness as a coach. In this chapter I look at some of the common traps for coaches and describe how to circumvent them.

As with so many other domains in coaching, this skill falls into the category of *simple but not easy*. One of my trainee coaches spoke for many others when she said:

> Intellectually I can accept the case for keeping it short and sweet and working from the client's agenda exclusively, but advice-giving is so entrenched in my mental concept of helping, that it's taken me a long time to see how loaded my questions are. And when I'm there with a real client, I panic and then I fall into my old default mode!

Successful coaching involves an intense awareness of the language you use and this does not come naturally to everyone. When coaching well, your language will have a purity and probably also a brevity that your everyday conversation does not normally have or need. Each word will count.

Knowing the traps

At the risk of appearing to emphasize the negative, I'm going to describe some of the most common traps, all of which I have been guilty of myself and seen many times in other coaches.

Here is an example, taken from a recording of a real-life piece of coaching:

Client: I need to work shorter hours. My life balance is all wrong.
Beginner coach: Have you tried asking your PA for feedback on where your time is going?

In this example, the client has named the issue on which he wants to work. The coach's mind immediately springs to a possible powerful solution: raising the client's awareness of how he currently spends his time by suggesting he asks his PA for feedback. This could be a good idea because PAs tend to see managerial behaviour in the raw.

This is how the conversation continued:

Client:	I need to work shorter hours. My life balance is all wrong.
Beginner coach:	Have you tried asking your PA for feedback on where your time is going? Her perspective would probably be very useful.
Client:	No, I haven't.
Beginner coach:	That would be really useful – often I find that my clients don't really know where their time is going and the PA is a day-to-day observer. As a starter for change it's really useful.
Client:	Well . . .
Beginner coach:	It's something you could do between now and the next session . . .
Client:	Well, I don't know . . .
Beginner coach:	OK, just a thought . . .

As a coaching conversation, this one is going nowhere. If we speculate about what each side was thinking but not saying in this very typical piece of dialogue, it would probably go like this:

Thinks but doesn't say		Actual dialogue
This is such a huge issue for me. I've been round and round it so many times. I wonder if she can really help me?	Client	I need to work shorter hours. My life balance is all wrong.
Oh help . . .! This is a biggie. Where on earth should I start? I know! That exercise where you ask the PA for their feedback. That will help him.	Beginner coach	Have you tried asking your PA for feedback on where your time is going? Her perspective would probably be very useful.
This sounds like a time-management course. I didn't come here for that.	Client	No, I haven't.
He's resisting, so perhaps I'd better push it.	Beginner coach	That would be really useful – often I find that my clients don't really know where their time is going and the PA is a day-to-day observer. As a starter for change it's really useful.
There's no way I'm going to do this. Just because her other clients find it useful doesn't mean that I will.	Client	Well . . .

Perhaps I'm not being persuasive enough?	Beginner coach	It's something you could do between now and the next session . . .
Absolutely not!	Client	Well, I don't know . . .
What on earth do I do now?	Beginner coach	OK, just a thought . . .

While the speculations about the client's thoughts are just that – speculation – the coach's thoughts are entirely authentic, because she described them to me in technicolor when, as her supervisor, we listened to the recording together.

Trap 1: advice-in-disguise questions

This coach, like so many others, has fallen into the trap of asking advice-in-disguise questions. These questions come from the coach's wish to be helpful through offering his or her own solutions, dressed up as questions. The give-away is the first word:

Have . . . ?	Was . . . ?	Is . . . ?
Haven't . . . ?	Wasn't . . . ?	Isn't . . . ?
Would . . . ?	Has . . . ?	Should . . . ?
Wouldn't . . . ?	Hasn't . . . ?	Shouldn't . . . ?
Do . . . ?	Did . . . ?	Were . . . ?
Don't . . . ?	Didn't . . . ?	Weren't . . . ?
Does . . . ?	Are . . . ?	Can . . . ?
Doesn't . . . ?	Aren't . . . ?	Can't . . . ?

For instance:

> Have you thought of . . . ?
>
> Would it be a good idea if . . . ?
>
> Should you check that out with someone else?

There are about 30 of these constructions in English, all beginning with a verb. These questions invariably come from the coach's agenda, not the client's. A sure sign that you are falling into this trap is to notice that your question can be answered yes or no. The questions suggest that there is a right answer and of course that is the one in the coach's mind.

Question: Have you done x or y?
Answer: Yes.

Apart from all the other disadvantages created by offering advice described in Chapter 3, there are two other, equally compelling ones for avoiding these questions. First, as in the example above, they can be readily deflected by a client who has two easy options: mindlessly agreeing immediately or abruptly declining to enter further into the debate. The client's energy is going into the evasion instead of into thoughtfulness and learning.

The leading question

An even more lethal version of advice-in-disguise is the leading question, as legendarily used by the lawyer who is cross-questioning a hostile witness in court:

> So would you agree that you have been lying, and you did commit this crime?

You can hear this sort of question asked every day on current affairs radio and television programmes by journalists whose basic position is that politicians are fibbing until proved otherwise. Since these programmes are a kind of theatre where each side knows its roles, it does not much matter. The politician says what he or she plans to have said anyway, and the journalist plays the role of ruthless inquisitor. The tradition is reinforced by the practice of parliamentary debate where differences are artificially emphasized. It is seen at its most exaggerated in Prime Minister's Question Time, the weekly ritual where the Prime Minister is subjected either to exaggeratedly sycophantic questions from his or her own party:

> Would the Prime Minister agree that this has been his wisest act yet?

or to overt attempts at sabotage from the other side:

> Would the Prime Minister not agree that it is time his government resigned?

This type of question has never been better mocked than by 'Mrs Merton', the 1990s TV chat-show 'host'. 'Mrs Merton' was a convincingly dowdy 50-year-old Northerner with a horrible perm, very unlike her alter ego, the much younger comedienne Caroline Ahearne. Mrs Merton's sly and apparently guileless questions frequently disarmed her guests, especially at the beginning of the series when the guests were often not in on the joke. One of her best was addressed to the glamorous and much younger wife of the magician and performer Paul Daniels:

So, Debbie McGee, what was it that first drew you to millionaire Paul Daniels?

Trap 2: the why question

When you ask the question 'why . . . ?' it seems at first like a benign, open question. In practice it is another trap. The question 'why . . . ?' invites defensiveness which takes the form of analysing and intellectualizing.

In this example, the client has raised the question of a highly unsatisfactory team meeting. This client already knows she has difficulties in chairing meetings and wants to improve.

Coach: Why did you decide to hold that team meeting when you did?
Client: Well, our policy on meetings is that we never let more than ten days go past without a team meeting and it was already nine days since the last one so I thought it was time . . . (*ramble, ramble, ramble*)

The coach's real question was about what was in the client's mind before calling the meeting and what she wanted to get out of the meeting. The coach has not had his real question answered here because by starting with the word 'why . . . ?' he has triggered a defensive response (see Chapter 2) which gets nowhere near the real issues for this client.

The 'why . . . ?' question is also unhelpful because it often focuses on the client's motivation. Nine times out of ten when you ask this question you will get the response 'I don't know', or 'It's just how I am'. If the client already knew what her motivation was, she might not be asking for coaching on the issue.

Coach: Why did you lose your temper with X?
Client: I don't know. I just seem to have a short fuse.

Similarly, 'why . . . ?' can seem like an interrogation or an accusation. For many people it reminds us of the kinds of questions that we were asked as children by our irritated parents:

Why did you get your trousers so muddy?

Why do you fight with your brother?

Why have you lost your bus pass for the third time this term?

When asked like this, it can easily be interpreted by the client as having the underlying meaning, 'Why were you so stupid?' The reply you get is then likely to be either the blank shrug that goes with 'I don't know' or a long-winded and defensive justification. In brain chemistry terms the word 'why?' alerts the amygdala (see page 31), the brain's alarm signal, the client feels attacked, is unlikely to be totally honest with you and cannot think clearly.

Trap 3: researching the data

This is a more subtle trap but it is a trap nonetheless. Let's suppose that you have a new client from an organization you don't know at all. The client begins his account of a problem concerning a poorly performing member of his team. The temptations might be to ask the client for an organization chart or to explain any unfamiliar acronyms he is using; establish how big the team is and how their roles relate to that of the problem member; ask how old the team member is and how long they have been in the job.

All of this is unnecessary. The client already has this data so it is pointless to ask him or her to give it to you. It will be far more important for you to take the client into areas that they have never considered and that means asking a different type of question. The most likely explanation for your behaviour is your own anxiety:

> 'Do I really understand this client's organization?' (Probably not, but you don't need to)

> 'How is this team like other teams I know in different organizations?' (Irrelevant – it may be or may not be)

The pertinent data – pertinent to the client, that is – will emerge when you ask the right questions. Anything else is simply postponing the moment when you get to the heart of the client's issues. When you find yourself searching for data, notice it as a sign that you are at Level 1 listening (see page 66), more concerned about whether you are asking the right questions than with truly listening to the client. Extra facts are usually a distraction and will take you away from the real issues rather than towards them.

On one of our coach training courses, my colleague Jan Campbell Young was working with Annie, a promising coach who had spent her career up until that point as a distinguished university teacher. Noticing how often Annie spent in a relentless search for facts in her practice coaching, Jan memorably burst out, 'Annie, you are not doing a PhD thesis on the client's problem!' I remind myself of this with an inner smile of recognition when I am tempted to start the equivalent type of questioning with a client.

Trap 4: asking about people who are not present

A client presents you with a puzzle. Let's say it is about how to harness the flagging motivation of their PA. The trap here is to ask about the PA's motivation or concerns.

> Coach: What does she feel about it?
> Client: Who can say?

None of us can ever know for sure what another person's motivation is. Clumsy probing about other people's motivation or feelings may confirm the client's belief that the other person is the problem, rather than looking at their own contribution to the problem. You may encounter another variation of this temptation. Let's say the client is thinking about a radical change of career. You know something of the client's personal circumstances through other questions you have asked. You now ask, 'What would your mother/wife/husband/partner/boss think about this?' Again, it is a distraction from the client's own responsibility to speculate about what the not-present other person might think. Interestingly, I notice that when we are tempted to ask this kind of question, the third party is often an authority figure. Asking about that person's views might therefore seem to be implying that the absent person has the final power to decide, and may have to be placated or manipulated in order for the client to have their own way. In this way, old myths and excuses could be unwittingly perpetuated.

Trap 5: long and double questions

As a coach, when you ask long questions you are at the risk of turning the spotlight of the coaching onto yourself. Long questions normally come out of uncertainty. Inside, the coach is thinking: 'What shall I ask next? If I go on talking I'll get to something eventually and it will cover up any pauses which might otherwise embarrass me . . .' As a coach, you cannot afford the luxury of doing all your thinking out loud. It will only confuse your client if your questions have long preambles followed by many dependent clauses, garlanded with phrases intended to give yourself time to think: *sort of, you know* and *I mean*. This coach found himself falling into this trap:

> So when you have this **sort of** problem, **you know**, with punctual-ity, and I know you've described it as baffling, and how it really, **sort of**, annoys your boss when you're late for her meetings, I wonder, **you know**, what the circumstances are – **I mean** whether it's when you're really hassled about everything else that's going on in your life? **Know what I mean**?

Not surprisingly, the client's response was: 'Yes – I mean no . . . I don't know. Could you repeat the question?' The question the coach was really asking was: 'What are the typical triggers for unpunctuality for you?' If he had asked the question this way, the client would have found it much easier to answer, though possibly also more challenging.

Buried inside the long question there are often two or even three sub-questions. An example would be:

> So tell me how you first came to feel concerned about this. Was it when you first joined the company or did it start later? And has that concern always been as strong as it is now?

This kind of question comes across as a barrage, however gently it is asked. It confuses because, as the client, you don't know which bit of the barrage to concentrate on. I notice that when coaches ask this kind of question, the client's most frequent response is typically 'Err . . . um . . .', or 'You've lost me there'. If you know this style of questioning is a particular trap for you, take a breath, give yourself a pause, gather your thoughts and only then ask your questions – one at a time.

Tactics that work

All these traps, and the types of question that go with them, have one thing in common. They narrow the search for answers, rather than broadening it out. They confuse and distract. They focus attention on one place rather than persuading the client to extend out to many places, including, often, the places they might at first rather not look. One way and another, they all lead to dead ends.

The coach's freedom

As a coach, you are in a remarkably free situation. You have the luxury of remaining detached from whatever outcome the client achieves. It really doesn't matter. You want the client to get an outcome which will make a positive difference in their life, whether it is greater clarity or a workable solution, but you are not attached to any one path.

You don't need to know the whole story, only the bits of it that matter to the client now.

The past is less important than the present and the future.

You don't need to be right.

You don't need to understand the context in order to be able to coach effectively. I often coach clients whose technical worlds are literally incomprehensible to me. A recent example includes a nuclear engineer who considerately asked me at one point early in our coaching whether it would help me if she briefly outlined the laws of thermodynamics. I reassured her that it would be a waste of our time. I might understand the individual words, but it would be unlikely that the whole sentence would mean very much.

Another client managed a complex overseas operation in a country whose political system is as different from the standard western democracy as it is possible to be, with internecine manoeuvrings, widespread corruption and a great deal of physical danger. This client was relieved to discover that he did not need to give me potted histories of the various factions involved. Whether or not I knew about them was irrelevant to our success. Similarly, I have coached theologians, lawyers, doctors, actors, IT specialists, interior designers, architects, retailers, academics, pharmacologists, sportspeople, finance directors, theatre directors, actuaries, civil servants, ambassadors, hospital managers, chefs and many others without knowing anything about their professional worlds except perhaps as a consumer.

In fact it is even more liberating than this. It is a positive help to know nothing about the context or the content. The more you know about the content, the more likely you are to be seduced into the role of expert. This case has been supremely well made by Timothy Gallwey in his *Inner Game* books, for instance *The Inner Game of Work* (2000). Gallwey worked for a time as a tennis coach and came to realize that the real opponent for a tennis player was not the person on the other side of the net. Rather it was the mental programming of the player. The real opponent was in the player's own head. A player without bodily self-awareness and further handicapped by lack of self-belief was almost bound to fail. Gallwey began his Inner Tennis courses with the explicit aim of coaching participants in the techniques of mental and physical self-awareness rather than in some preordained set of tennis techniques.

The contrast with traditional coaching is instructive. The traditional coach relies on his or her own ideas of what makes, for instance, a good serve: 'Watch me and do it like this,' or 'Keep your eye on the ball at this or that point.' This would be followed by feedback from the coach to the player: 'At the crucial minute, you let your arm drop and took your eye off the ball.' In this example, the coach is doing most of the work and the player is robbed of responsibility. The coaching turns into a performance to please the coach rather than the player taking responsibility for their own game.

In the Inner Game approach, the roles are reversed. The coach asks open questions aimed at raising the player's consciousness of their physical and mental states with the aim of the player taking the responsibility and doing the feedback on him- or herself:

What worked then?

What didn't work?

What was in your mind at the start?

What do you need to do now?

Where was the ball when you connected with it?

The results were startlingly successful, so successful that an Inner Ski school was started too, with coaches trained in the same technique. In his book *Coaching for Performance* (1996: 37), Gallwey's then collaborator, John Whitmore, tells a wonderful tale of how the ski coaches were able to coach people in tennis, in spite of knowing literally nothing about the sport:

> Several of our Inner Tennis courses were so overbooked that we ran out of trained Inner Tennis coaches. We brought in two Inner Ski coaches, dressed them in tennis coach's uniform, put a racket under their arms and let them loose with the promise they would not attempt to use the racket under any circumstances.
>
> Not entirely to our surprise, the coaching job they did was largely indistinguishable from that of their tennis-playing colleagues. However, on a couple of notable occasions, they actually did better. On reflection the reason became clear. The tennis coaches were seeing the participants in terms of their technical faults: the ski coaches, who could not recognize such faults, saw the participants in terms of the efficiency with which they used their bodies. Body inefficiency stems from self-doubt and inadequate body-awareness. The ski coaches, having to rely on the participants' own self-diagnosis, were therefore tackling problems at cause, whereas the tennis coaches were only tackling the symptom, the technical fault. This obliged us to do more training with the tennis coaches to enable them to detach themselves more effectively from their expertise.

Effective questions in coaching

The most effective questions in coaching have a number of characteristics in common.

- They raise the client's self-awareness by provoking thinking and challenge.

- They demand truthful answers by cutting through obfuscation and waffle.
- They are short.
- They go beyond asking for information by asking for discovery.
- They encourage the client to take responsibility for themselves.
- They stick closely to the client's agenda.
- They lead to learning for the client.
- They are more than likely to begin with the words 'what' or 'how'.

Some super-useful ('magic') questions

The easiest way to understand the difference between effective and less effective questions in coaching is to look at some actual examples. When I was relatively new to coaching, I was fortunate to get sent by my then boss to a course on organizational consulting run by Columbia University. There I encountered a set of questions which were so obviously special in their impact on people that I immediately adapted them to my coaching work. There is an equivalent in therapy – so-called 'magic questions' – from which these questions had probably sprung. Whatever their origin, I attached a crib sheet to my notebook and shamelessly kept it open during coaching sessions. I would explain that I needed the prompt, that the client would be the beneficiary and was welcome to see the list at any time (no one ever asked).

This list, much adapted, has proved its worth time and time again as an outline script, not just to me but to the many hundreds of other coaches I have now trained. It will work in almost any situation, regardless of the setting or the issue. There are several points to note about it:

- The questions are content-free.
- They are short.
- They do not include the word 'I'.
- They work elegantly as a natural progression, starting with asking the client to state the problem, going on to restating the problem as a goal, then to naming options and finally to first steps to action.

Here are the questions:

1   *What's the issue?*
    This asks the client to state the problem. It can often usefully cut through a client's lengthy account by asking them to summarize what the problem actually is.

2   *What makes it an issue **now**?*
    Issues that clients bring to coaching have typically been around in
    the client's life for a long time. But often there is some immediate
    provocation or development, even if this is in the form of anger or
    worry. This emotion will provide energy for change and resolution.
    That is why it is worth naming and surfacing it.

3   *Who owns this issue/problem?*
    If the client does not own it, there is no point in discussing it. You can
    only coach the problem owner. Some clients come to coaching in order
    to find out how to change someone else, whereas the basic assumption
    of coaching is that you can only change yourself. This question puts
    the onus back onto clients to own whichever bit of the issue is theirs.

4   *How important is it on a 1–10 scale?*
    If the problem is not important then why are you and the client
    wasting time discussing it? Importance captures the idea of issues
    with potential for major impact on a client's life. Anything the client
    scores at lower than 5 should be set aside.

5   *How much energy do you have for a solution on a 1–10 scale?*
    This question often draws an interesting response. The client may
    have told you the problem has an importance of 9, but then tells you
    that their energy for a solution is only 3 or 4. If so, you will want to
    ask a follow-up question such as 'What would need to happen to
    increase the energy to 8 or 9?'

6   *Implications: what are the implications of doing nothing (or of letting
    things carry on as they are)?*
    This question builds the pain created by contemplating staying stuck.
    When we are in the client role many of us like to imagine that the
    default scenario can continue for ever, whereas inside we know
    perfectly well that it cannot and that we are ignoring the discomfort
    the problem is creating. Naming out loud the likely consequences of
    inactivity paradoxically builds energy for change. You might want to
    follow this question with a further probe: . . . *and what would be the
    implications if that happened?*

7   *What have you already tried?*
    This question stops you offering pointless advice which the client has
    already tried or considered and it also lets you in early on the client's
    thinking. Most coaching problems have already been the focus of a
    great deal of energy and thought on the client's part. You need to
    know what this energy and thought has produced. If the client has
    not tried anything yet, that will also provoke an interesting discussion.

8   *Imagine this problem's been solved. What would you see, hear and feel?*
    Up until now, the client has been deep in the problem. You will
    typically see this reflected in the way the client has been sitting and

talking – often slumped or despairing. By asking this question you tap into their resourcefulness. Clients will sit up straighter, stop frowning and will look generally lighter. Note that the answer to this question reveals the real goal (see also Chapter 6). Asking the question at this stage prevents you coaching on the symptoms rather than on the underlying causes.

9   *What's standing in the way of that ideal outcome?*
    This question broadens out the client's thinking. Expect new insights to occur from this point on.

10 *What's your own responsibility for what's been happening?*
    An essential question. The client is always part of the problem as well as part of the solution. This question makes that assumption explicit and encourages clients to see how they have, maybe at an unconscious level, been sustaining the problem through their own behaviour.

11 *What early signs are there that things might be getting better/going all right?*
    However dreadful the situation, there is always something that is working. Identifying and building on it is part of the process of change and improvement.

12 *Imagine you're at your most resourceful. What do you say to yourself about this issue?*
    This question assumes that underneath all our typical confusion, at some level we do know what we should do. Another version of this question: 'If I could give you a pill which contained all the courage and insight you needed, what would you do?' I have yet to find a client who could not find an instant reply to this one.

13 *What are the options for action here?*
    Now that the question has been looked at from several angles, the client can begin to consider the options for change.

14 *What criteria will you use to judge the options?*
    Options are even more useful when you have criteria against which to judge them. Typical criteria might be: practicality, cost, fit with the client's values, time – and so on.

15 *Which option seems the best one against those criteria?*
    At this point you are narrowing down again towards action – including, of course, just pondering.

16 *So what's the next/first step?*
    The answer may be to do some more research, to have a conversation or to make a big life decision.

17 *When will you take it?*
    Asking for a commitment to *when* makes it more likely that the client will actually do something different as a result of the coaching.

I have seen this format, adapted of course to individual vocabulary and preferences, work time and time again. Not only does the format work; it also works at speed because there are few diversions.

Brevity

The most powerful coaching questions are often extremely short because they cut to the heart of the issue. The ideal question is between 7 and 12 words long. I believe the most powerful question of all is this one: 'What do you want?' Although another strong candidate is: 'What needs to happen to . . . ?'

CASE STUDY

Ros

Ros is a new chief executive who has inherited a less than ideal team. She expresses lack of confidence about her own ability to cope and also a rising level of concern about her finance director, Isobel. The coach encourages her to let off steam for a few moments.

Ros: . . . and then Isobel made it much worse by once again correcting me in a meeting and telling me that as I'm not a finance specialist, I had no idea what I was talking about and she couldn't really understand what on earth I was going to do about interpreting the accounts – on and on and on. I was so annoyed. And her manner with her team is awful – she's rude and she consistently loses her best people. We really can't have senior people behaving like she does.

Coach: What do you want?

Ros: I want her to go!

Coach: So what needs to happen to make that happen?

Ros: I've got to talk to my chair and get him on side and then find a civilized way for her to leave as soon as possible.

At last – clarity. Once these words 'I want her to go' have been spoken, the question then becomes how it can happen, not whether or not it is a good idea.

Sometimes the most effective question is a single word: 'So . . . ?'; 'And . . . ?'; 'Because . . . ?' Or even a questioning silence.

You could even say that any coaching conversation reduces itself essentially to three ultra-short questions: 'What?' (identifying the issue); 'So what?' (implications); and 'What next?' (action).

Summarizing

Summarizing is important. First, it shows that you are listening because you cannot summarize accurately unless you have been listening. Second, it reassures clients that you are keeping track of things. This is particularly important where there has been a period of intense and discursive conversation. Equally important, it keeps you in the frame and emphasizes your role. Also, it gives you a check that you really are understanding what the client is saying.

Summarizing provides punctuation in the coaching conversation. The coach's summary makes it a two-way and not a one-way conversation. When you feel you are getting confused by the twists and turns of a client's story, that is probably a reliable sign that you need to summarize. I now actually say to clients, 'I'm getting a bit lost here – can I try a summary?' Summarizing also helps us to get beyond the panic of Level 1 listening. If you know you can always summarize, you know you will always have something to say which is respectful to the client and helps you get back on track.

Genuine summarizing has these features:

- It does not contain any judgement of your own.
- It does not interpret.
- It uses the client's language.
- It ends with a question – 'Have I got that right?', or 'Is that a fair summary of where we seem to have got to?'
- It is authentically a summary and therefore brief rather than a polly-parrot rendering at the same length as the client's own account.

Some useful summarizing phrases are:

> I think it would be useful to summarize where we've got to here . . . There seem to be three or four main views that you have been putting forward . . .

> Can I check that I've really understood the points you're making here? What you feel is that . . .

> So, to summarize so far . . .

Or even the very brief, 'So you feel angry/sad/happy/confused about this?'

You should note that ending on a question (e.g. '. . . is that a fair summary?') often prompts further significant disclosure from the client. This is because it demonstrates authentic listening and therefore encourages the client to tell you more.

Getting to the crux

This describes the skill of asking a client to name what is ultimately at stake in whatever the issue is. The relief of being able to talk to another person who listens non-judgementally is such that clients will often begin to ramble. Signs of this are:

- the client tells you the same thing in several different ways;
- you begin to feel bored because you've already heard what the issue is;
- an instinct that the long story is a way of avoiding the main issues;
- the client starts way back in the distant past history of whatever they are describing;
- the client gets lost in all the detail: 'Where was I – I'm losing my thread here!'

As a coach, it is not a good use of the coaching session to let the client rove about in all the detail of a story. Getting to the crux is about pinning down what the real issue is – for you and the client. An example might be a client who has spent a long time describing her anger at what she feels was manipulative behaviour on the part of a team member. The client has ended up feeling stupid in front of others. This is not the first time this team member has done this. The conversation between you and the client has begun to take on a circular flavour. As the coach you intervene to say: 'So Barbara, the crux of it is that you're angry and fed up with this behaviour and want to do something about it?' Naming the real issue allows clients to address the nub and decide what to do about it.

Interrupting

Interrupting people is generally thought rude in our society. As children we learn that you never or rarely interrupt – it is part of being socialized. Hence, for instance, the mixture of horror, awe and amusement that the tougher journalist-presenters evoke: they break the taboo.

In coaching we also have to break the taboo. The client is paying us to get to the heart of things and coaching time is limited. Also, clients have already probably gone round and round the loop several times with friends. For many clients, there will be a well-rehearsed drone to the story. You will get to recognize the signs of this.

Interrupting needs to be done with discretion. There are always caveats to consider:

Potential for interrupting	**But . . .**
A client is going on and on, giving an enormous amount of detail which seems irrelevant.	The client may need to do this in order to get the story straight in their own mind.
The client is talking continuously about the past. Coaching is not psychotherapy where the purpose may be to reinterpret the past. It is about the future.	The client may need the catharsis of talking about the past.
The client gives the full script of every conversation. The give-away is lots of 'So he said . . . and then I said . . .'	This may be one of the client's ways of storytelling. The client may need feedback on how to be more succinct. If clients do this with you they are probably doing it with everyone and potentially getting the reputation of being a bore.

Why interrupt?

Clients often go on too long as a way of avoiding getting to the real point. Talking at length may be a conscious or unconscious tactic – a way of keeping the coach at bay. These clients may tempt you with distractions they know you will find alluring. This is nearly always because you are on the track of some nodal point for change. One British politician owned up to this tactic with his personal trainer:

> When I am under the cosh being pushed to my personal limit I might suddenly reveal a fascinating piece of low-level gossip to distract him or show intense interest in his life and welfare.

Sometimes, the same clients who play on your politeness may be the first to say later that the coaching was just a lot of pointless talking. Other clients may not know how long is *too long* for talking about an issue and will need your help in establishing this. Some people talk a lot when they are nervous.

Interrupting them will reassure them. Clients may know well enough that they are going on too long but may still have got into the habit of doing it. You do not need to know all the background in order to be able to coach effectively – in fact, often you need to know remarkably little, but clients may assume that you do need to know a lot of background. If they go on too long as a matter of routine, both they and you will potentially become dissatisfied. Interrupting in coaching is different from the annoying interruptions we experience in a social conversation because it has a different purpose. In social events people interrupt out of boredom or because they are queuing to speak and get fed up with waiting. Some interrupting is overtly crass and rude: it conveys, *'Now let's get back to the really interesting subject: ME!'* Coaches interrupt in the interests of the client and the coaching relationship.

How to interrupt

- Trust your intuition that it is time to do it.
- Set aside your worries about whether the client will dislike you for doing it – the chances are that they will respect you more. Coaching is definitely not like a polite conversation with a friend.
- Ask permission – 'May I interrupt you here?'
- Use body language to help – e.g. a hand held palm up (traffic cop style) to the client.
- Follow the interruption with an immediate explanation about your reason for doing it: for instance, 'I'm getting lost here' or 'I'm wondering if I really need to know all the detail?' or 'I'm going to pause you there because you used a really interesting word just then . . . and I'd like us to explore it'.

Assuming a positive outcome

The best coaches, like the best therapists, are naturally skilled at using language which assumes a positive outcome. In effect it is a hidden order. They consciously slip in the constructions which convey that success will be inevitable. This is the linguistic equivalent of the placebo effect in medicine. When the doctor conveys that he or she believes the placebo will work, the patient may get better, in spite of the fact there are nothing but inert ingredients in the pills. Hypnotherapists do the same: *when I count to 10, your arm will feel heavy.*

The unskilled coach conveys doubt and may say:

> *If* you *try* to learn how to control your nerves when you give a presentation *I think* you'll *probably* find that your problems with volume *may fade away.*

I have italicized the words which convey misgivings. As the client I will pick up this doubt – the coach is not certain that I can succeed, therefore I may not.

The skilled coach will use a different construction:

> *When* you've learnt to control your nerves, *you'll find* that your problems with volume will *disappear*.

I heard this exchange on a beginner coach's tape recently:

Client: (sounding very anxious) I don't know how to stop myself getting angry with Sharon. Every time I try to talk to her I get so annoyed because she witters on and on and I've given her hints that I don't like it but I'm afraid I may just have an explosion then she'll probably carry out her threat to lay a grievance against me for bullying . . .

Coach: Well, if you try to have the conversation in the slightly different way we've discussed before, you might find that it turns out a bit differently.

Client: (dubious) Mmm, I suppose so . . .

Coach: Yes, you ought to try it – you never know, it might work.

When you look at the dialogue you can see clearly that in trying to be encouraging and not too directive, through her convoluted and tentative language, the coach is actually conveying a belief that the suggested tactics will *not* work. When asked about this in supervision, the coach was amazed – 'But I did believe they would work!'

To counter this tendency, use phrases which assume success, such as:

> As you continue to improve . . .
>
> When you've learnt this . . .
>
> Once mastered, this will feel . . .
>
> You will feel better when . . .
>
> When you've practised this skill five or six times you will find that . . .

Similarly, beware of telling clients that something will be *difficult* or *tricky*. Essentially your role is to expect success because this way you will convey it to the client. This increases the chances that this is what will happen. When you label something *difficult*, you create the expectation of failure. One of my former dance teachers seemed to me to make life twice as hard for himself and his learners by announcing that we were going to find some particular sequence *a stumbling block*. Sure enough, we stumbled. Another teacher with a class of identical ability said nothing at all about whether it was easy or difficult but just took that same section a little more slowly, assuming that we would master it – which we did.

Naturally you need to temper all of this with pragmatism. It is not appropriate when you have serious doubts or when it would be unrealistic to raise expectations too high. But on the whole I find that grounded optimism gets much better results than doleful prediction of obstacles.

Encouraging clients to be specific

When a client is bewildered, angry or concerned about an issue, he or she may begin by explaining it through extravagant generalizations, assertions or comparisons. This is a sign that feeling has taken over from logic and also a signal to you that the issue is important to the client. Encouraging the client to be specific is often the swiftest way to begin unpacking what is really at stake.

Here are some examples of how to use the technique:

The client makes a comparison:	This is the worst boss I've ever had.
The coach surfaces the comparison:	Worst in what way? Or, Worse than what specifically?
The client makes a generalization:	She's always late.
The coach challenges the generalization:	Always? No exceptions?
The client makes a bald assertion:	I don't like the way this organization is going.
The coach asks for a specific example:	What specifically don't you like about the way the organization is going?
Alternatively, the coach asks for the opposite:	So if everything were going well in the organization, what specifically would be happening for you?
The client states implied rules which indicate firmly held beliefs:	We should know exactly how this recruitment programme is going to be organized.
The coach surfaces the implied rule and asks what the result would be of changing the belief:	What would happen if you didn't know exactly how the recruitment programme was going to be organized?

Look out here for *must* and *should*. For instance, if a client says 'I must have advance warning of changes in plans', the coach might reply, 'What does having advance warning of changes do for you?'

Can'ts may represent particularly strongly held self-limiting beliefs:

The client says: I can't hope to change the way I work.
The coach replies: What's stopping you?

Looking out for nominalizations

The study of linguistics has given us the ugly neologism *nominalizations*. Don't let the clumsy label put you off. A nominalization is a noun, adjective or verb which has been turned into an abstract concept. These words are used by politicians, preachers and advertisers all the time, precisely because they are vague. So a politician promises us *modernization* of the NHS, *excellence* in schools or *efficiency* in the Civil Service. A motivational speaker may talk about *values*, *happiness* or *truth*. To make sense of these words, we have to fill in the blanks ourselves. There is no behaviour specified. In fact, many politicians deliver speeches, whole parts of which are also entirely without verbs. Each listener will create their own meaning, lulled into a false sense of shared understanding. So clients may say they are locked into *misery*, or seeking *enlightenment*, or *paralysed by indecision*. If in doubt about whether you are hearing a nominalization or not, ask yourself if you could buy it, carry it away as a physical entity or see it in actual behaviour. If not, then you are hearing a nominalization.

When you hear nominalizations always ask the client to clarify. Here is an example:

Client: I feel a bit depressed about the state of my organization.
Coach: Depressed: that's an interesting word. What is depressing exactly?
Client: It's the way we as a senior team seem to be detached from what is really going on. We hide in our nice offices as if we're afraid to venture out – and I think we are! We know our people believe we've lost touch with them and I really don't know what to do about it.

Running the conversation like this will stop you assuming that when the client used the initial word *depressed*, he meant sadness, anxiety or clinical depression. What he really meant was something a great deal more particular.

The client's language

The effective coach notices and picks up on the client's language. When clients are talking about issues that really touch them their language changes: it becomes more vivid, sometimes more direct, often more metaphorical. It gives you clues to what really matters to the client and this is virtually always worth exploring.

> ## CASE STUDY
> ### Sean
>
> Sean, one of my BBC clients, constantly used military metaphors. His *troops* were going to *go over the top* in their *battle* with the *enemy*. This *battle* might be an enjoyable *joust* or it might *go nuclear*. When I pointed out this pattern to him, he was amazed and thoughtful. 'Well, yes,' he said, 'I see my department as being engaged in a life or death struggle for survival. We're fighting the independent production companies and our BBC bosses for commissions and if we don't win it will be the sack for all my producers.'

Metaphor and its importance

It is impossible to explore any abstract concept without using metaphor. In fact, metaphor saturates our conversation, even though we may be quite unaware of it. Possibly as many as 1 in 25 of our words are metaphors. Never underestimate how powerfully the language we use can affect how we think. This has been repeatedly demonstrated experimentally, most vividly in a series of experiments designed by two researchers at Stanford University, Paul Thibodeau and Lera Boroditsky (for a full account go to www.plosone.org). Subjects read accounts of crime in a fictional city, including statistics. One set of these reports contained the word *beast*, describing crime as *preying on* the city. The other used the metaphor of a *virus* which was *infecting* the city. These words were used only once. Subjects were then asked to recommend action to solve the problem. The group which had been exposed to the beast metaphor recommended vigorous police action (*hunting down, catching, imprisoning*) while the group exposed to the virus metaphor preferred *diagnosis, looking for root causes, cure* and *social action*. These results were only marginally affected by political affiliations. Intriguingly, few of the subjects attributed their reasoning to the metaphor. Most believed that they had been influenced by the statistics. This clearly has serious implications for any kind of political and social discourse – for instance, newspapers whose headlines use phrases like *immigrants flooding in* or *swamping* or which describe well-paid bosses as *fat cats* most probably have a profound impact on our attitudes. But there are also huge implications here for coaches. Just asking your client to describe the same story using a different metaphor may entirely change how they think and feel about the issue.

So in the example above, the essence of the dialogue went like this (shortened for the sake of brevity here).

JR: So Sean, I notice how many military metaphors you're using: *war, fight, nuclear, joust* . . .

Sean: (looking a bit startled) Yes, yes, I am, because that's how it seems.

JR: What's the evidence that it is actually a *war* or a *fight?*

Sean: (long pause) I suppose it's their behaviour. (he takes some time to describe the behaviour)

JR: Well, we haven't got them in the room, just you. How do you think it's influencing your own behaviour to describe it like this?

Sean: (another long pause) Probably a lot. (he describes it)

We then discussed how effective Sean thought these tactics were. Answer: not at all, in fact totally counterproductive.

JR: Let's just play with some language here. How else might you describe it?

Sean: Maybe a parley, a *negotiation*, a *conversation* . . .

JR: And how does it seem when you frame it like that?

Sean: (suddenly energized) Quite different. This is making me think! I need some new approaches here, otherwise I'm going to go down the same old path.

This conversation was a turning point: the beginning of devising a new strategy for the department. This was backed up by coaching in which Sean developed and practised the influencing and negotiating skills he had neglected for so long in his thirst for a fight.

Clean language

The concept of probing language, especially metaphor and simile, has been refined and made more elegant and accessible by neurolinguistic progamming (NLP) enthusiasts, notably David Grove, an outstanding therapist who built on work by Milton Erikson, a famous twentieth-century hypnotherapist. The ideas are well explained in the book *Clean Language* by Wendy Sullivan and Judy Rees (2008).

Essential propositions

- The coach must notice the client's exact language including their similes and metaphors.
- Using the client's exact words creates rapport: the essential foundation of any coaching or mentoring. Clients will feel understood at a very deep level.
- The coach uses phrases that are, as far as possible, 'cleansed' of any of his or her own presuppositions, interpretations and assumptions.

- The coach draws attention to any of the non-verbal signals that accompany the client's words – e.g. a raised arm, a hand on heart, a jiggling foot – without making any of the popular interpretations of so-called 'body language' (that crossed arms means defensiveness and so on).
- The coach directs the client's attention to their own gestures, metaphors and language and asks them to interpret these by expanding on them.
- Doing this enables the client to understand their own 'perceptual world' – for instance, their own assumptions, blocks and barriers – and to see how these link with behaviour, including the behaviour they would like to change.

Unclean language: an example

Client: I feel trapped in my job.
Coach: So how could you find a way out?

In this example, the coach assumes that the client *wants* to find a way out. The hidden instruction is that this is desirable and that the client should find a way out.

Clean language alternative

Client: I feel trapped in my job.
Coach: And what kind of trapped is trapped?
Client: It's a deep hole and I can't climb out.
Coach: And what happens when you can't climb out of this deep hole?
Client: I turn in on myself, I shut down. (client wraps arms around body)
Coach: (copies client's wrapped arms briefly) And when this happens and you turn in on yourself and shut down, what happens next?
Client: I stop asking for help – which I should!
Coach: And if you did ask for help, what would happen?
Client: I would feel far far better.
Coach: And then?
Client: I'd have other people involved and wouldn't feel so helpless and stupid.

In this case, the coaching turns to how to find help from others – a completely different topic.

How to do it

- The coach slows down his or her speech.
- There is an implied sense of wonder and curiosity in the way the questions are asked.

- The client's idiosyncratic emphases, pronunciation etc. are matched.
- Only the client's language, metaphors and similes are used.

Useful phrases

And what kind of < > is that < >?

And where does that < > come from?

And that's like . . . what?

And what happens next?

And is there anything else about < >?

Tell me more about < >

What does < > mean for you?

If you had < > what would be happening?

Occasionally, applying the principles of clean language can produce transformative moments for the client, as the example below shows.

CASE STUDY

Fran

Fran was referred to me by her boss who reported puzzlement about Fran's performance. Recently appointed to a leadership role, her early promise had fizzled out. Fran had lost the confidence of her team, was frequently turning up late for work and had missed an important off-site meeting with what seemed like an implausible excuse. The boss's attempts to find out what was going on had gone nowhere. Coaching was openly described to Fran and to me as a last chance to 'get your leadership style in order' before disciplinary action was started.

Fran's first session with me was intended to be about work issues, but in reality we spent the whole time on her private life and, thanks to that reliable tool, the Life Scan Wheel (see page 144), she made an unprompted sudden decision to pour out a tragic story. Fran, of British-Somali background, had married a Nigerian man. Cultural and personal differences began to damage the marriage and with no warning her husband took their two children to Nigeria, accusing Fran of a variety of gross moral failings. She discovered that he had not been paying their mortgage for some months and was heavily in debt. Their house was on the verge of being repossessed. Fran's psychometrics showed her to be an intensely introverted and deeply private person, avoiding disclosure and intimacy unless there was a high level of trust.

At this session we discussed the whole question of telling her boss what was going on in her private life and agreed that disclosure was essential. We also discussed how she could get legal advice about reclaiming her children and dealing with her financial problems. She left with a plan of action which encompassed all of these topics.

Some weeks passed. At her second session Fran reported that she had now told her boss and her team about her personal circumstances. Things had improved dramatically at work as a result. She was renting a small flat and was applying to the family court to get access to her children. I noted and fed back to her the striking change in her physical demeanour: more upright, more confident. I then asked her to reflect on how she would sum up her feelings about the whole experience.

Client: I feel I've been in a tidal wave.

JR: What kind of a tidal wave is that?

Client: Huge, overwhelming, a tsunami. I've been standing on the shore helplessly watching, seeing the sea roll back, knowing it's coming, unable to do anything to protect myself. (silence, several seconds) Feeling powerless, knocked over.

JR: Knocked over . . . powerless . . . and then?

Client: (very loudly) Yes, oh God, yes, that's exactly how it's felt, how amazing, I see myself there.

JR: And then . . . ?

Client: And then the tide's rolled in and I'm standing knee deep in water.

JR: Is there anything else about that water?

Client: (very energized) Dirty, full of wreckage, it's the wreckage of my life. Actually I'm in a house and the water has surged through it, leaving me standing. I'm just watching. When it all happened I couldn't run for the hills where it's safe.

JR: The hills would be safe. (short silence) You say you're still standing and the hills would be safe. Which way are you facing now?

Client: (sounding amazed) Oh God, I'm sideways, I'm sideways . . .

JR: Sideways. Which way would you like to be facing?

Client: Forward, forward, I'm going to be heading for the hills, yes I can see myself facing forward and away from that sea; even though that tsunami's not going to happen again, but the tide will still keep coming in and I need to get to safety.

JR: If you had that, how would that feel?

Client: (very slowly and quietly) A bit scary but a lot better, a lot, lot better.

JR: So better for you is . . . ?

Client: Feeling I'm in control for the first time for nearly a year.

I noticed Fran had a slight sheen of sweat on her forehead. She was sitting upright and forward in her chair and alternating smiling with a look of astonishment. She and I then discussed what had just happened. Her response was: 'Being able to say it all is brilliant, listening to my own metaphors and realizing how powerful they are; being able to tap into my feelings and say all this to someone who's not judging me. Feeling back in control!'

Two years later Fran was divorced, had recovered her children and had reached a reasonably amicable settlement with her former husband. She had moved within the same organization to a similar job in another city and considered that her life was back on track. In reviewing our work her comment was: 'Our tsunami conversation was a huge turning point for me – I'll never forget it. Everything improved for me from then on because I no longer felt at the mercy of stuff I couldn't control.'

Exploring feelings

This core coaching skill has the simplicity of the obvious, and, along with that, the risk of it being constantly ignored. Virtually all clients already know what the 'solutions' are to their problems. Examples might be:

Problem	**Solution**
I can't manage my time	Prioritize
I don't know what to do about my career	Take logical stock of your career and follow the rational path
My boss is difficult	Give your boss some feedback

The reason clients find it difficult to follow the apparently obvious path is that feelings are getting in the way. Many of us, but particularly people with a strong preference for logic and rationality, act as if we believe that logic will solve the problem. Logical methods of problem-solving are even taught on management development courses, but as the evidence from neuroscience shows that feelings precede logic by a long way in our responses to an event (see Chapter 2).

The logical solution may be obvious, but remain unimplemented. For the problems above, for instance, why can't the client take their own advice?

I could prioritize	but I am driven by assumptions from my early life about hard work and my identity is bound up in work
I could follow the logic of career choice	but I am terrified of novelty and change
I could give my boss feedback	but he frightens me, as all male authority figures do

This is why, along with looking at issues rationally, it is important to enquire into the feelings behind them. No client issue worth the focus of a coaching session will ever be without a 'feelings aspect'. As coaches our role is often to help clients articulate feelings that are there but go unrecognized, or to help them say out loud what they have kept inside.

Warning

When you ask a client about feelings, you will often get a *thought*. The symptoms of thoughts are clients who say, 'I feel *that* . . . this is exciting/interesting/ worrying': as soon as you hear the word *that*, you are getting a thought.

You are getting a *feeling* when a client says, for example 'I feel excited/ worried': point this difference out to the client and press for the feeling.

There are two natural places to ask for feelings. The first is at the beginning of exploring the issue. The second is at the end when the decision has been made by the client about what to do.

There are only a few questions in this area that the coach needs to ask and they can be asked constantly:

How does that feel?

Tell me about that feeling . . .

What does that mean for you specifically?

How does that translate into your behaviour?

Say more . . . ?

Moving the discussion on

Closed questions have their place in coaching, for example:

> Have we exhausted that topic?

This implies that the answer is yes and will allow you to move on quickly to the next part of the session.

Linking questions or statements are also useful here. Links combine a brief summary of the discussion that has just happened with a look forward to the next section. Here's an example:

> So in this part of the discussion we've looked at how the pressures on the business are affecting it in a number of ways [you then briefly enumerate them] and our plan now is to look in more detail at each of these. Is that OK?

For daily examples of how to do this elegantly, examine any live discussion programme on television or radio. Broadcasters call these links *segues*, meaning a technique of sliding seamlessly from one topic to another by making a link between them.

The simplicity that counts

The kind of language I have described in this chapter goes beyond technique, though technique is important. A 'coaching-aware' client may also be perfectly aware of any 'techniques' that you are using. A client of mine with whom I have worked for two years – so we know each other well – asked me in the course of our coaching how he could develop coaching techniques himself as a way of enhancing the performance of his team, and I taught him some questioning techniques. In our session recently, where I was pressing him on some issue or other, he suddenly said in mock exasperation, 'Couldn't you just ask me a closed question for once?' In agreeing that my question was entirely appropriate, we were reminding each other that coaching means fresh thinking for the client – i.e. hard work.

Language in successful coaching is the disciplined simplicity that comes from trusting clients to tap into their own resources. It is about paring down to the essence – having the questions but understanding that you don't need to have the answers.

5 Taking stock: the learning client

The process of coaching begins with an assessment of where the client is now. Our prime task as coaches is to facilitate self-awareness and learning for the client and that is impossible unless you and the client have a shared understanding of where the client currently stands. In this chapter, I look at techniques for making this initial assessment.

Clients bring a whole range of issues to coaching. These may show as urgent dilemmas or as nagging background puzzles. It would be quite usual to find that in any one client several major work and life issues present simultaneously. This should not be surprising because in coaching you are working with the whole person, not some subset – even if that is what the client initially assumes. Clients have many times assured me that they are completely different people at home from how they are at work. This, in itself, should alert you to potential problems.

Evan, for instance, vividly described himself as follows.

CASE STUDY

Evan

I say goodbye to my wife and son, heartily kissing them both, and set out on the walk to the station. I always feel melancholy leaving them. As I'm doing it, I feel a bit like a cartoon character. In the cartoon, I start as Domestic Man, a nice, mildish, smiley pussycat. Domestic Man is blinking slightly helplessly through his glasses, then he gradually transmogrifies into the dark and frightening Work Person who gets off the train in London. The briefcase, which would look a bit of an affectation for Domestic Man, has become a weapon of mass destruction. The glasses magnify the piercing eyes. The suit, which would look like an Oxfam donation on Domestic Man suddenly fits in all the right places. Instead of an amiable slouch, Work Person seems about seven feet tall, has a towering stride, and a don't-mess-with-me scowl to match.

Evan ran a directorate in a large public sector organization where his reputation was for intimidating and demanding leadership. In requesting executive coaching, Evan knew that something was wrong somewhere and saw coaching as a way to find out what it was. Initially he imagined that we would be looking exclusively at his work world. But part of the secret of finding the answers he needed was in looking at the connections and indeed disconnections between the two selves he so powerfully described when given the opportunity to talk about his whole life.

Whatever the issues a client brings to the coach, there will be a sequence of necessary stages through which coach and client must pass:

1   Where, who and what am I now – in my life, my work, my relationships, my skills?
2   Where, who and what would I like to be ideally?
3   Given those answers, what goals do I need to set for myself?
4   How can I achieve and sustain those goals?

I notice that some coaches want to hurtle over this first stage. They explain to me that they are anxious about wanting to impress the client straight away with their dynamism and willingness to work on the client's agenda. They fear that the client might feel, and possibly actually express, 'Why are we wasting time with all this preliminary stuff? I want to get on with the coaching.' When clients are paying good money for the work, many coaches, already struggling with difficulties in asking for a proper fee, may be tempted to omit these fundamentals. You have to judge each case on its merits of course. For instance, if you are simply offering the client two sessions to prepare for a job interview, then it is unlikely that either you or the client will want to invest in a session which is purely about background and self-awareness. But the longer the likely length of the coaching programme, the more important it can be to make the first session different from what follows. Typically I email clients in advance, alerting them to the format, making it clear that this is the only one where the process is laid down in advance.

A feedback-exclusion zone?

Beginning the self-discovery journey starts with a well-rounded scrutiny of where the client is now. Most of us live in a feedback-exclusion zone where the Scottish poet's well-known plea remains an impossible dream:

> Wud that God the gift wud gie us
> To see oursels as others see us.

> (Robert Burns)

Few of us really see ourselves as others see us. In the corporate world it is striking how isolated senior people can be and what a high cost both they and the organization can pay for this isolation. In her riveting account of the late 1990s crisis at Marks & Spencer, Judi Bevan lays it out with stark clarity. She compares Sir Richard Greenbury, the chief executive who led Marks & Spencer to the brink of complete collapse, with Margaret Thatcher, who did the same for the Conservative Party:

> Like Margaret Thatcher, Greenbury was an example of the classic leader who hung on too long. Surrounded by weak people who pretended at all times to agree with him, he was eventually pushed out by those he believed were his loyal lieutenants. The parallels with him and Thatcher were clear. Both possessed of towering egos, they had rallied the troops in times of crisis and then allowed themselves to be diverted, seduced by the perfume of power. They both failed to nurture a worthy successor, or to bring in new blood. Their increasingly irrational behaviour was tolerated by their acolytes, who found them inspiring on the way up, as long as the formula produced success. For Thatcher, the catalyst for her removal was the poll tax, for Greenbury it was the profits collapse and the attempted coup by Keith Oates. Both were great leaders whose tragedy was that *they failed entirely to appreciate the impact of their personalities on those around them.* They both tended to shoot messengers bearing bad news and so the bad news ceased to reach them – until it was too late.
>
> (Bevan 2002: 210, my emphasis)

This reminds me of being a young participant on a BBC management development course when the then reigning director general was invited to come and hear our possibly somewhat naïve proposals about how to solve the BBC's organizational problems. Most of the time he remained affable and politely interested. However, he suddenly flipped into glacial overdrive at the notion that there was anything wrong with the morale of the BBC's staff, then generally accepted as a major problem, snapping pettishly, 'Don't tell me staff morale has never been lower. Morale has *always never been lower.* Let's get on to the positive, shall we?' Needless to say, with self-preservation sensibly to the fore, our suggestions were made in a noticeably more timid way after that.

In general, the people around us don't tell us the truth. Leaders don't get told the truth by those around them. They don't get told the truth by their bosses and are even less likely to get told the truth by those they manage. They don't get told the truth about the organization and they don't get told the truth about their own leadership styles. There is no mystery about why.

First is the shoot-the-messenger tendency as described by Judi Bevan in her blow by blow account of what happened at Marks & Spencer. People who challenged Rick Greenbury would be treated to terrifying red-faced blasts. A respected journalist on the *Investors Chronicle* wrote what turned out to be a balanced and highly accurate forecast of troubles to come. She was treated to a 'Rickogram': a rude and ill-considered diatribe which the editor must have enjoyed publishing under the headline 'Fierce riposte from M&S's Mr Grumpy'. While a journalist can wriggle free from such attacks, it is much more difficult for colleagues who feel, rightly or wrongly, that their futures depend on the patronage of the leader. It is easier to buy time and whimper in corridors with fellow sufferers than to confront.

The fear of ejection is very real. We can see what happens to the majority of whistleblowers, large or small: they find it difficult initially to get taken seriously and when they do, many seem to end up leaving the organization. Giving feedback is a high-level art and in spite of the fact that it is a skill taught on more or less any management development course in the western world, it is still more often talked about than done. Giving honest feedback will name the pluses as much as it identifies the minuses, but it can still feel like making criticisms, and to do that face to face is uncomfortable. It can feel like attacking the person, and therefore we dread that it might be hurtful to the recipient.

One large study of US managers showed that only half of the sample had ever asked for feedback (Jackman and Strober 2003). Among the many reasons cited were a number of familiar avoidance patterns. These included:

> *Reawakened childish dependence*: being given feedback potentially awakens the feelings of being a child upbraided by more powerful parents. The feedback receiver dreads being chided for behaviour that falls short of the parental ideal.
>
> *Procrastination*: the subject of the feedback knows something is wrong but cannot bear the idea of exploring it.
>
> *Denial*: it might get better if just ignored.
>
> *Brooding*: the person has a morbid preoccupation with the negative and an overwhelming sense of foreboding. Dread of what they might discover becomes magnified.
>
> *Jealousy* in relation to others: the potential feedback subject fantasizes that others will emerge more positively from the exercise and hates the idea of being benchmarked in case this turns out to be true.

Self-sabotage: the subject looks for ways to make the expected negatives real.

Breaking through the feedback-exclusion zone

You could describe much of coaching as being about breaking through the feedback-exclusion zone because an essential preliminary to any successful coaching is increased self-awareness. However, for the purposes of this chapter I want to concentrate on some particular tactics and approaches that coaches can use to help the client with the very first stages of the coaching process. You will have your favourites. These ideas are meant as a menu of options – you will never have time to use them all.

The core questions at this stage are:

Who are you as you see yourself now?

How much do you know about your impact on others?

What are the pressing issues for you?

Autobiography: how did you get from there to here?

I have always regretted it when I have not asked clients for a brief account of their lives so far. If you are going to do it, the first session is your best chance. It builds intimacy and rapport and also establishes that you are interested in the whole person, not just the work person. The whole person has evolved from life experience, so hearing a client tell their life story is one way you begin to understand the client's world.

There are a number of other compelling reasons for doing it:

- For all of us our relationships with authority figures evolved from our relationships with our parents and parent figures such as teachers. Our relationships with peers will have been affected by how we got on with siblings and early friends. These influences on relationships at work will have important effects on approaches to leadership and to being a follower.
- Patterns of emotional response are laid down in childhood and have biological as well as psychological impact (see Chapter 2). It is worth looking for the common patterns (see pages 44–47) as a way of understanding the client's issues.

- What clients emphasize and what they leave out is always interesting and relevant to their view of themselves.
- You will begin to hear the limiting beliefs that clients hold because such beliefs will have been formed in childhood.
- Most clients have never told a complete life story to anyone previously and most enjoy the experience.

Some warnings

You are not doing psychotherapy or psychoanalysis in coaching. For this reason I encourage clients to take no more than 30 minutes to tell their story. If clients resist, do not press but always explain why you are asking, using the explanation above and reassure them of confidentiality. Be prepared for cathartic reactions in clients who have had a childhood trauma such as child abuse or the death of a sibling or parent and take such revelations calmly. It is not your role to make interpretations: leave that to the client.

Do not expect to get 'the whole truth' from this session – it is usually too early. For instance, a gay client may not tell you about their sexuality because they may not feel they can trust you at this stage. You will also want to develop different emphases depending on the expected nature of the coaching. For instance, clients whose expected focus is career coaching can usefully be asked more questions about their career choices to date.

Also, remember that you can overestimate the importance of early experience. Genes play their part in creating temperament. We no longer live in the relatively closed communities of our recent past. Mass migration, old and new media, the increasing importance of teenage and other peer groups, easy access to higher education – all these may have as much influence as the family of origin. Parents may sometimes be guardians rather than shapers of our behaviour.

A useful framework

You will not need to ask all these questions. Pick what appeals and develop your own versions of them, as you see fit.

- What was your place in the family – birth order?
- What effect has your birth order had on you – e.g. the experience of being an only child/the youngest of four?
- How did your parents' occupations shape the person whom you have become?
- How did you feel about school?
- What were you rewarded for as a child? What were you punished for?

- If you had to point to one outstanding experience in your childhood – one that had a really major impact on you, what would that be?
- How would you describe the relationship with each parent?
- How did you get on with your siblings?
- What effects have marriage/partner relationships had on your life?
- (For clients with children) What has the experience of being a parent done for you?
- How did you make your career choices?
- What helped you decide to move on from earlier jobs?
- What have been the highs and lows of these jobs?
- What themes and patterns do you see emerging in the story as you have told it?
- What are the links to the coaching we will be doing?

CASE STUDY

Annette

Annette was chief executive of a consultancy, a firm of which she was a founding director. She described herself as having had a lonely childhood with little overt affection. She was the daughter of two famous theatrical people, both of whom married several times before and after being married to each other. At the last count, she told me, she had three living step-parents, many step- and half-siblings, but no full siblings. Early recollections were of being *prinked up* as she put it, *to appear as a fashion accessory at glamorous parties*, followed by many bleak moments, including being sent to boarding school as a very young child. Her own marriage and children were important to her but she had chosen to work in London during the week while her husband worked on his own business from home, 40 miles away.

What patterns emerged for her in telling this story? She said that for the first time she understood how pervasive had been her lifelong feeling of being alone in a crowd, and that this had been a protective mechanism. It had toughened her up and she felt she could deal with any challenges in her professional life, including dealing with uncompromising and troublesome client organizations. Also, she felt that in telling her life story she had had a moment of insight into the performance aspect of her job: 'I enjoy making pitches for work. I enjoy preparing, I enjoy dressing well for it and I do it well. I've suddenly thought this might be something I've inherited from my parents, though I hate to say it! In fact even the rackety nature of my job could be a bit like theirs.'

And the links with the coaching on which we were just embarking? 'The main reason I'm here,' she said, 'is that I need to understand more about my style with my staff.' The firm was beginning to struggle in its ultra-competitive market-place and Annette had had hints from her team that part of the reason was that, as the founder, she hugged too much work to herself and was a charming but remote presence. 'They tell me they don't know what I feel about them,' she said. 'Mm . . . I wonder why I've never realized this before, that it's got a lot to do with protecting that little girl I used to be in those early days . . .?'

Understanding the pattern also creates a moment of potential choice for the future. *This is how I've been up until now. That was then, this is now. I can choose to be different.* Just occasionally it can feel as if the telling of the story is almost all that needs to happen. The most dramatic example I have ever encountered was that of Michael.

CASE STUDY

Michael

Michael came to his first session with one burning issue. His boss, Felix, had decided to expand his team from four to eight. Michael was deeply uncomfortable about this change, feeling that it was a strategic mistake and that it would make decision-making far more complex than it needed to be. Felix and Michael had a close relationship – in fact they had worked together for 10 years and Felix had brought Michael into their present company with him. Michael's role in effect was to be special adviser to Felix and he had helped him do what he described as 'keeping the stupidities of the organization at bay'. They socialized outside work and their families got on well together.

Michael's early life was unusual. He was one of eight children in a tightly-knit fundamentalist Christian household which held severe and inflexible views about mixing outside the exclusive society created within the tiny church community. He was one of a pair of fraternal twins in the middle of the family. He and his brother – at first subtly and then overtly – rebelled against what they saw as the strictures of the family's way of life, its religiosity, its harsh rules and its stifling lack of privacy. They even developed a special twins' language which their parents could not understand. As adults they had broken away, completely rejecting their faith. This had included 'marrying out' and being cut off from the family as a consequence.

As he was telling me this, Michael suddenly broke off, stared at me wildly, smote his forehead melodramatically and said, 'Oh my God, I've just realized . . .'

'You've realized . . .?'

'Eight children . . . eight is the size of the new team! Felix is not my brother is he! The team is not my family!'

Michael's realization that he had unconsciously brought a deeply shaping childhood experience into his work was a profound and liberating moment for him. He realized that he had been making false assumptions about the changes ahead and was thus able to think completely differently about the work situation.

Lifelines

An alternative way of building up an autobiography by simply asking clients to tell you their life story is to brief them in advance to draw it as a graph, bringing the result to the session. The horizontal axis represents years and the vertical axis represents the peaks and troughs of experience. This approach has the benefit of concentrating on the most important moments of the client's life, whether they are the moments of sadness and disappointment or of triumphant success and happiness. Also, as with any technique that bypasses verbal analysis, you may get to the core issues more quickly.

Alternative approaches to autobiography

A Life in the Day

When *The Sunday Times* newspaper began its colour supplement in the early 1970s, its then editor, Hunter Davies, devised a brilliantly simple but endlessly fascinating back page feature called 'A Life in the Day', often mistakenly described as 'A Day in the Life' and still going strong. The person who is the focus of the article is asked to describe a typical apparently humdrum day: what time they get up, what they eat and drink throughout the day, how they get to and from work – all the way through until bedtime. Asking clients to give me a life in the day is a wonderfully revealing and mutually useful exercise, especially where I know I have the luxury of working with clients over a longer period, so there is less time pressure.

The activity unearths a different quality of data from anything else I have tried. For instance, I discovered the following with these clients:

Clive feels so pressured by his job as a finance director that he unwinds by staying up every night long after his family have gone to bed. He surfs the internet for hours. Only then can he relax. His sexual life is suffering as a result and so is his energy, as he still has to get up at 7.00 a.m., regardless of whatever time he has gone to sleep.

Man Weh feels the pressure of being the only son of a first-generation immigrants from Hong Kong. His elderly parents speak little English and he visits them every day. He also feels obliged to devote a good deal of volunteer time to various support groups working for the London Chinese community.

Diane has six cats, four dogs, a guinea pig and two rabbits whose comfort she puts before her own. Her anthropomorphized relationships with them are probably preventing her putting energy into the more demanding area of human relationships.

Colin loves the rough and tumble of the undemanding male company that he finds in his local pub. This is refreshingly different from the competitive relationships he has at work. It also leads him to drink more beer than is good for his liver or his waistline. Divulging this aspect of his life allows him to speak out loud a worry that he might have an alcohol problem.

Some of my work is in the media sector and one of my clients, knowing that I sometimes asked for this story, offered to snap a series of pictures of a typical day for me, which he duly presented as an entertaining slide show with music, on his iPad. I thought this was a brilliant idea and now that digital photography is so easy and commonplace, have suggested it to other clients. However, whatever the medium – video, still photographs, writing, drawing, straight description – the discussion will be the same. What does this tell you and the client about the issues they are bringing to coaching?

360-degree feedback

I suggest this process to perhaps a third of my clients. When done well, there are few other ways as reliable of creating a platform for the coaching. Mostly in coaching we are dependent on *storytelling* from the client as the main source of data. When you commission a 360-degree process you are bringing the *observation* of others into play – hence its value.

This type of feedback is a planned process of soliciting comment from a selection of people in a range of relationships all around you (hence the label 360-degree). These people will typically come from whatever significant constituencies there are in the client's work life, for instance, peers, boss or other seniors, customers/clients, and people who are direct reports. I have occasionally had clients who suggest adding their partner or older children to the exercise on the grounds that these important people may see who they are even more clearly than colleagues. I have always agreed to these requests.

Where you are doing executive coaching, it is critical to make the compelling business case to the client for the self-awareness that 360-degree feedback can bring. It is not just another nice-to-have; it can also be critical to the success of the business. In his book *The New Leaders* (Goleman *et al.* 2002), Daniel Goleman quotes research into what distinguished the leadership of a number of highly successful US healthcare companies from the least successful ones. Positive performance was measured by return on equity, share price and so on over a 10-year period. He says:

> Tellingly, the CEOs from the poorest performing companies gave themselves the highest ratings on seven of the ten leadership abilities. But the pattern reversed when it came to how their subordinates rated them: they gave these CEOs low ratings on the very same abilities. On the other hand, subordinates saw the CEOs of the best performing companies as demonstrating all ten of these leadership abilities most often.
>
> (Goleman *et al.* 2002: 95)

So self-delusion was associated with poor company performance and a high level of self-awareness with company success. In one of Goleman's own parallel studies he also found that the more senior the managers, the more they were likely to inflate their own ratings. 'Those at the highest levels had the least accurate view of how they acted with others.'

There are a number of different ways 360-degree feedback can be done.

By the client

This is the simplest and most direct method. Ask the client to pick eight people and to contract with them for some private time and for honest answers to the following questions:

> In what ways do you think I am already effective?
>
> In what ways do you think I am less effective?
>
> What could I do to improve my relationship with you?

What would be the one piece of advice you would give me about how to improve my effectiveness?

Prime the client on how to encourage honest responses, pressing for examples and further clarity, and writing down everything their feedback-givers say without protesting, arguing or editing. This method has the tremendous advantage of people owning their opinions directly to the client and the client hearing them without any intermediary. However, it does depend on clients being able to stay in non-defensive mode when they hear things they don't like and to press courteously for examples, and it also depends on the ability and willingness of the feedback-givers to be straightforward.

Questionnaires

There are hundreds of commercially available questionnaires, most of which can now be delivered to respondents via the internet. The questionnaire should be based on unambiguous behavioural descriptions. An early version of a 360-degree questionnaire in one organization was widely greeted with snorts of derision because one of the items was 'behaves in a way that leads others to trust him/her'. To the sceptical audience at whom it was aimed, the phrasing was clear evidence of management gobbledegook. Actually, as a description of behaviour it was simply too broad for anyone to answer easily. The questionnaire should always be tailored for the organization, using its own language and linked to its particular organizational development needs to get around this kind of problem.

About 60 items is the right number. Most questionnaires have a five-point scale for rating effectiveness although recent research suggests that a simple 'traffic light' system of *yes/no/don't know* answers may give higher quality results. It's vital to have free-flow open questions at the end where people can write in their comments. This helps give the messages clearly and also explains why people have scored the client the way they have.

The client should always be free to choose the respondents. This guards against any tendency to hide behind the idea that the feedback is something that is being done *to* him or her. You need at least eight respondents to achieve a valid result, including the client's self-perception. Confidentiality is vital. This is why it is always better to have the collating process handled outside the organization. Although this feedback is better than nothing, I am dubious about how much value it adds. The graphs may look 'scientific' but there is no way of knowing whether all the 'raters' were using the same criteria when they scored the client. When many such forms have to be filled in within a short time period, for instance where a whole team is undertaking the same exercise, raters can become bored and sloppy, clicking on any old box just to get it over with. Most seriously, the free-form answers are often just hastily composed summaries and are easily dismissed as meaningless by the subject of the report.

Telephone interviews

This is the Rolls-Royce version of 360-degree feedback and much more valuable. Again the client nominates and prepares the respondents. You telephone them under conditions of non-attributable confidentiality, conducting the same structured interview with each, exploring areas such as creating direction, leadership style, performance management, influencing style, communication and so on. You then write a report for your client based on what you have heard. My reports typically run to seven or eight pages. The advantage of this method is that you can probe for examples and for clarification. You can also explore any interesting inconsistencies – for instance that the client's impact on more junior people is different from their impact on seniors. The disadvantage of this method is that it depends critically on your ability to ask good questions, to stay objective and to avoid convergent thinking at the same time as not missing the important themes, and to write the report in a way that your client can hear. For added objectivity you might want to commission a colleague who has never met the client to undertake this process for you or to partner you in it.

Debriefing

With either form of 360-degree feedback, the debrief is the place where the learning begins. Your role here is to:

- help the client look unblinkingly at the messages – positive, negative and middling;
- steady and reassure clients who only see the negative;
- challenge clients who are unduly complacent;
- remind clients that feedback is not an instruction to change: they can choose what they take notice of and what they ignore;
- help the client make links to how they see themselves and to other feedback they have received over the years;
- help the client make links to their own perceptions of their learning agenda.

I sometimes give clients a blank grid to take away, ponder and complete to bring back with them for the next session (see Figure 5.1). The impact of 360-degree feedback is usually considerable.

Use this grid to fill in what the main messages are for you:

Good news		
Not aware already	Pleasant surprise: over-modesty?	Affirmation: how can I carry on with the good work?	Already aware
	Shock/denial: how true is this really?	Challenge to action: how can I change and do the new behaviour consistently – if I want to?	
Bad news		

Figure 5.1 Responding to 360-degree feedback

CASE STUDY

Annette, continued

Annette decided that there was an information gap for her – she simply did not know what people really thought and felt about her, so she decided to commission some feedback from me.

Annette's feedback confirmed many of her own insights into how others saw her, but it also surprised her. People in her team saw her as calm, composed, stylish and aloof. Her team saw that her ability to make shrewd judgements about the future market and its trends was an important contribution to the firm's success – 'a natural strategist' summed up many similar comments.

Her composure, even in a crisis, which both she and others saw as one of her greatest assets, was also perceived to be a weakness. 'Does she actually have feelings?' asked one person exasperatedly. Similarly, her drive, another considerable plus, also had the power to alienate. 'I think she just sees us as invoicing machines' was how one person put it. Many people spotted her failure to grow a successor, pointing out that this was putting the firm at risk.

Similarly, they spelt out in painful detail how undermining they found her difficulty in delegating. The extent of their annoyance and frustration came as a shock to Annette. But perhaps the biggest shock of all was that when asked about what they perceived her values to be, the majority of the people filling in the questionnaire said they did not know. Others assumed that Annette's core motivation was making money, a big turn-off for the majority of her staff. While it was true that Annette was a natural entrepreneur, she had also chosen to build her firm aiming at non-profit organizations because she, too, shared these values. 'Surely they can see,' she asked mournfully, 'that I'd make so much more money if I'd decided to go for other sectors!' But alas, it was clear that people did not see this.

In discussing these results with Annette, we agreed that the agenda for coaching was:

- building on her strategic ability to reposition the firm against its competitors and to do this through involving her staff;
- rebooting her leadership style by learning how to describe her values far more clearly;
- learning to disclose her feelings, including talking more about her family and asking other people about theirs;

- adopting a coaching approach with the seniors in her team and then delegating a significant amount of work to them.

Getting 360-degree feedback was supremely useful for Annette. It allowed her to test her own ideas about what she needed to develop against what other people saw. Like many other clients, the majority of the criticism was about the overuse of her strengths. The process allowed her to make informed decisions about which parts of the feedback to pay attention to and which she could downplay.

Annette was a mature, focused client, already halfway there in terms of self-awareness. Sometimes you will coach people for whom this is not true. Here the 360-degree process has the potential for enormous shock because how the client sees him- or herself is so much at odds with the perceptions of others. Your role here is to stay steady, calm and compassionate. There is an ever-present danger of colluding. This could include some or all of the following:

It's not true.

It's their fault that they don't see your virtues; they are all less intelligent than you.

It was a bad day for them when they filled it in.

The methodology is flawed.

It doesn't really matter how people see you.

It's only the view of a few people, if more had been asked it would look different.

You used to be like that but of course you've changed

. . . and so on.

CASE STUDY

Malcolm

Malcolm was poised to leap to the most senior tier in his organization and initially asked for help in dealing with the promotion process. In discussing his agenda, it emerged that he had a number of pressing issues with his current job and we agreed to extend the remit of the coaching to include these. It was clear that 360-degree feedback would help. The dismally negative messages in the report alerted me to the need for extra care in the debrief. People saw Malcolm as an angry bully, impatient, prone to inexplicable rages, impossible to please and unable to develop any but the most able of his team. His saving graces were grudgingly seen as his intelligence and his expert knowledge. I emailed Malcolm a copy of the report a carefully calculated 24 hours ahead of our meeting, asking him to mark anything he thought would deserve special attention and suggesting he did not overreact to the contents because we would be talking them through together and putting them in context.

For someone others saw as a bully, Malcolm looked white-faced, shaky and shockingly upset when we met for our session. He was soon in tears. I asked what the tears were about. 'Shame,' he said. 'I've had an insight into what it must be like to be managed by me. I'd hate to be managed by me. They don't even like me do they? How could I have got to this?'

Most of that session was spent in constructing exactly what behaviour Malcolm's colleagues saw and why it had the impact it did. We got down to micro-behaviours: the way he sometimes darted forward in his chair; his piercing stare when puzzled; the jabbing finger when explaining his point of view; the way he raised his voice when confronted.

We also looked hard at the fear of failure that lay beneath all of this and how this fear drowned out perspective. In looping back to his autobiographical account, Malcolm made the clearest possible links to a childhood with a violent and alcoholic father. 'I learnt to fight back then, but what I've got to learn now is that I'm not fighting him – he's been dead many years in any case. I despised him but I'm doing the same kind of behaviour. It's urgent for me to learn to like myself and then to start liking others, rather than fearing how they might damage me unless I get in first!'

The next major question for Malcolm was his fear: fear that his behaviour was so ingrained that he might not be able to change.

Several years later, I met Malcolm in another context. He told me that he had never been so frightened in his life as he had been at the moment of receiving that report and that the jolting shock had been the painful but necessary stimulus to a fresh start.

Other useful data for the first session

Ask clients to bring along anything that they think might help give a rounded picture of who they are. This might include their latest appraisal, a staff survey involving their department or organization, and their CV. The CV for instance, may look like a bland, factual document, but actually it tells unerringly how that client sees themselves – or presents themselves to the world, not least what it leaves out. Where clients have already done psychometrics relatively recently, ask them to bring the results with them.

Psychometrics

As part of the 'know thyself' theme for clients, it is useful to be able to offer them a suite of psychometric questionnaires. Psychometrics means, literally, measuring the human mind and as a science it has been around for many decades. What is measured and how you measure it and which method is best will continue to be the focus of fierce debate. There are thousands of questionnaires available, many of dubious merit. I prefer to rely on the few tried and tested instruments which are backed by convincing research, are easy to understand and have proved genuinely enlightening to clients time and time again.

The case for psychometrics

Many of us assume that the way we approach the world is, plus or minus a few unimportant details, just like the way others approach it. Psychometrics offer a useful way to demonstrate in just what ways we are like and unlike others. Psychometrics give a short cut through what might otherwise take many hours of further discussion and the language of psychometrics can become a useful shared vocabulary, not just between coach and client, but between client and other clients.

Using two or three such instruments gives several different methods of approach because the starting point of each will be contrasting but valuable. Here are some popular choices for coaches. You can buy the starred items without being licensed:

> *The Myers Briggs Type Indicator*™ (MBTI),[1] first developed by Isabel Myers and her mother Katharine Briggs in the middle years of the twentieth century and constantly updated ever since. The underlying framework is Jungian. Clients emerge as having a preference for one of 16 different personality types. The Indicator highlights preferred thinking style and offers hypotheses about the behaviour likely to be associated with each style.

The FIRO-B™ (Fundamental Interpersonal Relationships Orientation-Behaviour), first developed by the US psychologist Will Schutz for the US Navy during the Korean War. The questionnaire produces scores against six dimensions of need and style in terms of how we typically behave with others.

The 16 PF (16 Personality Factors), first developed by the British psychologist Raymond Catell.

Big Five personality questionnaires. These are based on research combining results and thinking from many earlier questionnaires and identifying five overarching factors in human personality. Suites of questionnaires include the *NEO* and the *Hogan*.

The Belbin Team Roles Questionnaire. This well-known questionnaire identifies which of nine possible informal roles in a team the client will typically prefer to play.

The OPQ (Occupational Personality Questionnaire), developed and distributed by the British company Saville and Holdsworth, recognizably in the same genre as the 16 PF.

*Career Anchors: Edgar Schein's approach to uncovering career motivators. The basic proposition is that in every life there is one driving motivator. The questionnaire and booklet (Schein 2006) suggest a format for uncovering what this is. Especially useful for clients where career is the focus.

The Strong Interest Inventory. This is a vocational interests questionnaire, useful for people with career dilemmas. The Strong also has a long and distinguished history and has been updated many times since its first appearance in the 1920s.

*The Thomas-Kilmann Conflict Mode Instrument, first developed in the 1970s. Five typical conflict-management styles are identified, giving clients the opportunity to see which they tend to prefer and which they tend to avoid.

The Ennegram has until recently been an orally taught approach to personality, said to be based on Sufi thinking and incorporating a spiritual dimension. There are now questionnaires available which help identify which of the nine personality types represents your typical style. For a useful briefing on the general approach, read Palmer and Brown's book, *The Enneagram Advantage* (1998).

Using psychometrics skilfully

The most important question to ask is why you are using a psychometric questionnaire at all. Working with new coaches, I often observe undue interest in questionnaires such as the MBTI. We can all be attracted to these and other tools and techniques out of anxiety. The thinking goes something like this:

> If I have a questionnaire to administer and interpret, at least I will be on safe ground. I won't have to worry so much about what question to ask next. I'll have a structure to help me.

When this is your motive, recognize it for what it is: a way of exerting control over the client and over your own fear of incompetence. Using a questionnaire or any other coaching tool for this reason only postpones the moment of coming face to face with the fear and, paradoxically, ensures that you will stay at Level 1 listening (see page 66). You could also be tempted to use questionnaires indiscriminately, blind to whether or not the client really needs them. As the old joke has it, 'Give a boy a hammer and he'll discover that everything needs hammering.' Work on your listening skills and questioning technique first.

Don't meddle in this area without training. Licensing training is necessary for most tests: you can't buy them unless you are a registered user. Training prevents disrespectful misuse of such instruments, on the basis that they could come to seem like an interesting but essentially trivial exercise of about as much importance as a magazine quiz. Training may seem like an expensive and time-intrusive exercise, but repays the investment you have made, many times over.

The best time to use psychometrics is at or near the beginning of a coaching programme. Some coaches plan a half-day meeting for the second session where they debrief a number of instruments together or send them to the client in advance of the first session after a conversation about whether or not they might be useful. If you have the qualifications and experience, this is probably the ideal way to do it.

However wonderful a psychometric questionnaire is, and many are wonderful, it is never the whole truth about a person. First, the questionnaires are self-report instruments, so they are always potentially open to being filled in as we would hope to be seen rather than as we really are. High-quality questionnaires have safeguards against this tendency, but none is completely foolproof, so all questionnaires depend to some extent on the subject's willingness to take the risk of being candid. Results can also be affected by mood or by particular periods of stress or crisis.

Carl Jung, on whose thinking the MBTI is based, described his typology as 'compass points in the wilderness of human personality'. Those are wise words. Similarly, it can be tempting to assume that questionnaire results represent some kind of final judgement on a person, regardless of that person's own view of themselves. One of the most important questions in the debriefing discussion is, 'How does this seem to you?', or 'How does this tally with how you see yourself?' The client's answer here has to be the best and last word on the topic.

The feedback discussion is at the heart of the process. It involves:

- allowing enough time for a full exploration;
- asking how the client felt answering the questions;
- reassuring the client that you will be keeping their results confidential and that they will never be used for any other purpose (e.g. selection);
- acknowledging any scepticism or irritation as healthy;
- briefly explaining the underlying theory behind the questionnaire;
- asking the client to make an estimate of how they are likely to emerge against the various dimensions or factors;
- comparing this with the questionnaire results;
- establishing how far the results match self-perception and any other sources of feedback such as 360-degree;
- looking at examples of behaviour which match the reported results;
- seeking examples of behaviour which do *not* match the reported results;
- looking at strengths and development areas and agreeing how to take these forward.

In using psychometric questionnaires you are potentially disturbing the balance of power in the client–coaching relationship. In the normal run of a coaching conversation, the client has the information and you have the questions – in pursuit of a shared understanding. With psychometrics, you have expert information about the questionnaire. This could disadvantage the client and probably explains why many clients will express nervousness about completing a questionnaire with whose purpose they are unfamiliar:

> Will it tell you something about me that could be uncomfortably revealing?

Poor use of debriefing techniques can include what one of my colleagues dubs *psychological rape*: telling the client that they are something devastatingly unpleasant from the lofty pinnacle of your expertise:

> The questionnaire tells me that you are undemocratic in the way you run your team.

> You are at risk of imploding if you don't manage your stress better.

> You don't delegate very well do you?

This is why the principles of creating trust through respect must prevail here as elsewhere in coaching. If the client does not want to take a 'test' even after you have given them your best shot at reassurance, then don't press it. Taking any psychometric questionnaire should be voluntary. Watch out for any tendency in yourself to make arbitrary assertions about what a client can or can't do (jobs, skills, relationships) on the basis of the results of the questionnaire. No test has sufficient predictive validity to do this, but in any case such an assertion would be an abuse. Equally importantly, it's essential to resist the temptation to over-interpret. Your role is to explain. The questionnaire results are hypotheses only. Any interpretation should be left to the client. Finally, be alert to your own results on the same tests, sharing them with clients in the interests of equality and keeping constantly aware of the biases and blind spots which might influence how you work with your client on these same issues.

Note

1   This questionnaire, the FIRO-B, the 16 PF and the Strong Interest Inventory are distributed in the UK through Oxford Psychologists Press, which also runs accredited training courses.

6   Choosing the future: creating goals for coaching

In my role as an assessor for the Diploma in Coaching, I have listened to hundreds of hours of other people's coaching. Some of the candidates are experienced coaches looking for a benchmark qualification. More typically they are relatively inexperienced. I have come to see that this whole business of goal-setting is more difficult than it looks. If excellent questioning is one pillar of coaching technique, another must surely be setting robust goals. In this chapter I describe why it matters to set goals and how to do it.

Findings from research

Goal-setting as an aspect of motivation has been one of the most minutely examined areas of management and has been the focus of many hundreds of studies. It has also been the centre of many research projects in sports science – for instance, what part does goal-setting play in improving the performance of athletes? The outcome of these studies gives a remarkably consistent picture:

- The process of setting a goal directs attention and therefore affects behaviour.
- Setting goals improves performance.
- The more explicit and measurable a goal is, the more effective it is likely to be as a way of changing behaviour.
- Stretching goals, which also have intermediate, measurable steps, are highly effective in improving performance.
- Easy goals are not motivating.
- Goal-setting is at its most effective when it builds on strengths – so, *How can I be even better at something I'm already good at?* is more motivating than *How can I tackle a weakness?*
- Developing strategies for coping with the inevitable difficulties en route can make the difference between success and failure.
- It matters who sets the goal: a negotiated goal in which you participate in an unforced way is likely to have the biggest impact.

- There is a difference between *performance* goals, which are about avoiding appearing incompetent, and *learning* goals, which are about mastery. Learning goals are far more effective in enhancing self-esteem and in their long-term impact.

There is a firm match in these findings[1] with what we know works with goal-setting in coaching.

Goal-setting matters. Getting clarity on goals begins the whole process of change. It matters to the coach because without this clarity you will not be able to work with the client or measure the success of your coaching (see also 'Return on investment', page 236).

Where and how goal-setting goes wrong

When you are aware that a session has had an uneasily unsatisfactory feel to it, assume until proved otherwise that poor goal-setting was the cause. Here is some of what can go wrong and how it happens. My colleagues and I have made all these mistakes, and some of us were serial offenders until we realized our errors, but you can learn from our hard-won experience:

The coach assumes they know what the goal for the session is, but never clarifies it – and the real goal is something different

This phenomenon is well expressed in the reflective diary that Suzie submitted as part of her diploma portfolio. This was her second session with Janos, a 45-year-old former librarian who had been unemployed for a year, had said he was looking for a job but who, she had established, still yearned to recapture the modest success in the music industry that he had enjoyed as a young man.

> ## CASE STUDY
> ### Suzie
>
> I really struggled in this session. It seemed to start OK but as it went on I felt more and more worried. I thought I had asked all the right questions. He was very polite and so was I but the time went *sooo* slowly! When I asked him for feedback at the end of the session, he said he wasn't sure that coaching was right for him and that maybe two sessions were enough. I felt so hurt! I was giving him my time for free! I also felt

angry, though tried not to show it, but inside I was thinking, *Well why don't you get off your backside and look for a job, for heaven's sake, do you really want a job or are you content to sit around feeling sorry for yourself for another year . . .!* However, when I played the recording back, it all became so very clear what had happened. I had assumed that the goal was how to find a library job. But I had never asked the question that would have established whether this was the goal for the session or not. The real goal lurking there somewhere was whether he should have one last go at establishing himself again as a musician. I know literally nothing about the freelance music world. I worked in a local authority for years, so of course my assumption was that 'everyone' should have a 'proper' job and because I knew about our library services I assumed that he would want another job like the one he had held previously. Whereas for Janos, none of this turned out to be correct. I just didn't pick up his reluctance to pursue the 'proper job' option because I never questioned my own assumptions.

Suzie's experience is salutary and is also common. It is so easy to assume that you know what the client's goal is. This can happen with experienced as well as inexperienced coaches. In fact it may even be more tempting for those experienced coaches who have heard so many of the same issues before – or believe they have. *Oh yes*, you think, *this is my old friend better time management*, or, *It's that good old work-life balance issue again*. Whereas actually, it may be nothing of the sort.

The coach confuses the client's responsibility to set the agenda with the coach's responsibility to clarify and frame the goal

As Suzie's experience also shows, while it is the client's job to create the agenda, it is the coach's job to frame the agenda items into the goals on which coach and client can work. It is a mistake to assume that clients will arrive at their sessions with perfectly formed goals. Much more frequently, client and coach use the first part of each chunk in a coaching session to make clear exactly what that goal is. It is normal for clients to be at least a little vague or confused about the goal and for the real goal to emerge through skilful questioning on the part of the coach. In fact, if the client was already totally clear about the goal, they might not need the coaching at all. This is because clarity about the goal may already be generating the motivation that will sweep many of us towards achieving it.

The coach allows the client to chatter on about what has happened since the last session without intervening to agree goals

All coaching sessions will rightly start with a catch-up. *How did you get on with the actions we agreed last time? What else has happened?* But some clients can let this account run on seamlessly into the body of the session. This is what was happening to Janice in her sessions with Austin.

CASE STUDY

Janice (coach) and Austin (client)

I really enjoyed Austin's style. He was a senior manager and a high flier in a telecoms company and was well up for coaching. Essentially his 360-degree feedback showed that people felt he was a go-getting person, lively and conscientious, but that he was a poor listener who didn't always show good judgement. He was eager for 'homework' and would try everything, but all of it would prove to have generated other problems and further interesting issues. After some frank supervision sessions based on my recordings, I realized that the catch-up on action points was morphing into the whole session and that three-quarters of an hour or even an hour could go by with no goal set. Of course I also realized that Austin was amply demonstrating to me the very behaviour that had led him to coaching in the first place.

Like Suzie, Janice was making assumptions. The goals might have been implied in Austin's enthusiastic accounts but these assumptions were never tested.

Getting stuck on 'problems'

Typically what happens is this. The client presents his/her issue as a problem:

> I can't manage my time.

> My business is failing – we've got terrible results this quarter.

> I feel stressed all the time.

The coach's sympathy is aroused – she wants to help. She then dives into the many dimensions of the problem: how much, how many, how awful ... quickly feeling as hopeless as the client. Where you have the benefit of videotape or actual observation you can see both client and coach literally sinking deeper into their chairs with the misery of it all. Sympathetic chat, yes, but coaching, no.

Being asked to change someone who is not present

Here the client presents another variant of the problem-scenario. The client says:

> My boss is awful – I can't bear her.
>
> I've got this poor performer in my team.
>
> I'm working with someone who's cheating the company.

The trap here is to ask a lot of questions about the non-present person: how old are they? What is their role? What is the behaviour they do which is so upsetting? Soon, unless you manage it carefully, this leads into the realms of speculation: why do you think they behave like this? What are they thinking when they do this? How do you feel they might respond if you did this or that thing?

When you go down this track you are potentially colluding with the client, tacitly agreeing that the problem is *out there*, rather than *in here*. The only person you have in the room is the client and they are one half of the relationship. You can't coach someone who is not present. Nor can you coach a client on a problem which they do not own – only on the part which is theirs. So for the client who suspects that a colleague is cheating the company, the goal cannot be, as hinted by the client, to stop him cheating. But the goal might be, after discussion with the client, to assess the evidence that cheating is indeed taking place and then to tackle the dilemma of what to do about it.

The goal is enormous: far too big to work on in any one session

When clients have stored a high degree of misery and uncertainty inside themselves for some time, the relief of having someone to discuss it all with can be overwhelming. When asked about their goals for coaching, they may say something like:

> I want to know what to do with the rest of my life.
>
> I want to be happier.
>
> I need to develop a better leadership style.
>
> I want to know why I'm still single at 40.

While these are important underlying themes – in fact they are themes which underpin a great deal of successful coaching – they are far too big to manage in one session and must be broken down into smaller goals on which you can work, one chunk at a time. Also, the bigger the overall goal, the more likely it is that the mental blocks and barriers are substantial, will only dissolve slowly and that consequently the 'answers' will emerge gradually. It is most unlikely that the client will suddenly have a Eureka moment where an easy solution to a major and long-standing problem just plops into place, though to read some accounts of coaching you could imagine, as a naïve coach, that this is an everyday occurrence.

The client doesn't actually have any goals

This may seem odd. Surely every client has a goal – isn't that why they've come for coaching? But now that coaching has become a popular intervention in organizations, it is being widely offered to whole cohorts of staff – for instance as follow-up to a management development programme. I will never now take on a new client without a so-called *look-see* conversation the aim of which is to assess the viability of the relationship from both sides. It is healthy for clients to consider at least two possible coaches and as a coach to be prepared to say no if the client does not seem a good fit with you for whatever reason. Lack of goals is one of the main reasons that I will tell a client not only that I am not the right coach for them but that I doubt they need a coach at all. Be wary of any client, for instance, who tells you that they are 'curious about what coaching is' and wonders 'if it might be fun'. Or the one who says that because the organization has made it available, they may as well give it a try. Or, it's free, so why not? None of these is a strong foundation for future work.

A coaching conversation is unlike other kinds of friendly discussion in many ways, not least in the emphasis it puts on change. Where a client believes that nothing needs to change then there can be no coaching. Goals for the future are best created through identifying what we have and comparing it with what we want. If the gap is tiny then it is unlikely that we will have any appetite for change, and without this appetite there can be no coaching agenda. Even anger is better than apathy. The awareness of dissatisfaction is what creates our energy for transformation and improvement.

CASE STUDY

Jonathan

Jonathan was a newly-appointed ambassador and had just been through a five-day leadership programme at the Foreign and Commonwealth Office. He and his colleagues on the course had been thoroughly briefed on what coaching was and had been equipped with some suitable questions to ask us, expecting in their turn to be asked by us what they wanted to achieve through the coaching as a preliminary to making a choice of coach at a 'meet the coaches' event organized by the HR team in the organization. When I asked him what challenges his new role would involve this was how the conversation went, in shortened form:

Jonathan: Well, this posting is the apex of my career. It's a very important country strategically for the UK and I'm looking forward to going there. It's going to be great. My wife and I . . .

JR: (interrupting) Sorry to interrupt you, but coaching is really about working with you on the challenges that the new role will bring. What do you think those will be?

Jonathan: Well, I think I can take them all in my stride really. You see this is the apex of my career, and . . . (and on round the same loop several times).

When our HR contact rang me the next day to see which of the people I had met I thought I could work with, I asked her not to tell me whether Jonathan had chosen me, saying that I did not feel he really wanted coaching and therefore was not on my list. While it was perfectly possible that he could have benefited from coaching, he did not really believe he needed it because he seemed to have no immediate or longer-term goals that coaching could satisfy. Privately I mused that it was not the role of the coach to be audience to the client's theatre.

Don't misunderstand. This was a charming and able man, but I was willing to forecast that any coaching would quickly peter out and I was not prepared to live with the disappointment and frustration that this would involve.

There is a high price to pay for failing to tackle these problems. What happens inside the session is that it begins to acquire a going-round-in-circles air. This is because it is going round in circles. No goal has been set so the coach cannot ask the 'magic questions' (see pages 00–00) and gets stuck on what to say next. The client's real goal has not been identified so both parties are likely to endorse the polite fiction that they are engaged in coaching. But inside, both will have the feeling that something is wrong. Both may be blaming themselves – the coach for not knowing what to do to retrieve the situation, the client for failing in the role of client. Commonly, clients will believe that the session has run out of steam because they have not made it *interesting enough* for the coach and that the coach has become bored. Alternatively, either party may be blaming each other. The coach finds herself disliking the client for his vagueness and the client finds himself criticizing the coach for not bringing a solution any closer. By the stage that the coach has realized that something has gone badly wrong, she is feeling frantic: the client is not getting value for his time and money, it's all the coach's fault, so she has to find a solution for him. She's right back to Level 1 listening and her mental dialogue is panic: 'I'm a terrible coach. This client is probably feeling worse by the minute' (she's right, he is, or else just bored and annoyed). It's so terrible that, sooner rather than later, advice-giving kicks in and, subtly or overtly, the coach gives the client suggestions about what to do. The word 'I' intrudes more and more. At this point she will experience the energy swiftly leaching away from the session because the client will be stalling and blocking. What you notice when you listen to these recorded sessions from the calm and objectivity of your role as supervisor is that the coach gradually begins to do more and more of the work. She steps up her interventions in both frequency and length while the client seems to disappear from the conversation.

In a videotaped session of this sort, submitted for review by a very inexperienced coach, I noticed that the client physically retreated, shifting his chair inch by inch away and moving his body so that only his side and shoulder were facing the coach. As this happened, the coach became more and more desperate, pursuing the client by inching his own chair closer and closer, talking more and more loudly as he pressed on with his unwanted advice.

Solutions

- The first part of the solution is to notice what is happening: you do not yet have a goal you can work on. Next, remind yourself constantly that it is your job to provide *the process framework of the session*, meaning its mechanics such as goal-setting and timekeeping. Never leave this to the client or assume that, if you did, the client could or would want to do it.
- If you notice that the first 5 or 10 minutes have passed and that you have not agreed goals, stick at it with the client until you do have a set of proper goals for the session. Don't let the client wriggle out of it. Interrupt if necessary (see page 89). Be prepared to express your unease.

- Where clients present their issues as negatives, aim to flip the negative to a positive. You cannot work on a negative. For instance, it cannot be a goal to say that you would like to avoid losing at tennis. It is a goal to say that you would like to win your matches. So for instance, if the client says, 'I can't talk to my sister without there being a row,' you respond, 'So you'd like to be able to learn how to talk to your sister with calm on both sides?'
- Make sure the goal includes the phrase *how to.*
- If the issue is a dilemma, the goal may be how to get clarity on what the issues are rather than necessarily finding a solution on the spot, or it may be to weigh up all the alternatives and make the actual decision. So the client says, 'I don't know whether to stay in my present job or look for a managerial role.' You respond, 'So you'd like to use this session to get clarity about whether to stay put or look for a managerial role?'
- Where the client still resists, again express your unease and say, 'I'm still not sure that we have a real goal here.' Other useful phrases are:

> Assuming our coaching today is successful, what would have changed for you as a result?
>
> What's our goal for this session?
>
> What would an ideal solution here be?
>
> What help do you need from me on this?

- Distinguish the goal *for the session* from the goal around the *issue.* So the overall goal might be that the client wants to prepare for a job selection process, but the goal for the session might be to get feedback on how he or she is answering typical job interview questions.

A hierarchy of goals

I am aware that, when put like this, goal-setting possibly sounds tedious, mechanical and long-winded. It's actually a knack, and need take no more than a few moments, but like so much else in coaching the knack is acquired through a high level of self-awareness, plus training, practice and feedback from a more experienced coach or supervisor. Learning to do it properly will immeasurably increase the value your clients get from your coaching and therefore will also increase your own levels of satisfaction and confidence.

Note that after a while a few clients do realize the importance of proper goals and will begin to frame them in a way that means you and they can start work straight away. A short while ago, a client with whom I have worked off and on for some years, through several different jobs, leapt into the room and scarcely had his coat off before saying, 'I know you're going to ask me what my goals for the session are and I know you won't let me get away with anything fluffy. So here are my three goals for the session in priority order and I suggest we spend the first 45 minutes on that one and then see how we go.' Naturally, I agreed to all this with meekness, grace and good humour.

Transactional (performance) and transformational (learning) goals

In coaching we are working with two different kinds of goals, often simultaneously. *Transactional* or *performance* goals are specific tasks that a client wants to achieve. These are often externally imposed and have an emphasis on short-term performance. Sometimes they have the flavour of dodging failure or of avoiding looking incompetent. Examples would be:

- Enrol for the gym and go twice a week.
- Run my departmental meeting to time.
- Get through a job interview successfully.
- Recruit a new marketing manager.
- Deliver an effective presentation to the board next week.
- Carry out appraisals with all of my staff by the end of February.

There is nothing wrong with such goals: I work on goals like them with clients all the time.

However, *transformational* – or *learning* – goals have much more power. These are the goals that are about intrinsic satisfaction. They are internally focused and are about increasing capacity to deal with similar situations and dilemmas whenever they arise, rather than with achieving a short-term task. It really only needs a moment or two of reframing to help the client see the difference:

Transactional goal	**A transformational equivalent**
Enrol for the gym and go twice a week.	Discover what I enjoy and can sustain to improve my physical fitness and then commit to it.
Deliver an effective presentation to the board next week.	Increase my awareness of what constitutes effectiveness in presentations and apply it effortlessly whenever I have to give one.

| Carry out appraisals with all of my staff by the end of February. | Develop my understanding of how to manage performance well; develop the skills to do it every time. |
| Get through a job interview. | Present myself with impact and integrity in any situation where I am the focus of attention or competing with others. |

Concentrating on strengths, not weaknesses

Some clients may insist that they want coaching which ruthlessly targets their weaknesses. While clients clearly need to know what their weaknesses are, there is evidence that goals are more powerful when there is a different question:

What better ways might there be of working with my strengths?

CASE STUDY

Angela

Angela's great strengths were her outgoing personality, her sense of fun and her optimism. These had been severely repressed in the tension of worrying about whether she was going to be 'attacked' at meetings where, as a defence, she resorted to meek and unassertive behaviour. Instead of working on how to avoid being attacked, Angela's coach asked: 'How could your sense of fun be brought to the meetings?' He also asked her to monitor when she was consciously enjoying the meetings and to log those moments. Much to Angela's surprise and delight, bringing fun and optimism to the meetings did a great deal to resolve the problem of staying calm.

Business and organizational goals

When you are working as an executive coach, the whole process of goal-setting becomes at once more complicated and easier. It is more complicated because there is more to consider and easier because if you do it the right way, you will have a far better grasp of the real issues in the client's life. Executive coaching is fundamentally a business proposition where client and coach work together for the benefit of a third party – the organization. It is not enough to say to the organization, in effect, *Trust me to work with this client – it will bring value to the organization – honest!* If you do this, a number of undesirable things can happen. First, you are entirely reliant on storytelling – the client's view of things – as your main source of data and this is invariably one-sided, however open and honest the client may be. Second, coaching becomes a mysterious process – a secret between coach and client. And since the organization has no input into the purposes of the coaching it may become suspicious about its focus, let alone having any way of assessing return on investment (RoI).

When the coach is uneasy with business processes and maybe does not have a strong personal background as a senior manager, coaching can become more like life coaching where the emphasis is exclusively on personal relationships and personal goals. This may be a particular temptation for coaches who have come to the profession from a therapeutic background. I have occasionally inherited clients whose previous coaches have behaved in this way. One such client said to me, 'He kept bringing things back to my marriage and my childhood. My mother seemed to be of perpetual interest to him.'

The organizational context provides yet another source of significant pressure for change. It is easy to forget that a senior client for coaching does not come simply as an individual. The organization is part of their environment where there will be pressures from customers or users, competitors, regulators, or from technological advance. So, yet another important conversation that you need to have with the client is to establish just what these pressures are. Equally, that client is connected to the prevailing culture of the organization and to their team. It is improbable that any individual can be successful acting alone, so the behaviour and attitudes of the client's team are also an important part of the picture. All of these will then have an impact on the performance of the organization.

One way of representing this approach to goal-setting for executive clients is to see it diagrammatically, as in Figure 6.1.

Executive coaching is far more likely to fail when it concentrates exclusively on the circle labelled 'Leader's behaviour'. The more you and your client can include the whole system, the more effective the coaching is likely to be.

Three- or four-cornered contracting

I now make it standard procedure wherever possible to ask for a three-cornered meeting or conference call with the client's boss. Where you have a keen HR professional involved, it might become a four-cornered meeting. The purpose of the meeting or call is to get the organization's perspective on what they want the coaching to achieve for the client. The conversation will also give you invaluable insight into the culture of the organization and will prevent you getting too fixed on the client's version of events. This is how to do it.

Figure 6.1   A systemic approach to goal-setting

Before the meeting

Ask for the client's consent. Explain the benefits and ask him or her to approach the boss or sponsor. Set up the meeting or call, explaining that it will take two hours altogether and email everyone to confirm the purpose and timings.

Your role is to facilitate the discussion. You are not doing coaching even though you should expect this to be a meeting for which the client will be paying the full fee. Your aim is to clarify the organization's needs.

Stage 1: meet the boss

Spend the first 30 minutes alone with the boss. Encourage frankness. If your potential client is a problem performer, the boss will often be far more candid with you than they have been up until now with the potential client, but establish whether this is the case by asking, 'So how frank have you been about these issues with X?' True candour is remarkably rare. Useful questions to ask the boss have strong echoes of the goal-setting technique you will be doing with the client in due course:

So ideally, what will have changed for you if this coaching is successful?

What's at stake for the organization here?

How will we evaluate the success of this coaching programme?

Stage 2: boss, client and coach

Ask the client to join you and spend the next 40 minutes facilitating the same discussion. Encourage the boss to be as straightforward about the organization's aims as they were with you when alone. Ask the client how their perception of the organization's needs fits with what they are hearing from the boss.

Gain the agreement of the boss to be involved in the 'homework' between sessions, if appropriate – for instance, giving feedback on changed behaviour. The more open the client can be about what is happening in the coaching sessions, the better the outcome because the goals become transparent and public, thus increasing the chances that they will be met.

When it emerges, as it sometimes does, that the boss–client relationship itself seems to be the problem, I will offer a facilitated meeting for the pair as an alternative to coaching for one of the pair.

Be prepared to challenge unrealistic expectations and to agree alternatives.

Stage 3: client and coach

Ask for 40 minutes alone with potential clients to discuss whether they are up for coaching or not. This is especially important if it is the first time you have actually met. I cannot work with a reluctant client, so will usually say something like:

How do you feel about what you have just heard? (Expect that some clients may be shocked and angry.)

Your organization has made this time and budget available, but it's up to you whether you take advantage of it or not. How do you feel about going ahead?

What concerns do you have about this process?

How will you report on progress to your sponsor?

Stage 4: review at the end of the coaching

When the coaching is finished, negotiate a review meeting or conference call with boss or sponsor and client. The purpose is to enable the client to point out to the funder what has changed, what has been learnt and how he or she proposes to embed the learning into everyday practice. This is often a crucial part of the process. Bosses can have fixed ideas about the client, sometimes secretly believing that they cannot or will not change. This can be profoundly dismaying to a client who has made heroic efforts to change but has seen that these changes have not been registered by the funder. Don't comment on the content or process of the sessions, but do help clients articulate what they believe has changed and encourage funders to do the same.

You should note that some very senior clients initiate their own coaching programmes and are paying for them entirely out of budgets over which they have total control. They may resist the notion of involving *their* bosses, seeing this as pointless and intrusive. In such cases you should not press the idea.

Is the client coachable?

Finally you may want to consider how coachable the potential client actually is. Much of the answer will turn on their levels of self-awareness and motivation as well as how competent they are with the technical aspects of their job. The coach, writer and tutor Peter Bluckert has a framework in his book, *Psychological Dimensions of Executive Coaching* (2006), which I have adapted here with his kind permission. There is a much fuller treatment in his book. Many problems in executive coaching can be predicted and prevented if you apply this useful structure.

Ask yourself where any one of your more 'difficult' clients are in Tables 6.1 and 6.2.

Never be afraid to refuse the assignment if you can see that the client's level of coachability is low. Where this is the case, it is unlikely that the coaching can be successful and the client, or the client's sponsor, will first of all blame you and next blame coaching itself, thus damning the whole profession.

Identifying personal goals

My philosophy of coaching has an explicitly whole-person perspective. So it follows that the goal-setting process must encompass the personal as well as the professional. Coaching will then have a powerful double focus.

Severe psychological problems	Interpersonal problems	Perceptions by colleagues of client's behaviour	Threat of career derailment	Performance issues	Motivation for coaching	Coachability level
Absent	Absent/low	Excellent	Absent	Absent	High	1 Excellent
Absent	Absent/low	Excellent/good	Absent/low	Absent/low	Medium/high	2 Good
Absent	Low/medium	Medium	Low/medium	Low/medium	Medium	3 Average
Absent	Medium/high	Medium/poor	Medium/high	Medium/high	Variable: low–high	4 Poor
High	High	Poor	High	High	Variable: low–high	5 Inappropriate intervention right now

Table 6.1

Coachability level	Typical features of the client
1 Excellent	High-flier generally seen as being on the fast track; powerful hunger for learning; eager for challenging feedback; strong commitment to personal development. Admired as boss. High emotional intelligence.
2 Good	Possibly part of sheep-dip development course. Strong results drive but may struggle at first to identify an agenda for coaching and might not have thought of coaching without the stimulus of a third-party suggestion. Or may come for some purely instrumental coaching – e.g. interview skills. A little sceptical at first. 360-degree or other feedback often essential as platform.
3 Average	360-degree feedback has often revealed a problem – a surprise to this client who thought they were doing all right. Alternatively, a promotion may be turning out to challenge more than this client expected, leaving them lacking in important skills. Strong in the technical aspects of their jobs, may lack emotional intelligence. Motivation can go either way in practice.
4 Poor	Serious performance issues may mean coaching is the last chance for this client to retain their job. Often a low level of self-awareness. Outlook for coaching may be poor if the client is also struggling with technical aspects of their job. Sometimes sees self as victim. Essential: clarify that the organization genuinely believes the client is coachable.
5 Inappropriate	Client has serious psychological or medical problems. Colleagues do not want to work with them. Technical aspects of work also below par. May have been absent from work for a long period and now returning.

Table 6.2

CASE STUDY

Alastair

Alastair was running a hospital, taking over after the previous chief executive had been dismissed. He had inherited a large deficit and a demoralized staff, mortified that their hospital had been in the headlines for such negative reasons. However, Alastair also knew from his initial few weeks in the hospital that it had an inward-looking culture with doctors who were hostile to the managers, seeing them, rightly or wrongly, as their 'enemies'. Alastair's organizational goals, agreed in a three-way meeting with his chair and coach were to:

- reduce deficit to zero within 18 months;
- rebuild the confidence and competence of the executive team;
- reorganize the clinical structures through 're-engineering' based on 'patient journeys' rather than on the old functional structures; this project to be led by senior doctors;
- meet all the government-imposed targets;
- achieve the highest possible ratings by government auditors.

This was a formidable list. After working with Alastair in his first session there were also a number of personal goals, which included:

- finding a permanently sustainable way to reduce his weight;
- increasing his physical fitness and his energy;
- improving his ability to influence his peers so that he obtains commitment, not the compliance which had been a feature of the previous regime;
- delegating more effectively;
- establishing strong relationships of trust with his chair, commissioners and the Department of Health.

At the initial session, the coach's questions were:

What organizational targets are priorities in the light of our conversation with your chair?

How do your personal target areas link with the organizational ones?

How should this affect our agenda for coaching?

The answers to the last two questions were, of course, that the personal and the organizational were tightly intertwined. Alastair knew he was not, and never could be, the *rescuer* of his hospital. The three-cornered conversation with his coach and boss demonstrated very clearly that quietly inspirational leadership was fundamental to the organization's recovery and the first session alone with his coach demonstrated that staying physically fit and energetic was a vital foundation to all the other work.

He could only deliver on the organizational agenda through addressing his personal needs: developing his team through skilled performance management including delegating appropriately and learning how to coach them, and using positive influencing techniques to nurture the upward relationships, as well as building strong relationships with the doctors in the hospital.

Out of this conversation a further need emerged: to develop and implement a communication and patient-involvement strategy which Alastair would also lead. And he could only do this if he used the leverage of his already impressive communication skills both to inspire and to speak hard truths at large meetings of his staff. This created a rich and challenging agenda for the ensuing coaching.

It is true that organizations commissioning coaching are by and large only interested in the behaviour and capability of their staff. Their suspicion that executive coaching is really just therapy-lite, or life coaching in disguise, is often somewhere just below the surface. However, it is the whole person who comes to work and events in our private lives have an immediate impact on our performance at work and vice versa. As my own coaching experience has deepened and lengthened, I have also come to understand how frequently clients, often well-known people in extremely senior roles, can experience a sense of distress and dislocation. They will report a feeling of meaninglessness in their lives. Some are classic over-achievers who want to step away from the long hours and obsession with competence, but don't know how to do it. For this reason, coaching is always more powerful if coach and client can work in these areas as well as on the mechanics of behaviour in a work context. There are many hundreds of possible tools and techniques you can use to access this material and you will have your own favourites. I have picked several to describe here that I have found consistently useful.

The Life Scan Wheel

This simple, powerful and well-known exercise is rightly a favourite for coaches. Sometimes known as the Balance Wheel, or the Fulfilment Wheel, it asks you to assess your satisfaction with your life as it is now, comparing it with how you would like it to be. The centre of the Wheel represents zero fulfilment or satisfaction and the outer edge of each wedge represents total fulfilment (see Figure 6.2).

This exercise asks you to assess your satisfaction with your life as it is now. The centre represents zero satisfaction. The outer edge represents 10: total satisfaction. Rate each wedge on this 0–10 scale, then draw a line connecting each one. What kind of wheel emerges?

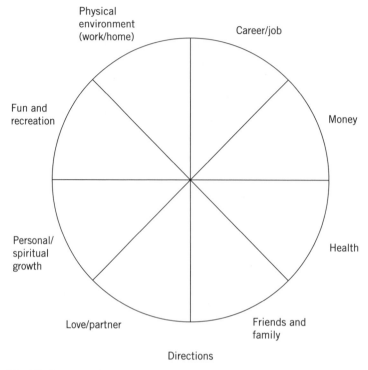

Figure 6.2 Life Scan exercise

The case for using this tool is that it encourages clients to see their lives as a whole – often for the first time. It conveys the expectation that, as a coach, you are as interested in the personal aspects of their lives as in the work aspects. Also, it is another way for clients to tell you about what is currently going on in their lives.

For many clients this is a relatively painless way to pass on important information to you. Here is one example.

CASE STUDY

Richard

Richard: I'm really proud of my relationship with my partner, Bernardo. We've been together for 15 years. I'm also keen to be seen as a good example of an 'out' gay man in a powerful position, but this also poses me a problem.

> Coach: How is this a problem?
> Richard: Because my company wants to move me to a country where
>   Bernardo would not be able to get a visa and we refuse to be
>   separated!

Using this tool allowed Richard to declare an important issue, his sexuality, in a swift and legitimate way, rather than having to find some other means of giving me such vital data.

How to use the Wheel

- Send it to clients in advance of the first session, explaining how to fill it in and asking them to bring it with them.
- At the session, ask clients to talk you through the thinking behind the way they have scored each wedge.
- Don't press clients who either say directly or indicate indirectly that they do not want to talk about any particular area, but log it privately for possible future exploration.
- Ask clients what links they see between the way they have scored the different wedges. An example might be that a client who has scored his satisfaction with work at 8 or 9 has also scored his partner relationship at 1 or 2. Sometimes when a client wheel looks like this, the client has poured everything into work at the expense of a marriage. It has become a negatively fulfilling cycle: work is enjoyable and rewarding so the client puts love and energy into it; the marriage is unfulfilling and unrewarding so the client dodges putting love and energy into it, thus ensuring that it becomes even less fulfilling and rewarding. This may seem like a simple and stunningly obvious connection, but it is often a point that the client has avoided seeing until that moment.
- Ask about how much energy the client has for change in any areas that show low satisfaction. Don't assume that a low score means a willingness to change, or even that your role should be to challenge reluctance to change a low score.
- Ask how the areas of satisfaction and dissatisfaction link to the client's initial ideas on goals for the coaching.

Alternatives to the Wheel

There are many alternative approaches which you might prefer. Another one I like invites the client to name and develop the categories. For this you need a large sheet of paper – a flip chart page is ideal.

- Hand the client a set of felt-tip pens and ask them to draw a pie chart in the centre of the page, leaving plenty of space to add further rings. This inner circle should represent how the client spends their time now.
- Add a second circle outside the first, allocating different proportions representing how the client would ideally like to spend their time, listing the benefits this would bring.
- Add a third circle, writing in each category what will need to change in order to bring these changes about.

CASE STUDY
Kevin

Kevin was a 53-year-old senior manager in an oil company. He was a 'lifer' – someone who had spent his entire working life in one organization. He had lost his zest for work. He was frustrated by his inability to devote time to the developing world charity which reflected his strong religious beliefs. In his inner circle he drew a number of wedges for work, indicating 'organizational politicking', managing his team, visiting chemical plants, going to conferences and travel.

Kevin's job involved at least 80 days a year of international travel, and he had increasing distaste for the stresses this created. His marriage was a longstanding, loving relationship and his wife had recently retired. A generous salary was matched by a generous company pension scheme, so money was not an issue.

His second circle showed a dramatic contrast: work reduced to a small proportion of the whole and the leisure pursuits much enlarged. Benefits included better health, increased time for relaxation, learning Spanish and enjoyment of his marriage. In the third circle, Kevin described what needed to happen to bring about the ideal. Essentially this meant talking to his employer about voluntary redundancy and moving to a consultancy role, refining his consultancy skills, learning Spanish 'properly' and concentrating on the work he really enjoyed.

Two years later, all of this had happened. Kevin now freelances for his old company and several others, and also gives free consultancy to his favourite charity, where his hard-won worldly wisdom is much valued.

Drawing your life

Many clients have endlessly analysed their situations. They can articulate exactly what is wrong yet somehow things still stay the same. For these clients, it can produce a much better response when they move away from the comfort of words and analysis and use the playful, creative parts of their brains.

- Hand the client a large piece of paper and a clutch of nice juicy felt-tip pens in a range of colours or use a drawing app on a tablet computer if you have one, promising to email the results to them after the session.
- Ask them to draw two pictures. The first: how your life is now. The second: how you would like your life to be.
- Reassure the client that no artistic ability is required and let them loose to draw.
- Talk through the results, asking the client what needs to happen to move from the present to the desired future.

An ideal day

Invite clients to tell you the story of their *ideal* day from the time they get up in the morning to the time they go to bed. What would be happening? What, specifically, would they be doing? Ask clients to use the present tense, describing the day as if it is actually happening.

An alternative which is especially useful for clients with life-balance issues is to hand the client a blank diary representing a complete week. Say:

> Imagine you have given up your present job. Fill in this diary with an ideal week of activities which do not include paid work.

Most clients find this an absorbing exercise – I usually ask them to complete it between sessions. The follow-up discussion will include topics such as:

> How difficult was it to fill all the time? (Usually it is impossible)

> What would it be like to live this life?

> What would it be like to live your life with this as the yardstick rather than fitting your private life around your work?

Identifying life purpose

Sooner or later in any substantial piece of coaching, one core question appears: 'What's my life purpose?' Underneath this question is the one virtually all of us must ask ourselves at some point: what meaning does life have anyway? A sense of pointlessness is often behind the initial request for coaching. It is why, even in the real and apparent trauma of sudden redundancy or sacking, clients can feel energized and optimistic. It is another opportunity to find out what this core purpose might be. If you never answer the question about life purpose then you will potentially feel a perpetual sense of something lacking. It will be more difficult to make either career or life decisions confidently and without 'buyer's remorse' if you make what turns out to be the wrong decision. By contrast, once you are clear about life purpose, such decisions are much easier. Any major turning point can be held up against the life purpose benchmark.

Don't pussyfoot with clients about life purpose. It sounds a bit of a portentous phrase – and perhaps it is. But introduce it confidently.

Some approaches to identifying life purpose

The simplest way is to ask a series of straightforward questions. Where you have already done an autobiography session with a client, these questions may usefully build on the answers the client gave you then.

- What's unique about you?
- What do other people constantly say that they value about you?
- If you are an invisible presence eavesdropping while some of your greatest admirers talk about you, what do you hear?
- What do you enjoy most about your current job?
- What skill or task do you perform so easily that you don't need to think about it?
- What do you enjoy most about your non-work life?
- What secret dreams do you have about things you would really love to do or try?
- What unrealized goals are there for you?
- What themes or threads run through your life?
- What quality or experience in your current life/job would you sacrifice last?
- What do you want to leave behind you as a legacy
  - in your current job?
  - in your life?

A postcard from the future

The instruction is simple. Imagine it's sometime in the future: choose your own time frame. Give the client an actual postcard, inviting them to write themselves a postcard from that time, saying what they love about it and describing what they did to get there.

Most clients quickly realize that true life purpose is as much about what they want to give as it is about what they want to take. It is the giving that bestows significance, not the taking. When you are focused on taking, you can never have enough of whatever it is you want to take, whether it is money, fame, power, glamorous possessions, houses, the thrills of chasing sex or of outwitting competitors. When taking is the concern you have to be constantly on your guard because others might steal or damage what you have, whether these are cheeky younger colleagues after your job, a rival for your love or feckless burglars after your possessions.

All of this is immeasurably bolstered by the myths and fantasies with which we surround ourselves. The most popular include:

I'll be able to slow down tomorrow.	Reality: unlikely. Working with manic energy becomes a habit.
Working long hours now will clear time for me later.	Reality: the longer the hours you work, the more you train others to expect those hours as your norm and they will obligingly fill up your in-tray for you.
Buying my children nice things will make up for the time I can't spend with them.	Reality: nice things can never replace parental time.
I am my job – they couldn't manage without me.	Reality: they forget you more or less as soon as you have left.

Asking about core life purpose cuts through all of this, and often comes as a shock.

Sometimes a simple reframing is all that needs to happen. The client is already in the right arena, doing the right sort of job and leading the right sort of life. What is missing is seeing the significance of the choices he or she has made. A well-known tale describes the work of three men laying bricks on the same project. Asked what he is doing, the first replies, 'Laying bricks.' The second man replies, 'Building a wall.' The third man replies, 'Building a cathedral.' It is not difficult to imagine whose work gave him most satisfaction. People's choices of life path, of partner, of job, of work sector and so on are rarely accidental. Part of our work as coaches is to make explicit what has always been present but partially hidden.

CASE STUDY

Mark

Mark was running a voluntary sector organization with a successful trading arm. There was a split in the organization between people who saw themselves as tough, commercially focused professionals and the people who had joined because they believed in the original campaigning mission and purpose. The commercially focused people saw the campaigners as 'fluffy' and the campaigners saw the marketers and finance specialists as cynical and opportunistic.

Mark straddled the two uneasily. He had grown up in a big Catholic family in West Belfast and as a boy had naïvely joined in riots and fighting 'because it was fun and exciting'. It had given him insights into what it was like to feel beleaguered and disadvantaged. Early on in life, Mark had discovered that he had a gift for advocacy. He had used it in the Students Union and it took him seamlessly into a series of what he called 'sub-political' roles – for instance working for an English MP as a researcher.

It was easy for Mark to answer questions about his life purpose. 'Righting wrongs' summed up his answers. He was never happier than when fearlessly acting as David against the Goliath of an apparently more powerful adversary. The stress for him was that his role increasingly seemed to be constraining him from drawing on his strengths.

The choices seemed simple: change jobs or refocus the job he had. He chose to refocus the job he had, feeling that the core purpose of his organization was indeed close to his heart and that he could easily reposition the role by creating a new role of director of operations, reporting to him, to manage the commercial parts of the business. This would leave him to concentrate on the external, ambassadorial role while also directly heading up the campaigning function inside the organization.

Now the commercial activities of the organization were aimed at supporting campaigning, rather than the other way around. Mark described himself as 'springing out of bed each morning, knowing I'm doing what I was born to do!'

Identifying values and drivers

Asking about life purpose takes you into the core territory of the being self rather than the doing self. It is saying to the client, 'What really matters to you?' You may get answers to this question through exploring life purpose, or you may prefer to look at it through activities explicitly designed to flush out the client's values and drivers. This approach is useful with clients facing career dilemmas because they start by identifying answers to the questions 'What do you really want?'; 'What's important to you?' rather than where so many clients believe they have to start, which is with 'Who will hire me?' Knowing what your values are is also a powerful way of reinforcing goals.

Being 'in the zone'

Sports people describe moments of maximum performance as being 'in the zone': a time when you just know that you are going to win, play or perform well, doing as well or better than you ever have before. And the wonderful thing is, it feels effortless. The same phenomenon has been called 'being in flow'. It has been described many times over the centuries, often linked with spiritual awareness, but in the twenty-first century the phrase is most associated with one of the founding fathers of the modern positive psychology movement, Mihaly Csikszentmihalyi (2003). These moments are characterized by:

- time passing quickly – your sense of time is distorted;
- a feeling of exhilaration – mind and body seamlessly joined;
- conscious happiness, a sense of playfulness and energy;
- clear goals that are tightly linked to strongly-held personal values and a highly focused sense of attention to the task in hand;
- confidence: no self-consciousness or embarrassment;
- a high level of immediate feedback enabling you to adjust your performance without difficulty;
- a feeling that the activity is *intrinsically rewarding*, so there is an effortlessness in it;
- a sense that you are achieving something stretching enough to be challenging but not so challenging that it becomes overwhelming; there is a feeling of being in control – you can do it, anything is possible.

I have yet to work with a client who cannot identify such moments. They may select a specific day or few hours, a whole project or an even longer period in a job role which was particularly satisfying. Knowing what these moments are is an immensely powerful lever for coach and client. They are, like identifying life purpose, the benchmark for decision-making and for planning the future.

To call on this approach, you will need to allow at least half an hour. (Some clients may prefer to prepare for this session in advance. You can email them a simple framework to help them structure their thoughts.)

Introduce the idea of being 'in flow' to clients and ask them to identify up to four such moments in their lives – more if you have the time and inclination. Encourage them to think about moments from their personal as well as professional lives and also moments that cover different phases or decades. By asking for several peak moments you will be creating a richer picture. Give clients enough time to think it through, perhaps while you refresh the drinks. Scribble down all the key words as they talk: don't edit what you hear. You could use a flip chart for this: it makes the themes easier for clients to see later. Most clients talk fluently about these moments. Prompt them with further questions such as:

- What made this moment or time special?
- Who else was present or involved? What were they doing?
- What was it that you specifically did that made it so important?
- What were your feelings then?
- What was achieved, done or learnt?
- How did you feel about that achievement or learning?
- What values and beliefs were you calling on?
- What need was it serving?

When clients have finished, ask them to mark the words that jump out for them and then to synthesize them into a list. Suggest possible links and themes, if they are struggling – sometimes such links may be easier for you to see than for them – then list the values and drivers that emerge. Now invite them to ponder the implications. Some possible questions here might be:

- Having listed these values and drivers, how do they seem to you?
- What is so important about them for you?
- What surprises are there for you in what is *not* on your list?
- What is it like for you when you are honouring these values?
- What is it like for you when you are not honouring them?
- What needs to happen to make these values real drivers in your life now?
- How prepared are you to make those changes?

This is a hugely enjoyable exercise. It focuses only on the positive and virtually always tells clients more than they first realize. Examples would be a client, one of whose peak moments was being godmother to her closest friend's first baby and realizing that uniting family interests, friendships and spiritual beliefs was not only a prime need but also something for which she had a talent. Another was the participant on one of our coach training courses whose peak moment was at last getting the opportunity to sing the part of the Angel in Edward Elgar's popular and moving oratorio *The Dream of Gerontius* in her local cathedral. The Angel guides Gerontius from this world to the next. Singing this role encapsulated her love of and talent for singing, her need for performance and limelight and also the need as a coach to do something for others that had profound meaning for them.

This exercise has multiple uses, especially where the focus is career. For instance, you can ask the client to assess how their current job or life stacks up against the criteria the exercise has revealed. Often there is a poor match and this can accelerate the client's determination to do something different. Or if the client is offered a new job but has doubts about whether to accept, it is always worth revisiting this list. And in any knotty dilemma that the client brings to you, you may want to say, 'Let's see how any decision would measure up against that list.' This can significantly shorten the period of vacillation.

Linking with action plans: making goals specific

Goal-setting is also about action planning – the changes that the client will implement in order to make the theoretical discussion of the coaching room a reality in their daily lives. The more specific a goal is, the more likely it is that it will be achieved. When you get towards the end of a piece of coaching around a particular goal there will probably be some action plan agreed. The client will want to try and then to practise something different and will report back on it at the next session.

Accountability

Accountability is about how the client will account during the coaching for changes in their life that they have agreed to make. The changes will happen outside the coaching session and that is why 'homework' is important. Sometimes thinking and pondering will be enough. Often it is not, and action will be required. Accountability is a tricky concept. It can seem too much like teacher–pupil or boss–subordinate if it is done in the wrong way. It does not mean finger-wagging if the client fails to carry out their commitment. I was shocked when a close colleague told me that his hypnotherapist, someone who also claimed to be a coach, had irritably terminated the relationship because he had not carried out some small piece of 'homework' as part of his attempt to give up smoking. A client also showed me an email he had received from a previous coach, a relationship that did not survive this communication, where the coach had baldly informed her that 'if you don't do your homework I shall be very displeased'. Accountability in coaching is totally different from boss–subordinate, teacher–pupil or parent–child accountability. It means that you, the coach, *hold clients to account for what they have said they wish to do to make changes.* It is their agenda and their ideas of where they want to change that is at the core but the clients design the items for accountability, not the coach, and the clients also design *how* they want to be held accountable. As a coach you have no attachment to whether clients have carried out their tasks/ homework. You want them to grow but you have no stake in their doing things to please you. There is no place for value judgements or blame as whatever has happened there will be learning in it. There may be exceptions when the client consistently fails to commit to what they have promised, in which case you will indeed need to discuss what is going on for them, but in a mature and respectful way.

Challenging and requesting

This technique is a further variant on goal-setting. It is usually light-hearted and enjoyable for both sides. It goes like this. Clients suggest an action and the steps they are going to take. Sometimes these may strike you as vague. You challenge the client to make them more specific or more challenging. The giveaway is when clients tell you they will 'try' to do something. 'Trying' is a cop-out and hardly ever results in action. You say:

> I challenge you to do x, y times between now and when we next meet.
>
> I'm going to make a request here . . .

The client can say yes, no or maybe. The client may agree to the task but not to the frequency, or may like the idea of the challenge but not the specific form it is taking. If so, that's fine.

Examples

- The client found it difficult to confront a mediocre performer in his team. Challenge: do it, using techniques practised in the coaching session, and do it tomorrow. Challenge accepted, but timescale negotiated.
- The client's problem was working exceptionally long hours. Sessions had initially focused on how to delegate more effectively. Doing this successfully had reduced his work hours but had exposed his lack of social life. Various ways of reconnecting with former friends were discussed in the session. Challenge: contact six of the friends we discussed, suggesting a night out and do so within the next week. Challenge accepted but number of contacts reduced to four.

Follow-up

I enjoy keeping in contact with clients between sessions and encourage phone calls, texts and emails. This can be especially useful if you and the client have focused on some important impending event in which some new behaviour will be tried. If you and the client prefer not to do this, in the next session, ask: 'How did it go on those action points we agreed last time?' When the client has achieved them all, congratulate them warmly and acknowledge whatever effort it will have taken to do it.

When the client has not achieved them, ask:

> What got in the way?
>
> What would you do in a different way another time?
>
> What did you learn from not doing them?
>
> What could help achieve them in the future?

While goals are important to client and to coach, there is also a toxic trap awaiting those who take them as the be-all and end-all. Eckhart Tolle makes the case potently in his book *The Power of Now* (2001). Commenting that our whole lives can be about waiting for the future, the book celebrates the liberating energy of living in the present. Tolle contrasts 'small-scale waiting' (in bus queues, in a traffic jam) with 'large-scale waiting' – for a better job or more prosperity. Large-scale waiting, especially without any of the action that will make the goal real, reduces the quality of your life now. The goals he associates with such pointless waiting he calls 'outer goals', all of which eventually end in failure. This is because outer goal achievements are subject to the impermanence of all things. He warns against waiting as a state of mind because it could mean that you only want the future while rejecting the present. Setting goals is important, but not at the expense of feeling alive now. In terms of the model of coaching I put forward in this book, he is warning against the doing self taking over from the being self:

> Your life's journey has an outer purpose and an inner purpose. The outer purpose is to arrive at your goal or destination, to accomplish what you set out to do, to achieve this or that, which, of course, implies future. But if your destination, or the steps you are going to take in the future, take up so much of your attention that they become more important to you than the step you are taking now, then you completely miss the journey's inner purpose, which has nothing to

do with where you are going, or what you are doing, but everything to do with how.

(Tolle 2001: 71)

And just in case we get too carried away with the seriousness of it all, I cannot resist adding the Woody Allen joke sent to me by Derek Adams, a thoughtful reader of the first edition of this book:

Q: How do you make God laugh?
A: Tell him your plans.

Note

1   For two helpful views in this area, see Bandura (1997) and Locke and Latham (1990).

7   Coaching clients through change

All changes, even the most longed for, have their melancholy; for what we leave behind us is part of ourselves; we must die to one life before we can enter another.

Anatole France

When clients come for coaching, they do it because they want their lives to change. But the desire for transformation is not the same as making it happen and there are few coaching clients who have not already tried all the obvious routes on their own. Change is complex because even when we freely choose it, there will be some loss. When I left my room at the BBC's undoubtedly grim buildings at Elstree for the last time, I looked at the trees outside, the only ones on the site, and felt a wrench, knowing I would never see them again. At the farewell party given for me by colleagues that night, I realized that this was probably the last contact I would have with many of the people there. I had eagerly sought this change, knew I had made it for the best of reasons and that the decision could not be revoked, but I still remember the poignant mixture of sadness and joy.

How much more difficult then is it to deal with what is imposed: redundancy, being obliged to take a less satisfactory role or to move house in order to keep your job, being left by a partner, facing a health crisis, getting dismissed, failing an exam, bereavement, the disappointment of not getting a job you badly wanted. These are the changes that you often could not predict or prevent, did not cause, can't control and can't avoid. Potentially they can lead to feelings of powerlessness and anger. You meet them again and again in the coaching room.

The Kübler-Ross change cycle

Elisabeth Kübler-Ross was a Swiss psychiatrist and teacher whose pioneering book *On Death and Dying* (1997), first published in the mid-1960s, revolutionized the way we look at death by challenging taboos and embarrassments surrounding it. Often described as a study of bereavement, in fact her first interest was in how people receive news they perceive to be catastrophic. The focus was on patients with terminal illnesses but her ideas quickly came to be seen as equally useful for people coping with any kind of loss or change. Her theory stands the test of time as both profound and simple. I have found it useful in two ways: as a constant reminder of the psychology of change and loss with which we and so many of our clients struggle, and also as a framework to teach to clients so that they understand their own processes better.

Her work identifies six typical stages of grief, represented as the change cycle in Figure 7.1.

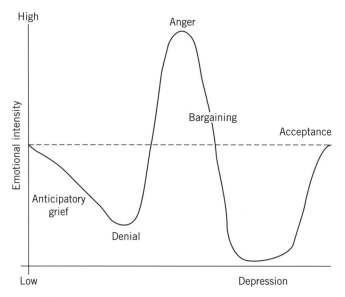

Figure 7.1 The change cycle

Anticipatory grief

You know that something has changed for ever, but it is not yet over and may not be for some time to come. You feel overwhelming and most probably silent sorrow for what you know will be lost, yet you feel guilty and possibly self-indulgent about the intensity of your emotion. Typically you bottle it up. It feels wrong to express it.

CASE STUDY

Francis

Francis was a charismatic performing arts specialist working with me on making the change from a professional to a managerial role. He knew he had to give up many of his previous shocking habits – gossiping, manipulating, having favourites – if he was to move from amusing, talented maverick to respected leader. He was an eager learner, confessing readily to his faults, both amazed and delighted that there were actually well-tried methods for motivating people that did not depend on coercion. When we did the Life Scan exercise (see page 143), he told me, his entire demeanour changing, that his wife, Mia, had endometrial cancer. At our third session he told me that Mia's cancer had spread to her liver. Her condition had deteriorated rapidly and she now needed a wheelchair.

'I've been able to cope up till now,' he said, 'but the wheelchair is a symbol of what is to come. I know she can't recover but I don't know how long she can live. The marriage is over to all intents and purposes. I have already lost her. I feel desperate but I can't show it to her or anyone else and especially not to the children.' His melancholy dignity was moving and the rest of our session was spent working out some better tactics for coping than simply turning his grief inwards.

Denial

At the Denial stage we are numb. We know, intellectually, that the change has happened: the company will be taken over, we will lose that job, a partner has left, an adored parent has died, but emotionally we cannot yet take it in. To outsiders it may look as if we are adopting head-in-sand tactics.

CASE STUDY

Eira

Eira ran a small organization which had to merge with a competitor and she had just been told that she was not a candidate for the chief executive role in the new company. In her coaching sessions where the planned aim was how to get a new job, Eira described with bafflement that she was continuing to run her organization as if nothing had happened. 'I'm still doing my weekly meetings, I'm still going through my usual routines. I can't feel anything though I think I should. It's as if I'm outside it all. I'm actually still working on a business plan for next year. How bizarre is that?'

Of course it was not bizarre at all, merely the normal protective mechanism of the human response to change kicking in.

Anger

At the Anger stage we look for someone to blame. This horrible event must be someone's fault so this person should be punished or at least say they are sorry. We will tend to divide people into goodies and baddies – there are no in-betweens. Often enough, the anger may be well justified – some corporate behaviour is beyond belief in its callousness and cowardice: dismissing people through text messages, or, as I read in one newspaper recently, emptying a store of its customers by sounding the fire alarm in order to tell staff that they were all redundant. Or we may cast ourselves as one of the baddies, assuming inappropriate personal responsibility for what has happened – 'if only I'd . . .' Sometimes there is indeed some culpability in the client's past behaviour. If so, encourage them to express their guilt at the same time as helping them put it into perspective. Remind them that most probably they did the best they could on the data available at the time, that mistakes are inevitable because we are only human and it is unlikely that any blame will be theirs alone. Asking clients what they have learnt, that they can apply to similar situations another time, is also a powerful way of coming to terms with the painful responsibility for a failure.

I have found that very occasionally, clients, in the temporary madness of their anger, may propose dangerous remedies – for instance, taking their organization to court in a case they could not win, or stalking their boss. Where you can see, because you are outside it, that this course of action would be catastrophic – or against the law – it may be time for plain speaking. Offering some perspective through a coaching conversation may be the client's best hope of avoiding a personal disaster.

In the early days of therapy it was assumed that anger should be expressed. Hence, clients were encouraged to beat cushions, shout and rage. However, it seems dubious now that this is helpful. Rather it is more likely to fix the enraged person into anger as their default mode. Anger can be addictive; we can enjoy the righteousness of our rage. In reality it increases the likelihood of making the false logic of black and white thinking more permanent. Clients can take refuge in claims that they are only seeking 'fairness' or 'justice' when it may be nearer the truth to say that most anger is about what *I need* versus what *others need*. People who are in a high state of emotional arousal are not calm enough to be coached. The more primitive the emotional state, and anger is a primitive state, the less likelihood there is of learning and of the prefrontal cortex, the seat of logical thinking, being brought into play. You may find it more helpful to calm an angry client and then to work with them on how to manage their anger than to encourage them to vent their rage in the session.

Sometimes, however, the client will tell you that release through expressing anger is exactly what they need in order to move on.

CASE STUDY

Marie

Marie had lost her job as a result of a highly-publicized major incident in the hospital at which she was chief executive. An inquiry later exonerated her. Although in subsequent sessions we worked on how to frame her CV, how to prepare for an interview, how to network and how to settle into the new job she soon got, at our first session she wept more or less continuous, angry, hot tears as she told her story. Although I stopped many times in that session to ask her if she really wanted to go on the answer was always 'yes'.

Her later reflection was: 'Letting me cry was the most amazingly healing thing. I got it out in that room in a way I couldn't do anywhere else. I couldn't worry my husband by letting him see how devastated I was because I was and am the breadwinner. I knew I just had to do that howling before I could move on. By letting me do it you conveyed far better than any words could that how I felt was legit. You conveyed that I was OK and I would get over it.'

Mostly, when a client is recognizably at this point in the change process, it works simply to acknowledge the anger and to explain that it is a normal part of the adjustment to change. Ask:

Who are you angry with?

If they were here, what would you like to say to them?

What would it take for you to move on from this anger?

Accepting some personal responsibility

When the black and white thinking of the anger phase is passing, it is often useful to help clients distinguish between blame, guilt and personal responsibility. We will usually have contributed something to the change and in the interests of learning and moving on, it can be therapeutic to consider calmly what that might have been.

CASE STUDY

Hilary

Hilary had worked for a hotel chain for 12 years as their learning and development specialist, getting positive feedback on her own training courses and believing that she was playing a valued role in the company. She had no clue that her post was about to be made redundant and when the news came she experienced it as a wounding personal rejection. Her feelings of anger were still strong four months later. In her second coaching session we looked at what responsibility she had for what had happened. The answer was that she had stayed in the same post well past her real interest in it because it had allowed her to be home by three o'clock in term-time to collect her children from school. She had not kept her bosses informed about the strategic value of her work. Instead, her tactics had been to get on with her work quietly, believing that its merit would speak for itself. Understanding the nature of this private bargain with herself was the key to moving on, including accepting that no one but the individual concerned can ever manage their career.

Bargaining

Bargaining is a good sign, although it may not seem so at the time. It means that we have accepted, at least in part, that the change will happen. In the original work with dying patients, it was described as bargaining with God: 'If I pray really hard, and promise to live a pure life, then maybe I'll survive.' In coaching work we are more likely to see it in the kinds of desperate compromises that clients suggest. For instance, one client, whose wife had left him for another man, offered to move house if she would come back. A client who had been sacked by his company instigated a grievance procedure in an attempt to stave off the inevitability of the formal letter ending his contract. Another client, sorely disappointed by her failure to win the job she wanted, proposed a new role as deputy to her successful rival. It is unlikely that any sustainable solution can be produced by bargaining because it is most probably a forlorn bid to deny the inevitability of the change. As coaches our role may be to offer reality-testing by asking questions like:

How far would this solve the underlying problems here?

What would be the balance of upsides and downsides?

Imagine yourself a year from now living inside this solution. How do you think it would feel?

What would need to happen to make this solution work for you?

Depression

We feel paralysed. We are indecisive. The anger has gone but has left behind a sense of powerlessness. This is a difficult stage for the coach as well as for the client. Clients may cancel their sessions and have too little energy to tell you why, even if they know. It may look as if they have lost interest in coaching. Contact them if you suspect this is happening and express your willingness to continue. Be prepared to follow up with more emails or phone calls if there is no response. I sent one such client, someone I knew well, an email with tick boxes that he could return with minimal effort and with five choices:

> I am fine and don't need any more coaching but thank you for what I have had.
>
> I am fine for now but might need some coaching in future.
>
> I am feeling too miserable to contact you right now.
>
> I am miserable but could be persuaded to have another session though not yet.
>
> I am miserable but a session would help and if Angie [my patient PA] would arrange it and contacts me, it would be useful.

His later comment on this possibly over-cheeky email was:

> It was so wonderful to get that. It broke the frozen skin of my sadness. I thought, why am I sitting here so wrapped up in ME? And someone does care. I got on the phone to Angie straight away and booked my session.

The underlying cause at this stage in the change process is that we have fully realized what has been permanently lost and with it goes a withering of belief that anything we do can have a positive impact. We doubt that we can be happy again. This is particularly true for clients whose identity has been tightly bound up in their work and who have lost their jobs or for a bereaved client who feels as if the centre of their lives has been squeezed out by the death of someone they dearly loved. Where the client does appear for his or her sessions, the event may have a lifeless air. When you see this happening, name it. Work at the feelings-level first and avoid intellectualizing. Ask the client what would help both in terms of how you run the actual sessions and on practicalities. The answer is often to design the small steps which work towards healing and renewal. And of course, if you recognize that you are in the presence of a serious mental health problem rather than just sadness, your coaching must be aimed at encouraging the client to find medical help.

Acceptance

Acceptance and adjustment are close partners. The change has happened or will happen. We begin to experiment with new behaviours. Cheerfulness creeps in occasionally and cautiously. We begin to believe that we can live with what has happened and that life will go on. Confidence trickles back. The coaching springs to life again.

Beware of believing that this change cycle is a rigid process. It is not. We may pass through its stages in any order or miss some out altogether. Typically it is literally a cycle: so a client who has apparently reached the acceptance stage may return many times more to anger, bargaining or depression. These labels are simply useful tools to gain understanding about what is happening.

As a coach you should also look out for clients who get stuck at one point in the cycle, most often at Denial or Anger, returning again and again to *what-ifs* and *if-onlys*.

Dealing with transition: William Bridges' model

The writer William Bridges has another useful framework for making sense of change. He describes it in his book *Managing Transitions* (1991) where the focus is on change in organizations. It maps well on to the Kübler-Ross change cycle. He suggests that the formal process of the change and the psychological adjustment to it are two different phenomena. This is because although the formal change has been made, the psychological adjustments have yet to happen. So, for instance, I have noticed that clients who have been forced to leave their jobs will frequently speak about 'we' and 'our', unconsciously talking as if they are still at their old workplaces.

Bridges describes three phases of change, suggesting that their boundaries are messy and overlapping and that this is what causes the delay in adjustment (see Figure 7.2).

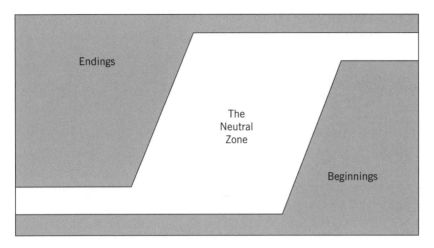

Figure 7.2 The three phases of transition

Phase 1: Endings

A change has to take place, but before this can happen at the psychological level, not just at the legal or physical level, the old has to be let go. That is what we find hard. It is no good stressing what benefits the new regime will bring if what has been lost is not acknowledged. Something will always be lost, whether it is the comfort of our old familiar ways of doing things, our status, our previous good health, our beliefs or our expectations. The immediate focus is on ourselves: how will this affect me? Questions linked to this are:

> Who now has the power?
>
> How are decisions being made?
>
> Which of the old rules still apply – and what are the new ones?

Working with clients at the Endings phase
All of these will help clients adjust to the new reality:

- Establishing what will change and what will stay the same: ask clients to distinguish between the two.
- Getting involved: the more you stay outside the change, the more it feels like something being done *to* you. Ask clients how they could increase their involvement in the change.
- Encouraging mourning by naming what has ended: for instance, ask 'What will you miss most?'

- Celebrating the ending: just as a funeral helps the survivors realize that the person really is dead, so will parties and rituals in other circumstances where something is irrevocably over. Where people will be leaving an organization – or a relationship for that matter – some celebratory marker will help.
- Preparing for the new, even before the old is completely over.

Rose is one example of a client who managed this phase with textbook expertise.

CASE STUDY

Rose

Rose had narrowly missed promotion to a senior job in a pharmaceutical organization. In our sessions she allowed herself private rage at the 'patronizing' feedback from the HR director about how wonderful her presentation and interview had been. She also anticipated the 'synthetic sympathy' of senior male colleagues who might be secretly pleased that a woman had not got the job.

At our next formal session we weighed up staying put against the energy it would take to find something else. This put Rose back in control and began the process of restoring her self-esteem.

With Bridges' helpful framework in mind, I asked Rose, 'What has really ended here?'

'My career in this organization,' she promptly replied. 'I really have to move on.' We discussed how she could contact head-hunters and reinvigorate her network of professional contacts. Within a few months Rose had been offered an impressive new job and had decided to take it. Now her questions were about how to leave. Her instinct was, as it so often is, to slink off. I had already described Bridges' model to Rose and asked her what she thought might be applicable to her at this Endings phase.

'Well, I have to have the big party, even if I don't really want it – you know how I hate all that tired speechifying and ritual? But I have to have it for others as well as for me.'

'Yes, I think you do.'

'And I have to treat it as an important event.'

I gladly accepted the invitation to a magnificent formal party and watched from the sidelines as Rose delivered the speech she had rehearsed with me: a generous acknowledgement of the strengths of the organization and a confident look towards her own future.

Some clients cannot manage the Endings phase with this degree of graciousness. They are tempted to indulge their desire for revenge and to express their disappointment in violent terms to whoever will listen. At one farewell party many years ago, I remember that the leaver had created a 'graffiti wall' out of flip-chart paper, inviting his guests to fill in the 'bricks' with harsh messages for the managers who had dispensed with his services. The embarrassment of his guests was palpable. It is sometimes hard for clients to see that recklessly expressing their anger at what they see as betrayal will have instant backwash on the person who gives vent to it so publicly. When clients do describe such a wish, I will typically ask, 'When you've been on the receiving end of this kind of unloading, how has it felt?' The answer, invariably, is some mix of the following: awkwardness, pity, dislike. This is usually enough to deter a client from pursuing such an unwise path.

Phase 2: the Neutral Zone

This phase has something in common with the Depression phase of the Kübler-Ross framework. Bridges describes it as feeling as if we are in continuous whitewater. Energy disappears. We withdraw and become self-preoccupied. We are more prone to illness and accident. We are unsure what has ended and even more unsure about whether the new beginning has actually started. Old weaknesses resurface. The essence of the Neutral Zone is ambiguity. However, maybe for this very reason, the Neutral Zone is also potentially a time for rethinking and creativity because at this stage we have an overt longing for answers. I have come to believe that it is an essential part of making a successful transition. It is often the point where client and coach make first contact.

CASE STUDY

Kees

Kees had made London his home when his Dutch company had acquired a UK competitor. But now, yet another acquisition had made his own director job redundant. Underneath this familiar explanation of why a job move was necessary, there lay the less palatable truth – that Kees, though popular and likeable, was a problematical colleague. His insistence of doing everything himself created decision bottlenecks for his staff. His obsession with detail meant that he often focused on the smaller picture at the expense of wider strategic need. With 25 years in one company, it would have been understandable for Kees to have felt aggrieved at his fate or frightened at the prospect of having to start again. But this was not the case. Coming for coaching at the point where his formal notice to leave had just been issued, Kees loved the concept of the Neutral Zone. He embraced the tough messages of his 360-degree feedback with courage.

'I see this as a time when I can learn all over again,' he beamed. 'I'd got stale, been in one place too long. I know I can tackle all this stuff that's driven people nuts and I can't tell you how ready I am to learn how to do it better! I am a very lucky man to have this opportunity.'

Kees and I worked on what he described as a *triple track*. Track One was an assessment of his whole life and led to a realization that he needed to pay more attention to his family and friends. Track Two was job search and started by identifying his strengths, many of which, for instance his fluency in five European languages, had been underused. This linked tightly with strongly-held values about the importance for him of being 'A Citizen of Europe'. Track Three was re-learning how to be a leader, revisiting past dilemmas, avidly reading articles and books and, at his insistence, arranging meetings with other clients from whom I anticipated he could learn. Every one of my many emails from Kees ended with a smiley face symbol. When he sent me the email to tell me that his bid for a job in Zurich had been successful, there were three jolly emoticons attached – 'One for each Track!'

Working with clients in the Neutral Zone

- Explain its value to clients, reframing its inevitable discomforts as a positive opportunity to learn.
- Encourage the thought that the common complaint about 'having nothing to do', or even, in dying organizations, 'too much to do', is rarely true. Business-as-usual may have ceased, but the task now is to concentrate on preparing for the future, for instance through training or job search.
- Encourage clients to create a Neutral Zone for themselves – for instance, if they are tempted to go straight from an Ending to a Beginning. Taking even a few days' holiday can create a valuable mini Neutral Zone.
- Help clients pay attention to the importance of networking and of keeping their social connections alive to offset the ever-present danger of Neutral Zone isolation.

Phase 3: Beginnings

The formal start and the psychological beginning are two different processes. Even though the beginning may be eagerly sought, it can feel daunting. There may be doubt about whether the beginning is 'real' or not. There was comfort in the meandering pace and low stress of the Neutral Zone. It was pleasant to get up late, please yourself and to feel free of day-to-day pressures. The decision to take a new step may still feel provisional, even though all the formal procedures, such as contracts, have been completed. The new is unknown – what will it take to succeed? It is normal to feel doubts about competence and capability at this stage. It is also normal for there to be a dip in confidence a few weeks when the reality of the new situation begins to become clear.

Working with clients on Beginnings

- Encourage planning – gathering information, imagining, visualizing, thinking, preparing – they all help with coming to terms with whatever is about to start. Ask clients to imagine a typical successful day under the new regime: what would be happening?
- Ask clients what new skills they anticipate the beginning will need. How many of these skills do they have? How could they acquire any that are missing? How could they boost and develop the skills they do have?
- Encourage the idea that in the first few weeks the task is to learn what the task is rather than to do it.
- As with every other aspect of managing change, getting involved counters feelings of lack of control. Ask clients: how could you be wholly involved with every aspect of this new life?
- Explain the value of early quick wins – these not only emphasize that the beginning is happening but create useful opportunities to underline what has changed and what is now starting.

The limits of 'models'

Writing about models such as these and encouraging their use has some dangers. Deeply painful experience is not readily packaged and explained away. It can rip into us, resisting labelling. A sensible, mature and gifted client whose life had, as she said, 'folded into despair' was still struggling to come to terms with catastrophic losses two years later, despite counselling and coaching. In one 18-month period her husband had died, her daughter had developed a brain tumour, she had lost her job and had been forced to sell her house. Grief, especially, is hard to manage.

Dr Johnson, who himself never ceased to mourn his wife, put it so well: 'For sorrow there is no remedy'. In a harrowing account of his baby's death, Aleksandar Hemon (2011) wrote that grief for him and his wife was 'now an organ in our bodies, whose sole function is a continuous secretion of sorrow'. In such cases, people will speak of their grief less and less, appearing to 'move on', but they never 'get over it'. So beware of expecting or wanting clients to reach the apparently sunny stage of 'adjustment' because sometimes it cannot happen.

Self-limiting beliefs

Change can be daunting. Part of the client wants the status quo because even if things are uncomfortable there is comfort in the familiarity of the discomfort. This is why we all cling to self-limiting beliefs, even while we are proclaiming our wish to transform ourselves.

Self-limiting belief has been given many different names. Timothy Gallwey (2000) (see page 82) calls it Self 1 to distinguish it from Self 2: the confident human being full of potential and capacity. Self 1 is the know-it-all who doesn't trust Self 2. Self 1's voice is always ready with self-condemnation, predictions of failure and gloomy comparisons of self with others. When Self 2 can silence Self 1, potential can turn into achievement and growth. Richard Carson (1987) coined the term 'gremlin' for the same phenomenon: a nagging critical inner voice always ready to sabotage success.

We all have these voices; they are part of growing up and they cannot be coached because they are not rational. They cannot be dismissed or killed off because they are inalienably a part of who we are. The challenge is to unmask, name and manage them, particularly with humour. This way they become less powerful.

The essential things to remember about the sabotaging inner voice is that it wants to preserve the status quo because it is scared all the time and its function is to hold you back through fear. It does not like publicity or humour, so exposing it to view and to laughter immediately reduces its authority.

Self-sabotaging statements

Here are some sample self-sabotaging statements:

> I'm only (able to do a little . . .)
>
> I'm no good at . . . other people are cleverer . . .

Don't stick your head above the parapet . . .

A person like me could never . . .

I'll wait until the time is right before I . . .

I should be . . . (better, stronger, nicer . . .)

I shouldn't be so . . . (silly, needy . . .)

I mustn't because (I might be successful; people might laugh; that's for other people, not for people like me . . .)

Listen out for these phrases. Usually they have originated in childhood and you will have probed for them when asking clients for their autobiographical accounts (see page 107). I remind clients that, as children, their parents or carers probably meant well enough in the limiting beliefs they passed on. Mostly such nostrums were designed, however simplistically, to keep us safe, or on track. As children they may even have done so, but as adults they are rarely useful.

CASE STUDY
Michael

I grew up in a working-class environment where fear of authority was very real. My parents had learnt to be docile with teachers, the council, the police and so on. It was important to 'keep out of trouble'. I was told all the time to *keep your head down, be seen and not heard, people like us don't show off.* I internalized these messages to a high degree and I suppose they did help because I did keep my head down and I did work hard and I got to a good university. One of the main benefits of coaching to me was learning that what may have helped as a kid was completely getting in the way as an adult. Through the coaching I learnt to see that failing to speak up was leading to colleagues believing that I had nothing to say or else was 'aloof' and that not challenging senior people was letting them think that I was a bit of a pushover. Through coaching, I had to learn all the skills associated with doing this stuff well, because I had never learnt them as a young man.

Spotting other flawed thinking patterns

Many of our clients have already identified some typically unhelpful *behaviour* patterns. Far fewer are adept at recognizing their typical *thinking* patterns. Often these are flawed. They represent distortions of reality and this is what causes the misery or ineffective behaviour. Listen carefully for these patterns. Note that when under stress from change, a typical small distortion in thinking can become magnified. Here are some of the most common.

> *The pessimist*: terrible events can and will happen and human beings have no say in whether they happen or not. I hear of some risk or potential danger and immediately assume it will happen to me or my family: terrorist attack, nuclear war . . . once I know it's possible, I believe it is likely. Anything good that happens is temporary whereas bad things are permanent.

> *It's all my fault*: if something goes wrong, it's all down to me. Others did not contribute, nor did the system. I am responsible for the health and happiness of everyone around me.

> *Other people can make me happy or sad*: I hold others accountable for the horrible things that have happened to me or for their failure to make me happy. If only they would see the misery they have caused, but somehow they don't.

> *My past defines me*: if there was some sadness, tragedy or uncomfortable event in my life, I will never overcome it. It will always be with me because it was and is overwhelming. I become a person defined by the event (e.g. abused child, widowed young mother, mugging victim).

> *Super-competent-me*: I have to be super-competent at every single thing I attempt whether in my work or personal life. Not to be competent is a disaster. Failure is unthinkable. I am my role. If you want a job done well, do it yourself. It is appalling to admit to a mistake because people might discover that there is nothing behind the mask.

> *No-such-thing-as-grey*: things are either perfect or a disaster, black or white, right or wrong. As a person I am either great or awful and so is everyone else.

> *It's not fair*: I expected everything to be fair but it's not. Other people get away with things that they shouldn't get away with. They should

be severely punished but often they're not. Someone should always take the blame.

I can change people: I believe it's possible to reform or rescue people. I try everything I can to make them see the error of their ways so that they will do what I want and take my needs more seriously. I give them advice and it's exasperating that they won't follow it.

The disciplined perfectionist: my language is peppered with *musts, shoulds* and *oughts*. I work from rigid rules about what has to be done. Where there are actual rules in my organization I believe they should be adhered to, even if everyone else ignores them. If only everyone (myself included) were disciplined about life, all its problems would be solved. I judge harshly when there is any falling-short.

The self-sacrificer/compulsive carer: I believe that you must always be virtuous by putting others first. Life should be about service. My reward will be that others offer service back. Disappointment and anger must be denied when this doesn't happen.

Everything should be peaceful and harmonious: conflict is scary and always destructive. I must do everything I can to keep the peace. If you expose conflict, nothing will ever be tranquil again. It's better to ignore the danger signs because if you do nothing, it might all go away.

You have to be tough: life is hard. I have to be tough and look out for myself because if you're not, other people will take advantage so it's better to strike first. Competition in human life is inevitable and healthy. Showing any vulnerability and tenderness means showing weakness and this is fatal.

The narcissist: the world exists to service my needs. I am the centre, I am special and have a sense of entitlement to attention, success and admiration. I'm not really that interested in others' feelings. Underneath, my ego is fragile but this is concealed in the super-confident way I feel I must present to the world.

As coaches, the most helpful things we can do are to:

- Spot the pattern.
- As in every other transaction with the client, commit to dealing respectfully with what you observe.
- Name or ask for the pattern:

I notice that several times in our conversation today you seem to have reduced your choices to either/or (you then describe what you have heard and noticed)
Or
What 'rule' are you applying here? (usually one about cause and effect: 'If I do *this*, then *that* will follow . . .').

- Ask the client if they recognize the pattern:

    I'm wondering whether this is a common pattern for you? Can you think of other examples?

- Challenge the generalization that lies beneath the pattern:

    Let's think about what alternatives there might be for instance to resolve (whatever problem the client has raised).

- Ask the client what useful purpose the pattern has been serving for them.
- Work with the client to spot it every time it occurs.
- Introduce the client to greater flexibility in their thinking.

CASE STUDY

Ed

Ed was working with me on his relationship with his boss. He was rehearsing how he would raise the subject of a salary increase. I had already noticed that Ed preceded almost every statement about what he wanted with a self-effacing qualifier, such as, 'I know I'm already well paid but now that I'm doing more responsible work I feel I should be getting at least 10 per cent more.'

In discussion, it emerged that Ed's underlying 'rule' was that you are more likely to get what you want if you imply modesty. His self-sabotaging voice, learnt in childhood from a crushingly critical father, was that people will punish and mock if you praise yourself. As a child, Ed's 'rule' had appeared to keep him safe from the perils of boastfulness and indeed it was true that he presented himself with a charming modesty. The flawed thinking pattern was that it is *always* better to keep the peace than to risk conflict. A further belief is that you cannot mix modesty with speaking up – the two are mutually exclusive. The combined impact of these mental habits conveyed the impression that Ed was not serious about his requests or could easily be out-manoeuvred.

I pointed out to Ed what I had observed. We discussed the likely impact on the other person of hearing a statement which is communicating such a double message: apologizing for being well paid and at the same time asking for more money. We looped back to our discussion about his childhood, revisiting the likely usefulness of some of these beliefs.

Every time I heard Ed make a statement like this (frequently), I doggedly pointed it out, or asked him to give himself feedback on the same pattern. Ed began to realize that this clarified much that had baffled him in his leadership role – for instance it could well explain why when he asked people to undertake a piece of work they frequently didn't deliver on it.

All of this may sound easy but it is not. First, the coach needs the courage to challenge. Second, the client needs to be able to see that far from being the rational truth they believed it to be, this aspect of their thinking is irrational. Ask clients other questions such as:

Are you sure that's *always* true? *Always*?

What is the evidence?

What do you notice that contradicts this assumption?

What other explanations could there be?

What would it be like to believe the opposite?

What belief would you rather have?

Be alert also to the danger of initiating a side-tracking debate about competing world views. Your own thinking could be as unsound as the client's and you might like to look at the list above to see if you can spot your own actual or potential weaknesses.

Identifying self-limiting assumptions

Nancy Kline recommends a method of getting at underlying limiting assumptions in her enjoyable book, *Time to Think* (1999). She suggests asking the client to identify the opposite of the limiting belief – note that the client does the actual identifying of the opposite, not the coach. This is then followed by asking the client what it would be like to know (note the present tense) that the opposite is true. Let's suppose that your client has said that they want to learn how to swim. Your questioning exposes the assumption that they would inevitably drown if they took their feet off the bottom.

Coach: So what would the opposite be of believing you're bound to drown?
Client: (laughs) That I'd be a confident swimmer.
Coach: So if you know that you are a confident swimmer, how would that feel?
Client: Absolutely brilliant!
Coach: So stay with absolutely brilliant – how does it feel to be absolutely brilliant as a swimmer and getting fitter?
Client: I can flip up and down the pool, I can do freestyle, I can swim 1000 metres without getting puffed, I have total confidence that I'm as good as anyone in that pool.
Coach: So, holding on to that belief and that wonderful set of feelings, how could you get there as a confident swimmer?
Client: I noticed an Adult Groundhogs Special at my health club the other day – very small classes for non-swimmers. I could enrol for that.
Coach: Will you?
Client: Yes!

Sometimes, as Nancy says, people will offer what she calls a 'possible fact' as the limiting factor. For instance, in the example above, the answer might have been, 'I did try once and all the children in the pool laughed at me.' This reply, although possibly true and a fact, still hides the limiting assumption. Nancy's comment is that this makes a further question essential: 'That's possible, but what are you assuming that lets that stop you?' This, as she comments triumphantly, will always slide beneath the possible fact and will capture the bedrock culprit: the ultimately limiting assumption.

Discounting

This useful concept comes from Transactional Analysis (TA). It elegantly codifies the many ways in which we can deny reality and resist change. We may *discount* any evidence which threatens our beliefs about ourselves, the people around us or the environment in which we live and work. Discounting represents distorted perception and it happens outside conscious awareness. The amount of fierceness with which we cling to a discount is directly related to the intensity of the perceived threat. In this way we protect ourselves from the disturbance and fear that acknowledging the reality might create. One way of describing an essential part of the coaching process is that it removes discounts and replaces them with healthier awareness because, by doing so, the client is likely to be in a stronger and more autonomous position. Discounting may happen at four levels:

1 *Discounting the* existence *of a problem*

> A smoker may continue to believe that smoking is not harmful. Here the facts established by 75 years of research are denied because to admit the validity of the facts would create enormous anxiety.

When coaching clients discount at this level, they may, for instance, deny that their job is under threat in spite of clear evidence that it is. They may deny strong evidence that there is a problem with their performance or that a central relationship in their lives is at risk. A client with a dishevelled appearance may discount the unflattering inferences others draw. A married gay client may discount his true sexual preferences, dismissing his occasional flings with men as trivial deviations from an essentially heterosexual existence. Signs that clients are discounting at this level might be a continuation of old behaviour in the face of obvious threat. Good coaching questions here might be:

> What are the known facts?
>
> What evidence is there that this is a problem? How often, how much, how intense?
>
> How reliable is the evidence?
>
> Who might confirm or deny it?
>
> If there are information gaps, how might you fill them?

2 *Discounting the* significance *of a problem*

> The smoker may admit that smoking is harmful but may believe that his own genetic inheritance will somehow protect him. He will support this belief by quoting a grandparent who lived to 95 and smoked 60 cigarettes a day.

When you hear clients discount at this level they may for instance have had uncomfortable 360-degree feedback but be inclined to blame others or the methodology. Or they may brush it aside by telling you that the people who gave the feedback don't really matter because they have no power to affect the client's future. A brand manager may discount declining sales figures by attributing them to predictable ebbs and flows in the market. At this level, discounting continues until the underlying feelings of fear, disappointment, loss, anger and insecurity have been expressed. We hide under the shelter of rationality because we are afraid of the intensity of our feelings.

Useful questions here could be:

> If this were true, what impact would it have?
>
> How did you feel when you first heard this?
>
> Where does it fit or not fit with other messages/evidence?
>
> How could you check out how much this will matter?

3 *Discounting the* solvability *of the problem*

> The smoker acknowledges that smoking may severely damage his health but believes that all the usual remedies – nicotine patches, going cold-turkey, hypnotherapy – will not work in his particular case.

Coaching clients may express views suggesting that the situation is out of their control – they are helpless. They may retreat into the apparent safety of being victims. Look out for black/white either/or thinking and phrases like 'I can't' or generalizations such as 'I always . . .' This kind of discounting has a lot in common with the Depression (or paralysis) stage of the Kübler-Ross change cycle. Useful questions here can be:

> When you've encountered this sort of situation before, what did you do that worked?
>
> When you've seen other people deal well with this situation, what seemed to work for them?
>
> Who might be ready to offer useful help?
>
> What other resources are available?
>
> What skills do you have that you can bring into play here?
>
> What criteria might you use for finding a solution?
>
> What partial solutions might there be?
>
> What could you live with here, even if it's not the perfect solution?

4 *Discounting the* ability *to change*

> The smoker knows that all the usual remedies would work on him, but doubts his capacity to live without cigarettes.

Here the client has accepted the facts, understands their significance and knows that there are solutions but discounts his or her personal ability to react differently or to live with the consequences. Executive coaching clients may say things like, 'This is who I am – I can't be different', or 'It's all very well for other people, they're younger' (or more adaptable or more employable).

Effective coaching tactics at this level are usually about re-establishing the importance of the goal (see Chapter 6) and its accompanying vision. What will work here are techniques such as drawing, visioning, imagining a day spent in a positive future and refocusing attention onto positive outcomes rather than wallowing in problems. It can also help to develop best- and worst-case scenarios and then to look at what it would actually be sensible to expect. Good questions might be:

> What's your overall strategy here?
>
> What will the benefits be of achieving it?
>
> What first small steps towards the goal might you make?
>
> What additional training or other help might you need?
>
> Imagine you can cope: what would be happening?
>
> Who could support you?
>
> When you've learnt something new in the past, what did you find were the best methods?

Identifying the pay-off for staying stuck

One of the reasons that we can stay fixed in a problem is that there is some pay-off from doing so. It is worth exploring what this might be.

However miserable clients are about feeling stuck, there is always a benefit. The prison of misery may be horrible but at least it's familiar. Asking the client to identify how the pay-off works can often be a moment of enlightenment. Ask, 'What is it doing for you to stay stuck here?' Typical pay-offs may include:

- Controlling and manipulating others by engendering guilt.
- Creating some personal space and 'reward' for yourself.

- A moment of 'high' and pure enjoyment.
- Giving away your power, which means that you can't fail because you can always say that if you'd tried you could have succeeded. As that well-known sage Homer Simpson comments: 'You tried your best, and you failed miserably. The lesson is, never try.'
- Forcing others to take responsibility for you, which means that you never have to blame yourself if something goes wrong.
- Focusing all your problems and fears into one package – as is the case, for instance, with phobias.
- Avoiding facing up to actual weaknesses.

One dramatic example of a pay-off was the research conducted by Neville Kay (reported in 'Legal fight is pain in the elbow', *The Times*, 22 November 2003), a hand surgeon who discovered that in some patients with tennis elbow, surgery was ineffective, as were steroids and physiotherapy. Surgery normally has excellent results. The predictive factor in recovery was whether or not the patients were suing for compensation. His conclusion was that even the best treatment will not work if patients literally have an investment in their pain.

When it's always someone else's fault

There are some clients who can seem fixed in the role of victim. To have a client determined to blame others for their own disappointments invariably takes me to the boundaries of my skills. Suggesting therapy is always a possible alternative, but many clients are not so obviously extreme in their distress as to warrant this tactic or might dismiss the suggestion that it would help. What can be done for clients like Carys?

CASE STUDY

Carys

At the time we worked together, Carys was a disappointed woman. As a senior accountant in the City she had expected to get the finance director job in her organization. It had gone instead to a colleague whom she liked but whom she also judged to be less competent than herself. Our work initially focused on getting another job as Carys felt she could not stay in the original organization – it would have felt too humiliating.

I encouraged Carys to contact headhunters and to alert her networks to her wish to move. Soon there were two potential offers on the horizon, both of which paid much the same as the job she had failed to get. Carys took one of these jobs, but as our coaching went on into her new job, it was clear that a sense that 'it was unfair' still pervaded her life. She complained about the new job – it was lonely, the office was stiflingly hot, the chief executive did not appreciate her. In every session it seemed that we would inevitably come back to the unfairness of not getting the finance director job in her old organization, even a year later.

Some possible approaches

First you must *notice the pattern*. The give-aways are:

- coming to coaching looking for a way of changing someone else;
- evading questions about what they, the client, have contributed to the situation;
- a lot of sentences beginning
  - If only they would . . .
  - If only it hadn't turned out like it did . . .
  - My life would be fine if only others would let me . . .
- generalizations suggesting that mostly other people are getting things wrong around this client: 'They always . . .'; 'They never . . .'
- a constant sense of weariness and disappointment, whatever good things seem to be happening – nothing is ever quite good enough.

The next step is to *offer the client feedback*:

> Carys, I notice that in this session as in so many others, we keep coming back to that old sore of the finance director job. You've mentioned it twice in this session, just as you did in our last one. What's going on here for you?

In Carys's case, she was ahead of me. 'I must be a very annoying client because I'm always blaming someone else, aren't I?' So Carys could intellectualize her dilemma but still could not move on.

Now ask the client *what they are contributing to staying stuck*. Some clients will deny that they are contributing anything. The therapist and author Irvin Yalom (2002) suggests saying something like, 'OK let's accept that 99 per cent of this is someone else's fault. Can we work on the 1 per cent that's yours?'

Now e*xpose the fallacy* of devoting time and energy to the goal of having a better past. The past has gone and can never be rescheduled, reworked or remodelled. There is only now.

For most clients one or all of the approaches I describe here will work, one way or another. If they don't, I will have one last tactic to try: *expose the client to your own dilemmas* about how to help them. So with a client like Carys, having tried all of the above tactics without any apparent success, I might say:

> Carys, I feel at my limit here. I really want our coaching to succeed for you, yet I'm feeling frustrated by my inability to help. We've tried a number of things, yet I notice you still seem attached to that original dream of the job you didn't get. What would you advise me to do?

Note that the risks here are of a client like Carys believing that I, too, am persecuting her and will be about to reject or abandon her. I will refuse to play that game, stressing my continuing support for her as well as putting half the responsibility for our relationship back on her.

In general I find it challenging to work with clients who protect themselves by adopting a victim mentality. If I suspect that this might be what is going on I will probe in the look-see conversation, asking an initial, cautiously-put question about how far they believe they have responsibility themselves for whatever their situation is. A client who gives me some variant of 'none – it's all about other people' is giving me fair warning and I will usually politely decline the assignment at that stage. I know such people to be vulnerable, despite what is often an appearance of certainty and confidence. My refusal to work with them is based on experience that whenever I have taken on such clients, despite my doubts, the coaching usually comes to an abrupt end at the point where their view of themselves as helpless victims is challenged.

Beware, too, of believing that the client should or can make an instant, radical swap of an old, limiting, faulty view for a new wonder-view. Human psychology simply doesn't work like that and it would be worrying if it did. If the suggested fresh thinking appears to contradict some fiercely-held value, the client will dismiss it, even if they politely agree to try it. What is more likely is that clients will experiment small step-by-small-step with new ideas and behaviour. Old ways of thinking have a way of resurfacing – why wouldn't they? The client has had many decades reinforcing them.

The Immunity to Change approach

Everything in coaching is about change. Our clients want to change and we want to work with them on the changes they say they want to make. And yet, if you're honest, how many times as a coach have you wondered if you are really just working transactionally with clients? Do you have a private suspicion that what you're doing is tinkering, working at the behavioural level but not getting to the heart of it? For instance:

- client A vows to delegate, and yet he still seems to be doing his team's work for them;
- client B is ashamed of her weight and knows she has to shed three stone, yet she's still fat;
- client C's life is all work and no private life. His marriage is at risk, but he still puts in 12 hours at the office every day.

Things may have improved – a bit – thanks to your coaching, but the main problem may remain untouched. One way of tackling this has been suggested in the book *Immunity to Change* (2009) by Robert Kegan and Lisa Lahey. Kegan and Lahey propose that we skilfully create our own 'immune system' to change, invariably sabotaging ourselves. The solution is to make three assumptions:

1 The client has something vitally important in their lives that they wish to change: without this motivation nothing will happen so the issue must be one that has potential to transform their lives.
2 Both thinking *and* feeling must be involved – either on its own will not work.
3 Learning new adaptive steps will take time and is best tackled in small stages.

The Immunity to Change approach proposes a four-stage grid. Try it on yourself first.

Filling in the columns

Column 1: commitment to improvement
This is essentially about your growth as a person. Look for ONE BIG THING that would have power to transform your life. It must be important to you, have impact for radical improvement in your life and should matter to others who are important to you: if you don't know what this might be, ask them. However, it must primarily involve you: the area for improvement is yourself. It should not be something technical like a skill and should not involve a personality transplant – stay with the person you are at the core. The goal should be stated in the positive – in other words, not be phrased as something you want to give up, or stop doing.

Column 2: what you are doing or not doing instead of achieving your goal?
Write these as actual behaviours, not as attitudes or beliefs, or states of mind, and be honest. Enter everything you do that is working against achieving your

1 Commitment: improvement goal: phrased in the positive	2 What do I do/not do instead? (Actual behaviours)	3 What are my hidden competing commitments? When I think about doing the opposite of what is in Column 2, what fears do I have?	4 What big assumptions am I making (e.g. what assumptions might a person who listed whatever is in their Column 3 be making about their world and themselves)?
I want . . .	What I actually do to prevent my commitment being fully realized . . .	I am afraid . . .	I assume . . .
What commitments does your improvement goal imply?	What I don't do . . .	By engaging in the undermining behaviour what worrisome outcome are you committed to preventing?	

goal and don't worry about why you engage in this behaviour or about plans to stop doing it. Go for the behaviours in all their embarrassing glory.

Column 3: revealing the hidden or competing commitments

This is the worry area. It shows the hidden dynamic, the immunity to change, a set of competing commitments. To fill in this column, take each of your Column 2 entries one by one and ask yourself, *If I imagine trying to do the opposite of this behaviour what is the most worrying, scary or uncomfortable thought that comes to me?* This thought should have the power of Yuk! Experience the power of this feeling. If you don't experience it you are not there yet. You should feel at risk in some way. People frequently identify an early negative feeling (e.g. 'boredom' or 'twitchiness' or 'impatience'). This is not the answer – dig below it – what is the awful feeling that lies beneath? What is the risk? Typical fears are of:

Being incompetent

Being humiliated

Helplessness

Being unloved

Hurting someone we care about

We therefore protect ourselves from feeling such horrible things and find ways of dealing with the anxiety. Our Column 2 behaviour is a way of keeping anxiety at bay and of protecting us, often very effectively. This is what keeps us stuck and prevents us making any progress on our goal. In the space headed 'I am afraid', write down your fears: 'I worry I will . . .' Underneath, write:

'So I am committed to . . .' (e.g. not being humiliated, not feeling out of control).

Column 4: the big assumptions
You don't disrupt the behaviours in Column 2 by just 'trying' not to do them. You do disrupt them by identifying the big assumptions. To do this, look at your Column 3 entries. Now brainstorm all the assumptions a person who had such commitments might be making. Ask yourself how far you are making them generalizations – things that are ALWAYS true regardless of circumstances – and ask yourself how strong the hold that they have on you actually is. Where did this assumption come from? What is its history? What were the critical turning points? Write them down under 'I assume . . .'

Designing tests of the big assumptions
Kegan and Lahey emphasize – and I agree – that such enormous assumptions are never dissolved overnight. Most of us hug our most profoundly self-limiting assumptions – we believe them to represent an absolute truth. We also believe that they are protecting us, which is why we cling to them. They are best dismantled step-by-step through cautious experiment. The way to do this it to ask: what behaviour change would make for good information about the accuracy of your big assumption? What data might you collect to test it? Now you create a safe, modest test – an experiment designed to test the assumption. This should be something you can do immediately and not in the far future. Remember it's an experiment – a *test* – and does not commit you to anything.
 Some options might be:

- Alter a behaviour from Column 2.
- Perform an action which runs counter to Column 3 commitments.
- Challenge directly a Column 4 assumption.

Assessing the different behaviour

- What did you do?
- What happened? How did others respond?
- How might this challenge your big assumption?

Using this approach with clients

You can show clients the grid and work through it with them if you wish. Or you can simply learn it yourself and use it to talk them through the process. It is useful to explain the essential concept of 'immunity' and the apparently baffling way we can sabotage ourselves. Designing different behaviour fits well with the action/accountability part of the coaching process and also assumes that we will be working with a client over a long enough period of time to be able to make a steady difference.

CASE STUDY

Sandra

Sandra came to me for help with giving presentations. She had a senior role in a manufacturing company. The HR sponsor told me that Sandra seemed 'uptight and nervous' whenever he had seen her perform and that this skill was intrinsic to her work. An expensive presentation skills course had made no discernible difference. The behavioural approach to coaching would be to deliver what is in effect one-to-one training, perhaps using a video camera for practice and feedback. This is what Sandra told me she expected. In fact, no video camera was ever used in finding the solution to her problem. Instead, we looked at the paradox of how she desperately needed and wanted to be better at giving presentations, already knew exactly what it was she had to do, yet through skilled self-sabotage was making it impossible to achieve.

Using the Immunity to Change approach, we identified clearly what behaviour she wanted to change: this involved developing a confident, racy style of presentation unique to her. Column 2 discussions revealed a skilled pattern of avoidance: refusing invitations to speak, then, when it was impossible to avoid them, resorting to mumbling, to last-minute preparation or none, preparing elaborate PowerPoint slides and staring at them throughout the presentation, and keeping the whole thing as short as possible. In Column 3, the hidden competing commitments emerged. We explored her belief that the remnants of a West Country burr and the fact that she had gone to an 'ordinary' and not a 'posh' university made people conclude that she was 'stupid'.

Then there was the deeper belief that she had nothing to say that others would wish to hear, starting in childhood where as the youngest of six and the only girl, she was routinely referred to as 'Fat Piggy' and at any family gathering ordered to 'Shut up because who'd be interested in what you've got to say?' She had been literally silenced. In Column 4, her deepest fear was of exposing herself to the possibility of finding out that those childhood taunts represented the truth about herself, that despite her professional success she was stupid and incompetent. Together we designed a series of safe experiments to test these destructive assumptions and slowly, over the next few sessions, began to assemble a different 'reality': people did not care a jot about her accent (which was in any case barely noticeable); she did have in-depth expertise in her subject; she did not need to be cleverer than her colleagues, only clever *enough*; she was already an expert storyteller and could and did bring this talent with profit into her presentation work.

Fear is the enemy

Ultimately, we are held back from change by fear. The fear is about loss of control and of being unable to cope with the unknown. Fear is the real opponent in coaching. Fear ruthlessly targets the most fragile spot, starting as faint doubt and, in the right conditions, growing quickly to terrifying proportions. As neuroscience now proves, logic is often no help because fear crowds it out, reducing it to a parody of rationality, becoming in quick order anxiety and panic. Yann Martel's character puts it wonderfully in his Booker Prize-winning novel, *Life of Pi* (2002), a profound, surreal, audacious and funny novel about a man who survives a shipwreck in a lifeboat with a Bengal tiger for company:

> Fear . . . nestles in your memory like a gangrene: it seeks to rot everything, even the words with which to speak it. So you must fight hard to express it. You must fight hard to shine the light of words upon it. Because if you don't, if your fear becomes a wordless darkness that you will avoid, perhaps even manage to forget, you open yourself to further attacks of fear because you never truly fought the opponent who defeated you.

In coaching what we are doing, with the client's full assent, is peeling back the surface of apparent logic to expose the vulnerable core protected, as it so often is, by irrational defences. Naming the fear, looking its underpinning assumptions in the eye, challenging and supporting, offering alternatives, building new skills, working in small steps, being alert to the psychology of human change, showing that you believe the client's life could be what they want it to be: this is what will make the difference. To be successful as a coach you need to be open, warm, curious, honest and unafraid. These qualities are never more necessary than when working with clients on change.

8 Bringing pace and interest to the session

When I watch and listen to recordings of other people's coaching sessions, I am, of course an eavesdropper after the event in a different role and for a different purpose from either of the two players. Even so, with some coaches, I find that my attention can drift off with the soporific drone of the conversation. I long for some action, some change of pace and, yes, some drama. Everything in my experience tells me that this will make for better learning. Sitting still for two hours of the same kind of question and answer can be deeply dull. When appropriate, there are many techniques that can accelerate learning as well as providing a change of pace and that is the focus of this chapter.

Changing the physical pace

Sometimes the simplest interventions are the best. Stopping halfway through a session and suggesting another cup of tea or coffee will often revitalize a flagging discussion. Similarly, suggesting a quick stand-up and physical stretch can achieve the same thing. Drawing is useful because it bypasses the tendency of highly articulate people to intellectualize their problems, so activities like the Life Scan Wheel or drawing pictures of your life as it is and as you would like it to be also have this extra value (see pages 143 and 146). Depending on the weather and the location of your coaching room, a walk can also be a wonderful way of adding pace and variety to the session. I was working with a client on a longer-term programme whose aim was to establish himself as a self-employed consultant in his field. At the time of the session he had, only a few hours before, returned to London from San Francisco. It was a luminously sunny, fiery July day. About 10 minutes in, he suddenly said, 'Jenny, I just can't concentrate – it's no good, I'm hot, jet-lagged and distracted.' Within moments we were out of the office and had set off on a walk around the attractive buildings and surrounding gardens of one of the ancient Inns of Court, a few minutes away from my office in central London. We kept going on a circular route for the best part of 90 minutes. Indeed, there is often something to be said for a conversation where you are side by side instead of face to face – there may be more candour because you are released from the relentlessness of the eye contact involved in a conventional conversation and being outdoors in a pleasant place creates a different atmosphere.

I have a flip chart in most of the rooms I use for coaching. Getting up to draw, write, explain useful 'models' and theories, or have the client explain them to you, and standing side by side while you do it, is a less dramatic but nonetheless useful way of introducing a physical change of pace.

Overtly managing the time

I like to make the principles of pace and timing explicit to clients. So although I always have a clock just over the client's right shoulder, so that I can glance at it covertly, and am also expert at reading the client's watch upside down, I also do a certain amount of pantomime time management. This could involve rolling back my sleeve to look at my watch, or saying out loud, 'Now what time do we have left?' and then glancing at the clock, as well as agreeing a rough schedule for each of the items on the client's list at the outset of the session. It can also help to draw attention to the need for a change of pace by saying something like, 'We've spent a long time on that rather heavy and sobering topic, how about we go now to your lighter one?' A two-hour session often has an energy dip after 90 minutes. So at that point I might say, 'So we've got half an hour left. What would be the best use of that time for you?' If a session has run out of steam altogether, never prolong it for the sake of finishing exactly at two hours, or whatever your allotted time is. Be prepared to agree to end early, or to spend the remaining minutes in overtly social chat. In the first session, as part of your contracting conversation, you might like to ask the client how they feel about the proposed length of the session. For some people, two hours of sitting still is agonizing. So when I met a young client, a professional sportsman, whose presenting issue was how to cope with the many stresses of his life, I noticed that his right foot was busy waggling throughout the first 15 minutes of our first session. Creating a little pause in the conversation, I said, 'So, Derren, I notice that your right foot seems to have a life of its own. What's that about?' His reply was, 'I'm feeling anxious right now and also I've never been able to sit still without wriggling, but I'm trying to be polite.' This led to a productive discussion about how to manage our time so that we built in frequent breaks, did some of our sessions outside as walks and worked in 90- instead of 120-minute blocks.

'Stepping into it'

This activity asks the client to *walk through* an issue instead of just talking about it. Standing up, walking it through and experiencing the feelings and sensations at each stage can give clients powerful insights into why they behave the way they do and can also create motivation for change.

There are many variations, but one that works well is to set out a series of sheets of A4 paper in a line on the floor of the room, labelled in this order: Environment, Behaviour, Capability, Beliefs, Identity and Wider Implications. The framework is a variant on the many techniques developed by NLP practitioners where the assumption is that by changing your position and imagining yourself in a different place, mentally and physically, you will alter your beliefs and behaviour.

Explain the purpose of the activity and ask if the client is up for it. Assuming the answer is yes, ask the client to stand on each sheet in turn, answering a series of questions around each 'stepping stone':

> *Environment*: Where are you when this happens? Who else is with you? What's it like being there?
>
> *Behaviour*: What's your usual response? What do you typically do? How does it feel?
>
> *Capability*: What skills and abilities are you using in this situation?
>
> *Beliefs*: What beliefs do you hold around this behaviour? What's driving it?
>
> *Identity*: Who is this person, e.g. [client name] The Perfectionist, The Saint, The Rescuer?
>
> *Wider implications*: Knowing what you know now, what are the wider implications of this?

Now work your way back down the line on the other side, asking at each stepping stone a series of questions based on more resourceful thinking:

> *Identity*: Who could you be?
>
> *Beliefs*: What could you believe about yourself and the situation that would be more positive and hopeful?
>
> *Capability*: What skills and abilities do you have that you could use here?
>
> *Behaviour*: How then could you respond?
>
> *Environment*: Imagine yourself fast-forwarding to the next time you're in this situation. How will the outcome change?

Brainstorming

At some point in the coaching programme, virtually all clients describe feeling stuck. The 'stuckness' will be around finding a more satisfactory solution to a long-standing problem than the ones the client has already thought of. The client is clear about the goal, maybe thanks to your expert clarification and questioning, but cannot identify how to get there. Typically, the client has gone round and round the same thought processes without coming up with an answer that feels right:

> I don't know how to tackle an underperforming member of my team – he seems immune to all my feedback.

> My weight gain has got out of hand but I hate exercise and I know that diets just make you fatter in the long term.

> We can't afford to move out of our company's premises but they're so shabby and unsatisfactory and in completely the wrong location.

> I want a holiday but my husband wants to buy a car instead.

Brainstorming[1] works well as a technique with this kind of dilemma because it typically engages the right hemisphere of the brain (see page 45). It is a simple but powerful approach to generating ideas, and the great thing is that as a coach you can join in. So where you have been longing to offer ideas, this is one legitimate place where you can do it. However, you have to stick to the rules, the most important of which is that while you are in the idea-generating stage, no evaluation of any kind is permitted: no raised eyebrows, sighs, self-censoring of the 'Oh, that's a stupid idea so I'm not going to say it' sort. This rule applies equally to you and to the client. Brainstorming only works if you say whatever comes into your head without editing.

How to do it

First you ask the client's permission:

> I feel that it might be useful to brainstorm some ideas here. Is that OK?

If the client says it isn't OK, then of course you drop it. However, it would be rare indeed for a client to say no – anything that would break the deadlock is probably welcomed.

Next, get clarity around the question. It needs to be reduced to something simple and straightforward, normally a question beginning 'How can I . . .?' or 'What ways could there be of . . .?'

Now you explain the rules. A lot of people think they know what brainstorming is but in practice they often start evaluating the ideas as soon as they have been uttered – the self-defeating habit that brainstorming is designed to prevent. Explain that at this stage any idea, however silly, outrageous or off-the-wall, is welcome. All ideas will be written down: ideally on a flip chart. Standing up and working side by side while you do this seems to help because, again, it breaks the trance of the seated conversation. Encourage humour, wildness and silliness. You explain that you will be giving yourself permission to join in because this is not advice, only idea-generation.

When the ideas have clearly been exhausted, turn to a fresh sheet of paper and ask the client what criteria they will use to evaluate the ideas. Now you are back in strictly coach-mode. The criteria will normally cover areas such as practicality, cost, fit with the client's core values, time, realism, likely impact on relationships – and so on.

Put the two sheets of paper side by side, hand the client a pen in a different colour and ask them to highlight any of the brainstormed ideas that look interesting enough to explore further. Review these ideas against the list of criteria and move to action in the usual way.

CASE STUDY
Alan

Alan enjoyed good food and wine. He hated exercise because he said he was 'the class fat boy' at school and fended off jibes from other boys by clowning about being fat. He also loathed being fat and had recently become even fatter: 'I went to Marks & Spencer to buy a suit and found that they didn't do Size Huge.' Along with a number of goals relating to his leadership style, one of Alan's goals for his coaching was to lose three stone. He frequently had to represent his organization on television and he described himself as acutely embarrassed to be so obviously overweight: 'I'm not a good advertisement for us looking the way I do.' Additionally, he had some underlying anxiety about health. His father died young of heart disease and Alan had a nagging fear that he might also suffer premature death.

His learning goal in this area was to find a way of permanently sustaining increased fitness and weight loss by making changes in his lifestyle. He knew every diet: Atkins, Rosemary Conley, Slimfast,

Weightwatchers, Lighter Life, Dukan, Slimming World, detox, low fat, high fat – 'You name it, I've tried it.' He also knew that long-term successful weight loss is about steady, undramatic shedding of pounds and that this comes from eating less and exercising more.

Alan's coach helped him understand that his overeating was really about giving himself 'rewards', so part of the coaching tackled this theme. But Alan also highlighted a powerful need to get fitter through exercise, recognizing, too, that exercise is an excellent way of shedding the stress of his high-profile job. This is where the coach used brainstorming. The question was, 'What exercise could I do that will help me lose weight, get and stay fit?'

The brainstorm went on for about six minutes. Ideas generated by both Alan and his coach included: scuba-diving, jazz dancing, entering for the London Marathon, walking to work every day, cycling, swimming, taking the stairs instead of the lift to his apartment, joining a gym, getting a personal trainer, learning Pilates, buying a home treadmill – and many more. And what were the criteria he would use to judge any of these ideas? Alan was clear: it had to be something that involved other people, probably something 'blokeish'. It probably had to be competitive, he had to be in charge of it and, strange as it may seem for a self-labelled 'lazy' person, it had to involve the major effort of running because cross-country running was the only sport he ever enjoyed at school. A moment later Alan made a hurrumphing noise. None of the brainstormed ideas was quite right on its own. However, he had a moment of epiphany. He now knew exactly what he was going to do.

He started and then organized the 'Big Bellies Running Club' for other 'blokes' at his workplace. Soon this was the club everyone wanted to join, regardless of whether they were overweight or not. Running a total of 20 miles a week in a London park at lunchtime with a pack of other beefy men suited Alan just fine. Perhaps he could have got there with another sort of discussion, but there was something about the pace and fun of the brainstorm that for him, as with so many other clients, freed up his thinking.

Empty chair techniques

These approaches appear in a number of different therapeutic traditions, but most particularly from Fritz Perls of the Gestalt school, and are also invaluable for coaching.

Essentially they all work on the same principle: physically altering your point of view and seeing things from a literally different angle can bring useful insights and can lead to changed behaviour.

The first time I experienced this as a client was with my colleague Phil Hayes, who talked me through one such exercise when my elder son, Luke, was a 17-year-old coming up to important exams. Luke's approach to homework was to postpone the moment of torture when he had to begin the wretched task for as long as possible, to do the homework or exam revision with both his CD player and the television on and maybe a girlfriend in the room as well, and to do what appeared to be the absolute minimum. This contrasted with my own experience of being a girlie swot at the same age, obediently pleasing my parents by putting in many hours of nun-like undistracted hard work in order to pass my A levels. I found it unbearable to watch Luke apparently frittering away his talent and risking his university place. The result was a great deal of well-intentioned maternal nagging. Phil talked me through a version of the *meta-mirror*, a classic empty chair technique. Within 20 minutes, I had seen how my behaviour looked to Luke. I had experienced the futility of my tactics, indeed seen how counterproductive they were, and had decided how to approach him differently. It's possible that Luke would give a different version of events, but from that day on I stopped nagging. He got excellent A levels and duly went to university. Whether these two phenomena are connected, I don't know, but I do know that my relationship with him, already good, was immeasurably improved from that time on.

Essentially all empty chair exercises work on the same principle. You set up two empty chairs. You ask the client to sit in one of the chairs and to imagine that the empty chair is occupied by the other person in the relationship. The client describes how they feel about the imaginary person in the other chair. You then ask them to change chairs and to think themselves into 'being' the other person, this time looking at an imagined version of themselves. 'As this other person, how do you feel about X?' (the client).

Probably the most useful versions of empty chair work involve a relationship that is problematical in some way. It need not be a relationship that is in crisis; it could be one that is already pretty good but could be even better. A more important criterion is that the present and future health of the relationship should matter. Typically the coach will then ask the client to 'be' the other person, to imagine their feelings as the other person, and to look through the other person's eyes at him- or herself.

The meta-mirror

One classic exercise, mentioned above, is called the meta-mirror. Start by setting up two empty chairs and invite the client to position them in a way that represents the relationship, for instance, close together or far away, angled or face to face. You stand – or sit – at the client's side throughout.

> *Stage 1*: invite the client to be 'themselves', looking at the other chair and imaging the person sitting opposite. You ask the client: 'How do you feel about this person?'
>
> *Stage 2*: invite the client to swap chairs. Say, 'Now you are the other person looking at an imagined version of yourself sitting in the other chair. How do you feel about [your client's name]? Encourage the client to reply as if they are the person with whom they are having the relationship.
>
> *Stage 3*: now invite the client to stand a few yards away and look at the two empty chairs, imagining *both* people (the client and the other person) sitting there. Tell the client they are now in the most resourceful version of themselves. Ask them: 'What strikes you about this relationship from this distance?'
>
> *Stage 4:* either move even further away, asking the same question as at Stage 3 or return to the original seating and coach around whatever emerges.

Essentially, the meta-mirror asks a client to enter into a state of maximum empathy with another person and then to identify and draw on their own insight and resourcefulness. By physically moving around, the client 'breaks state' – that is, changes both the physical and mental dynamic – and gains new insights and energy. The physical movement of the exercise also enables the client to see the relationships from different perspectives – literally looking at them from another point of view.[2]

This is a potent activity. I have used it many times with clients and there has never been an occasion where the client has failed to enter an intense and concentrated state. There is a stillness and deep absorption, which is quite unlike the usual run of coach–client conversations. Of course, there is no way of verifying the accuracy of our perceptions of what the imagined other person in the chair is feeling unless we check with them later – which some clients do – but my sense is that the insights from the perspective of the other chair are often spookily close. Most of us *can* actually access the cues others give us about their feelings towards us in the right circumstances, and this is what empty chair activities can provide. Perhaps most valuably of all, the technique allows us to understand and experience how we are contributing to the problems in a relationship.

There are many variants of empty chair techniques. They can be introduced simply and spontaneously and take little time. Here are some examples.

CASE STUDY

Sonia

Sonia felt puzzled about how to speak up sooner at meetings. Her coach set up the two chairs, explained the protocol and said, 'In the other chair I want you to imagine the part of you that wants to be confident and extroverted at meetings versus the more restrained person you feel you normally are . . . Get up from your own chair and sit in the more confident Sonia's chair. Now tell me how you feel.' Later the coach asked, 'What advice would you give the more restrained Sonia about what she could do differently?'

CASE STUDY

Brian

Brian was in a dilemma about which career path to choose. He had two good offers and felt paralysed about making the decision. His coach explained the exercise and invited Brian to sit in one chair at a time, imagining he was in each of the jobs, exploring how it felt.

An even simpler variant is one where the client is puzzled or troubled about the behaviour of another person in their lives. As ever, remind the client that you cannot work on the other person, only on the person you have in the room. Ask them to stand up and look at their empty chair. 'Imagine you are that other person looking at yourself. What would you see?' Most clients will get at least some insight into their impact on others by doing this.

'Pebbles'

Another way of working on relationship issues is to ask the client to identify the 'system' in which they are operating by representing it through a set of physical objects.[3] On a shelf easily to hand in my coaching room, I keep a bowl of pebbles of different shapes and sizes. They are nothing special – no polishing or 'crystal magic' is involved – in fact I chose them somewhat carelessly and impatiently from the decorative trough on the balcony of my apartment.

How to do it

Invite the client to pick pebbles which represent him- or herself and the other important people involved. They can use a nearby table-top as the base, or the floor if they prefer. The task is to arrange the pebbles so that they visually represent the nature of the relationships. Hand the client a washable felt-tip pen and suggest that they draw arrows or little faces on each pebble to show which way the people are facing. Physically handling the pebbles and choosing the right size or colour for the 'people' is something that clients usually enjoy. Now ask:

> Which pebble represents whom?
>
> Tell me why you chose the various pebbles you did to represent them (e.g. differences in size, colour and shape).
>
> Tell me what the distances between them represent to you.
>
> Some people are facing away from each other, or from you – what's that about?
>
> You've put yourself [wherever]. Tell me what your thinking is there.
>
> How does it feel looking at this system?
>
> In relation to the pebble representing yourself, how does that feel?

Then, depending on how the client has answered, invite them to rearrange the pebbles so that the pattern (system) feels more comfortable and then to talk you through the whole thing again. Then ask:

So what needs to happen to make this improved system a reality?

CASE STUDY

Tiffany

Tiffany was in the first weeks of her first chief executive role. She described the experience as being like scaling a mountain without any of the correct equipment or team support. We explored what that might mean for her through the Clean Language approach (see page 96) and what emerged was that the new job meant she had moved to a totally new country, had lost her network of close friends and neighbours, had to make a relationship with a seemingly prickly new boss, the chairman of the company, and had inherited an organization where her executive team was far less competent than she had realized, with one of its members going off sick and another instantly lodging a grievance against her. At the same time she was without her husband because he had stayed behind to sort out the sale of their house. She chose a small round pebble to represent herself and placed it slightly off-centre on the table. She arranged pebbles representing each of her team with two of the six facing away from her. Her chairman was placed nearest her and was the biggest of the pebbles. Her husband and former friends were on the extreme edge, her husband facing towards her, the friends facing away. These were her comments on the exercise.

'It was bleak doing this, but it brought home to me like possibly nothing else could, that I was socially and professionally isolated. That poor little round pebble! I felt sorry for it. I understood immediately that my feelings of incompetence and of being out of control could only increase unless I changed my attitudes and behaviours. When you asked me to rearrange the pebbles so that they represented a more satisfying arrangement and I did, I felt better straight away. You will remember that I also introduced some new pebbles, one of which was a PA, as I did not have this vital role filled at the time and I'd let the vacancy drift. I also realized that I had been invited to join a pan-European chief executive 'academy' and that this would give me support and challenge from peers. I added more pebbles close to me to represent the new friends I needed to make – people who had nothing to do with my work – and another one to represent an as yet unknown personal trainer who could make sure that I got exercise back into my life. It was a brilliant insight. I felt better immediately and it was the start of planning a whole set of new approaches.'

Note that this activity does not 'cure' the problems. What it does do is to highlight what they are and to create motivation for change. In Tiffany's case it was one of the foundations of the work we continued over several months.

Guided visualizations

One of the many amazing aspects of the human brain is its ability to use imagination (see also page 39). It seems as if the brain does not distinguish too readily between imagined and real – a disadvantage when we dwell on our fears, an advantage when we create a positive alternative because we are then laying down the new neural pathways that could lead to different beliefs and behaviour. If you are attracted to this approach, you will want to develop your own script, but all of the many variants of such scripts have the same core elements: you ask for permission and briefly explain the benefits. If the client is dubious, don't press it: it's not right for everyone. You ask the client to enter a light trance state. Some coaches prefer not to name it as such because of the poor reputation of stage hypnotists. If you believe a client will resist if you name it as *trance*, then don't. I do because in fact trance is a commonplace human experience. We can all enter it at will and often involuntarily – for instance when driving on a monotonous motorway or going for a lengthy jog. Trance is characterized by unawareness of time passing or of the intrusive effects of the physical environment. Believers in religion will enter it through prayer or meditation and you could well experience it at a concert. The theory is that when you are in a light trance, your mind is more open to suggestion. You reassure clients that they are in control at all times and invite them to enter the state through physical relaxation and closed eyes. This leads to a matching mental quieting. Your voice remains quiet, gentle and monotonous. You are aiming for a pleasant drone. You speak very slowly, using linking words like *and* . . . or *so* . . . You use only positive suggestion, so, for instance, you would say 'you feel calm' rather than 'you don't feel tense'. Saying the word 'tense' invites tension because what the mind focuses on is what expands. You build the content around what the client needs, of course, as a result of asking the right questions. This enables you to create the specific content that will help. All visualizations start with settling the client down by asking them to get comfortable and close their eyes.

A sample script

Get yourself comfortable in your chair. Sit without anything crossed – no crossed legs, feet or arms. If you'd like a cushion to support your neck, that's fine.

First let's establish some relaxed, steady breathing. Take a deep breath in from below your waist and feel your lungs filling and expanding and pushing outwards. Hold for a few moments; now let the breath out and feel your chest going in again. The out-breath is going to be much longer than the in-breath. Take the in-breath with your mouth closed and breathe the out-breath out slowly and steadily through an open mouth. [Do several such breaths with the client, counting slowly with each breath.]

Close your eyes and let your body relax.

First let your feet go floppy – let them feel as if they are completely free. Unclench any muscles that may have tightened in your toes. Wiggle the toes and let them relax.

Now do the same with your legs. Let the knees flop and now your thighs. Let your legs feel loose and very relaxed. They may start to feel heavy – if they do, that's fine. They may tingle a little and feel warm.

Now let your hands go loose. Shake out the fingers a little and let them relax so that they feel floppy. And now feel them getting heavy. And now the same with your arms. Let them get heavy and feel very, very relaxed. They may feel warm and tingly. If they do, that's fine.

Keep the breathing slow and steady, breathing in . . . and then out . . . in and then out. [Time this with the client's breathing, matching it with your own.]

And now your shoulders. Let them drop so that the muscles are soft and floppy. And now your neck. Let go of any tension in it. Now the same with your chest and stomach. And let the centre of your body relax. Feel a soft, warm feeling creeping through your whole body.

And now your face. Feel the facial muscles relaxing so that your skin is smooth. Let the muscles around your mouth go soft and floppy. And do the same with the muscles in your forehead.

Feel your circulation relaxing and your heartbeat steadying to a quiet, steady, relaxed beat. And feel whole, feel well, feel relaxed.

And now I'm going to ask you to imagine yourself in a pleasant place. It could be a real place that's special to you or an imaginary one. Call up how this place feels to you and the sensations it creates in your body to know that you're there . . . remember or imagine the sounds you can hear . . . and the views you can see. Enjoy all these sensations . . . Relax even more deeply and let go while you experience yourself in this place . . .

Where you take it after this depends on what the client wants to achieve. I have used it myself in a number of ways and also collected these examples from fellow coaches.

Client situation	**Coach response**
Chronically nervous before a job interview.	Suggests client imagines themselves in the interview room, totally calm but alert, doing well, seeing and hearing the interviewers and responding positively.

Now divorced from physically and mentally abusive husband but still haunted by fear of him.

Coach asks client to imagine how the ex-husband looks. Response is that he was like an outsize goblin. Coach suggests shrinking him down to garden gnome size. Then asks what client would like to do with him. Answer: 'Stuff him at the back of the garden centre where no one can find him.'

Afraid of speaking up at a large meeting.

Coach suggests client imagines the room, places herself in the best position to catch the eye of the meeting chair, sees self performing in a sparkling and confident manner.

A patient at a dental clinic who has chronic facial pain as a result of a dentist-inflicted accidental injury. Pain cannot be cured by any known means.

Coach is a doctor (but not a specialist in dental problems). Over eight 50-minute sessions, coach invites client to tell her what the pain looks like. Answer: a giant crab whose claws are stuck into her check from the outside. Coach suggests shrinking the crab and diminishing the grip of the claws. Session by session the pain lessens to manageable levels.

Afraid of the future, perplexed by how to find life purpose.

Coach invites client to imagine life five years on; to see a friendly, confident figure approaching – their future self – and to listen to what this self has to say.

Wanted to give up smoking; had tried patches, going cold turkey, willpower.

Coach creates scenario where client is exposed to all the situations where she usually smoked (as described by client) and sees and experiences herself happily free of the need for cigarettes.

Could not get to sleep easily; client described 'racing thoughts'.

Coach and client discuss general preparation for sleep tactics, including avoiding stimulants, cooling the bedroom down, reading a pleasant book. Coach teaches client progressive relaxation techniques first, including how to control breathing, and then does the visualization.

CASE STUDY

Stephen

I came for coaching with what now seems like a laughably mundane request: I wanted to know how to influence my boss, the chief executive, and how to get a better grip on my job which was specifically like a sort of bag-carrier role for him. He needed someone like me to smooth his path, write his speeches, make sure his flights were booked, deal with the press – and so on. When I did this visualization, I saw myself very clearly five years ahead. The other people with me were my wife and young children.

At the time of doing the exercise, I didn't have a wife, only a girlfriend, and I definitely didn't have any children! I was also aware in the visualization of how I was earning a living. I saw myself directly running a major part of the organization and running it in a particular way – very differently from the bullying standard leadership style I saw around me every day. It was a complete wake-up call. I suddenly felt I had been wasting my time in a highly paid but totally pointless backroom job, frittering away my energy in a playboy bachelor life and this wasn't what I wanted at all. The advice from my future self was: 'Get real mate!'

The coaching took a completely different slant as a result of that activity. Five years later I am on my way to that senior job. I realized how much I loved my then girlfriend and how mad I would be to lose her. We married within a year and have one and a half of the two children I saw in that meditation. I refuse to do the 12-hour days I see my colleagues working – getting a proper life balance is important and I'm not going to put any of that at risk again.

These are powerful activities. They can work better than anything else in the right place and with the right client. Don't necessarily expect one iteration to be enough. The doctor-coach dealing with facial pain, for instance, did a version of the visualization every time she and the patient met. I also recommend recording the visualization and then emailing it to the client so that he or she can play it as many times as they wish.

Using technology

Technology now makes it easy to use all kinds of aids in a session. I always have my iPad to hand and the awe-inspiring range of apps is a constant source of useful ideas. So, for instance, I have a drawing app which I use to invite clients to make drawings or notes which I can then email to them. I use TED, which stands for Technology, Entertainment, Design, a non-profit organization devoted to 'ideas worth spreading' (www.TED.com) with clients who want help on speaking at conferences, at job interviews or in the boardroom. Most of these clients need ways of getting away from the grinding boredom of so many PowerPoint presentations and TED, with its ever-varying range of speakers, shows brilliantly how this can be done. There are many apps which allow you to record your own voice, and some that will turn this into text. So clients can experiment with voice and style if they wish. I use the brilliant '3-D Brain' app to explain brain functioning to clients.

Next, my fellow coach Dr Amy Iversen describes here how she uses the ingenious Flip camera with clients:

> Every now and again, new technology comes along which really adds value to clients. The Flip camera is a credit-card sized portable video recorder capturing high quality video at the press of a button which can immediately be viewed on the big screen via a USB connection. As a coach I have found this invaluable as a way of allowing clients access to the 'meta-stance' – to see themselves as others see them. Clients can discover for themselves how they really look (clothes, make-up, facial expressions, their posture and gait), how they speak (voice, accent, tone, inflection, vocabulary), and how they come across (greeting, handshake, general demeanour).
>
> I have found it a powerful tool in two ways. The first is that it can help a client to bring into awareness something important which they may not have noticed, and can subsequently address (e.g. a tendency to avoid eye contact, or to interrupt). This can be powerful information for clients who are preparing for interviews, exams or assuming a new leadership role in which they need to influence others. Often just watching the video together and using some Socratic questions brings up some really powerful reflection; allowing clients to do this in the third person and inviting them to 'watch this like you are watching a video of someone you don't know' works even better (e.g. what do you notice about this woman?).
>
> The second is that it can help clients who have become very concerned or preoccupied about a certain aspect of their appearance and behaviour to get real-time feedback on just how important this feature is to the average person who meets them. In this case, the client and I produce a short video and some stills and construct together a survey of questions that the client would like to ask of others. I recently worked with a client who had started antidepressants and was concerned that he came across as 'drugged up' – to the extent that he was turning down opportunities to speak in public. With his

permission, 100 volunteers were emailed a short video clip of him speaking and were invited to comment on his appearance, with specific reference to whether they had noticed anything unusual about his voice and face. Evidence that not a single one noticed anything abnormal provided powerful new information for the client and enabled him to move forward.

Role play

This is another invaluable way of accelerating learning as well as of introducing a change of pace into the conversation. Some people have embarrassing experiences of role play from courses, where they claim that the artificiality of the exercise has created their extreme aversion for the method. Usually they are referring to staged and artificial scenarios where people who are not actors have to act. This is why it is probably safer not to label the activity 'role play' but just to do it without giving it a label at all.

Role play means that the client rehearses or revisits an important conversation. Normally the client 'plays' him- or herself and you 'play' the other person.

Why role play is useful in coaching

Some clients seem unable to move past their usual ways of behaving. Some cannot see how others see them. Role play is a safe way to experiment. Where you have grown the trust between you, clients can make themselves vulnerable without feeling that they will lose face if they get it wrong and it also gives you opportunities for feedback to the client. I find that role play is the best way of rehearsing for a challenging conversation that clients describe as being on their agenda soon, and also an effective way of reviewing a difficult conversation in the recent past. Role play is invaluable for clients who describe many different types of people behaving in much the same way to them. In such cases it is one of the ways for clients to find out that the response we get is as much to do with us as with the other person. For the same reason it is useful for clients who come to coaching hoping to change another person. Role play is a way of finding out that the only way to change another person is to change ourselves first and it is often useful to remind clients of that old cliché: 'Behaviour breeds behaviour'.

How to do it

No real acting ability is required for role play to be successful, but it does help if you are able to change your own normal pace and delivery to become a little like the person you are playing.

First, ask for a briefing:

> What kind of a person is this?
>
> What do they look like?
>
> How old are they?
>
> How do they typically respond when X or Y happens?
>
> Tell me about a situation where there was a difficulty – give me some of the dialogue.

This briefing need not be extensive – a minute or two is all that you need. Now say: 'OK, let's assume I'm the other person, and you're back in that situation. So you said . . .?'

You then respond as you have been briefed the person would typically respond. Let the conversation run for a few minutes – or for however long seems useful. Three minutes is usually enough.

The debrief

Role play has no purpose without the debrief. Ask the client for permission to give them feedback.

- Ask for the client's view on how it went first; log how accurate the client's self-perception seems to be and explore any over-modesty or unrealistic self-acclaim later.
- Ask how like real life the role play was. Usually clients will tell you that the way it went was exactly like the real-life incident went – or could go. They will often say: 'You must know this person – you're just like him/her!' The later learning to be gleaned from this observation is that the client's typical behaviour is shaping the response they are typically getting.
- Tell clients how it felt to be on the other end of their style. You are not analysing here, just *noticing* and trusting your own emotional responses.
- Be very specific. You are looking here to feed back your micro as well as your macro observations, your objective as well as your subjective impressions, so you will need to note these while the role play is happening. Nothing is too small to be noticed and fed back. The objective impressions are likely to include posture, voice, facial expression, language and so on:

When you started telling me about the project being at risk, you leant forward and raised your voice. I felt you were really authoritative at that point, but only a moment later your voice dropped and I noticed you put your hand slightly over your mouth.

- Your subjective impressions are about the impact of the behaviour on you. To do this you imagine yourself in that person's shoes. Use 'I' all the time: 'When you did/said this . . . the effect it had on me was . . .':

  So at first when you were looking authoritative I felt wary, but later at that point where your voice dropped and you put your hand over your mouth, I felt certain you would back down. The impact on me was that I felt that if I hung in there I could get you to agree to what I wanted.

- Ask what the client would like to change or experiment with.

Always do a re-run if the role play has not gone well, to give the client the chance to experience success. Look for all the small and large gains which will tell you that the client is beginning to learn how to behave in a different way.

Swapping roles

Here you play the client and the client plays the other person. Again, I will typically introduce this activity without labelling it 'role play'.

CASE STUDY

Felicity

Felicity told me that she couldn't understand why people were constantly hinting that she was *intimidating* when she met junior colleagues casually in walkabouts through the organization. 'I'm a friendly soul,' she said. 'I just don't understand. I'm an enthusiast for my work – is that the problem?'

'OK,' I said, 'so let's stand up. You and I have just met in the corridor. I'm a young colleague very new to your team. How do you greet me?' As we stood up, Felicity gave me her typical booming greeting, gripping my arm like a tourniquet and beaming her wide smile. As a tall and substantially built woman she seemed to take up a lot of space, including some of mine. She launched immediately into an intense discussion of 'my' work and how it was going.

We had no discussion of the behaviour at that point. Instead, I suggested reversing our roles.

'Right,' I said, 'so let's swap over. Now I'm you and you're me.'

I then gave as good a version as I could, without too much exaggerating, of what I had observed. Felicity was staggered.

'How did that feel for you?'

'Oh no,' groaned Felicity, 'that is one overwhelming woman! Am I really like that? I felt you were interrogating me – and do I really grip people that tightly?'

Our debrief discussion then looked at other ways of behaving that were still true to Felicity – she was never going to be less than a powerful presence – but also likely to be less intense for the other person. After the discussion we then practised again, this time with Felicity 'playing' herself and me playing the casual corridor contact, followed by more feedback and discussion.

Role play as practice

A role play may last just a few minutes and be introduced with little fuss and no labelling. Alternatively there are circumstances where it can be usefully extended. These will include areas such as job interview coaching, preparing to face the media and learning to enhance presentation skills.

CASE STUDY

Gareth

Getting on shortlists was easy for Gareth, but landing a chief executive job eluded him. After four failures in quick succession, he realized he needed help. First we worked on how he mentally approached the interview process. From his language it was clear that he saw it as the equivalent of an academic examination:

JR: What is an interview like for you?

Gareth: It's a viva – it reminds me of the verbal grilling I had to go through to get my PhD.

JR: So you see it as a place to demonstrate your knowledge?

Gareth needed to learn that a job interview is a social and not an academic event. Interviewers would most probably take his knowledge for granted. Displaying it at such length was not answering the main question that potential employers had in their minds, which was always, 'What would it be like working with this candidate?'

Together we worked on a new set of skills for job interviews, this time emphasizing the social aspects of the interview situation as well as Gareth's leadership experience and skills, his approach to influencing, his motivation for wanting the job, and so on. There are only about eight core questions that can ever be asked in a job interview and we set about practising how to answer all of them. Working in five-minute blocks, I took the role of interviewer and he gave practice answers. Then we debriefed the answers with feedback from me, sometimes using video recordings. This way Gareth could see for himself how he was coming across. His own ruthlessly honest feedback, seen through the dispassionate lens of the camera, was all he really needed: 'I look too cocky there', or 'I seem a lot more confident when I sit up', or 'I'm more convincing when I answer the question more briefly and directly', and 'I seem like a nicer person when I smile'. Within two months Gareth had the chief executive job he wanted, and has since moved on successfully once more and is now a well-known figure in his sector.

For clients like Gareth, already very senior, it can take courage to make yourself vulnerable enough to come forward for help. *Talking* about the interview may be useful so far as it goes, but only grounded practice with feedback will really make it clear what the blocks are and how they might be overcome.[4]

Similarly, a surprising number of clients describe themselves as handicapped by lack of social confidence. Inside their organizations, or in structured situations where they can feel in control, everything is fine. Put them in a room of strangers without the carapace of their role and status and they can freeze. Here, again, identifying from observation (this could be a homework assignment) or discussion of how socially confident people behave in such situations is the starting point, followed by bite-sized chunks of practice and feedback.

Shadowing

There is usually a strong case for seeing the client at least once on his or her home territory. When you do this, you meet the rest of the cast, people the client mentions who otherwise will remain vividly described but fantasy figures to you.

Shadowing means that clients invite you to accompany them for a day or half day, being with them as unobtrusively as possible. The idea is to see clients in their own setting. In this way you will get to see how they interact with others at the same time as getting a first-hand taste of the organization's culture. Virtually all clients forget how weird the organization seemed when they first joined it – they have become immune to its funny little ways. However, you will notice. Feeding this back, along with everything else you notice, can be an invaluable source of learning.

Setting up shadowing

It takes a brave client to do this but I have found that a surprising number are up for it.

Explain the benefits for the client. Discuss how the client will explain your presence to others. Total openness is really the only option. Most clients can see that their visible willingness to be open to such a high degree of feedback models exactly the behaviour that most organizations need so badly. Far from appearing 'weak', such clients appear robust and confident.

Be clear with the client – and others – that your role is *observer*.

Encourage the client to negotiate both permission and confidentiality boundaries with the colleagues who will be present during the day. Telling such colleagues that the spotlight is on the client, not on them, is usually enough to assuage any fears about being judged by the coach.

Ask the client on what he or she needs particularly to have feedback. Typical choices would be: delegating and briefing conversations; running meetings; interactions with a PA; time management; decision-making. Leave plenty of time at the end of the shadowing (typically a half day) for feedback and discussion.

You may be able to organize some shadowing within a normal coaching session, depending on the client's issues. Here is an example of a coach who came up with an unusual piece of improvised shadowing by seizing the moment with style and humour through a perfect piece of provocation.

CASE STUDY
Ravi

Ravi grew up in a big family but described himself as chronically shy. Self-consciousness was the hallmark of his interaction with others when they were not part of his close circle of family or friends. In spite of his striking good looks, Ravi found it impossible to initiate conversations, so at the conferences which were an increasingly important part of his professional life he lurked on the perimeter of the room feeling miserable. Ravi's goal was to build his capacity to network confidently and this meant learning how to take the initiative with people he didn't know.

Ravi's coach seized the moment, knowing that her coaching room was in an area surrounded by crowded sandwich bars. It was coming up to lunchtime. Ravi's challenge was the following:

Coach: Ravi, I challenge you to collect the lunch orders from others in the office, to go into six different sandwich bars, striking up a conversation in each with a complete stranger. It doesn't matter how banal the conversation is – it can be about the weather, the food, the sandwich bar – anything at all. I will be by your side, giving you feedback and encouragement on each one. I expect you to flirt whether you're talking to a man or a woman.

Ravi: (utterly taken aback) You are a very wicked woman! Is this what my company is paying all this money for?

Coach: (shrugging) Yes – dreadful isn't it, don't tell them, will you?

Ravi: What will my wife say?

Coach: Tell her the company paid this crazy woman to teach you how to flirt with other women.

Ravi: (helpless laughter) OK, I'll do just that.

After recovering from his shock, Ravi accepted, collected the orders from the somewhat bemused office staff and set off with his coach trotting at his side. At each stage, his coach gave him encouragement and some further tips – for instance, about his eye contact (sometimes avoided), his smile (dazzling when he used it), and asking him questions about what was working and what wasn't. The effect was astonishing. Within 20 minutes Ravi had discovered not only that he could overcome 30 years of waiting for others to speak first, but that he actually enjoyed it because of the response he got.

Observing

When you visit a client's premises, observe everything. Notice the state of the building: what is on the walls, the condition of the lavatories, the kind of food in the restaurant and how it is set out. Notice how you are treated as a visitor. Notice what surprises or impresses you. For instance, making a visit to a training college for one of our uniformed services, I immediately began to understand more about how my clients would be likely to think and behave.

The college was in the middle of velvety English countryside, but I was received by a uniformed guard. The grounds were crowded with people, most of them men, smartly turned out in full uniform, including hats. The noisy canteen was set out with long refectory tables topped by a high table with linen table napkins – a striking contrast to the cheap paper versions supplied for everyone else. The food was wholesome, plentiful and definitely in the school dinner mode. I was received with immense and elaborate courtesy by everyone and treated as an honoured guest.

This suggested a number of things about my client's organization that helped me in working with them. There was an easy camaraderie to life in this organization – a hugely supportive network of colleagues who enjoyed spending time together. Hierarchy, clarity about roles, rules and a smart appearance were also vital factors in the culture. The more senior you were, the more physically comfortable your life was likely to be, perhaps as a straight and visible reward for the notably stringent responsibilities for command you were expected to bear uncomplainingly. I also understood that to appear to be threatening the camaraderie in such an organization would be difficult and painful. So, for instance, when one of my clients faced the ultra-tough challenge of having to investigate fellow officers, I immediately knew something of what courage and steadfastness this would take.

Real-time coaching

This approach to coaching is only for the bravest client and the bravest coach. It involves you as the coach working 'live' with the client and his or her team and takes the process beyond shadowing. Here, you contract with clients to give them on-the-spot feedback about how they are working by coaching them on the basis of what you see in the moment.

When to use real-time coaching

- Clients describe getting constantly snarled up in repetitive and unhelpful patterns.
- Clients do not see what these patterns are and will often blame others or express enormous frustration with their own lack of ability to make things happen on their terms, sometimes stepping up the very behaviour which has led to the problem in the first place.
- Clients espouse openness as an important value.
- Clients are self-confident learners, prepared to make themselves vulnerable.

CASE STUDY

James

James presents as dynamic and self-assured and has come to his role through his expertise and reputation in the sector rather than through a standard management route. Gathering 360-degree feedback for him reveals that his team sees him as talented, inspiring, enthusiastic, exasperating and capricious. The feedback suggests that he see-saws between involving the team on the one hand and then making what appear to be high-handed and inexplicable decisions on the other.

Initially, James cannot interpret this feedback – it baffles him. Mostly he tends to blame the members of his team for his own frustration – the common human response to avoiding taking responsibility for the reactions we provoke in others. His meetings can, and often do, run for four or five hours at a time, with critical decisions left hanging and unresolved and personal issues unnamed, leading to an unhealthy level of corridor conflict outside the meeting.

As his coach, James and I agreed that a lot was at stake for the business: holding on to scarce talent was vital in the organization's competitive market; slow decision-making was paralysing the organization and the team's preoccupation with itself was sapping energy that should have been spent on beating off external competitors. James and I had worked together for six months and there was a high degree of trust between us. We agreed that I would work with him in 'real time' during planned breaks in the meeting as a way of spotting and then potentially changing whatever patterns he was using to maintain these unhelpful dynamics.

What real-time coaching is – and is not

It is important to be clear about what real-time coaching is and is not. You are not facilitating the meeting. You are not helping others in the meeting directly to understand your client. You are not addressing any comments to any other person there nor eliciting their points of view. You are not taking decisions for the client. You are working solely with that client, but either in front of his or her team (the truly scary option) or in the private conversations during breaks.

How to do it

- First you agree with your client what the goals for your session are. Two or three tightly defined goals are better than 10 fuzzy ones.

- Next you contract for the degree of honesty that will be acceptable. Part of the contracting process is to discuss how your presence will be explained to the rest of the team.
- Alert the client to how and when you will make your interventions by giving an example.
- Encourage the client to be explicit with the rest of the team about the goals they intend to work on in the real-time session, and also encourage them to ask the rest of the team to comment on the relevant behaviours during the meeting.
- Emphasize that your sole aim is to build the capacity of the client to solve their own problems, so you will be working in coaching mode throughout. Your role is to boost your client's authority, not to damage it.
- Offer the client the chance to back off at this stage if it all seems too challenging.

CASE STUDY
James, continued

James invited me to his standard weekly management team meeting. His goals were to discover how to:

- shorten these meetings without losing quality;
- involve people more evenly;
- make swifter decisions which everyone could endorse.

I sat immediately behind him and he explained the process to the group and also his goals: 'I want you all to help me with this – stop me and point it out if you see me doing things that go against them.'

So in the various pauses and breaks, I was able to ask James about his impressions of who was doing most of the talking in the meeting, what his own patterns of interaction were, including how often he interrupted people or did not seek to involve them, and how far he imposed an end to unhelpful iterations of decision-making which in effect tried to keep 100 per cent of the meeting 100 per cent happy with everything rather than asking what people could live with (much more practical).

This type of coaching has enormous potential for change in the client. The stakes are high – for you and for the client. As with any kind of observation, you alter the dynamic simply by being there. However, by working in effect on the client's default behaviour, there will be plenty of material. It is even more important than in any other kind of coaching situation to work respectfully and courageously. You have to keep yourself out of the way and yet be prepared to speak at just the right moment, so exquisite judgement is essential. Knowing how to give feedback skilfully is vital (see page 251).

Possibly the most powerful outcome of all is that in making themselves so vulnerable, and by making their commitment to change so public and specific, clients model boldness, openness and willingness to learn. The process itself demystifies coaching and also sends the most robust possible message to the rest of the team about what is expected of them in turn.

In general the way I think about any coaching session has been affected by my earlier career as a television producer. In any programme the producer knows that it is important to start with something that will grab the attention of the audience. This needs to be followed by subtle or overt changes in pace throughout the programme. There need to be fast parts and slow parts, points where there is laughter and others where there is room for sadness or thoughtfulness, light and shade, long sequences followed by short ones. Even the simplest kind of DJ-driven radio show will alternate fast music with slow, sweet ballad with upbeat cheeriness. Understanding that the same principles apply to any coaching session will immeasurably help both you and your client.

Notes

1   I am assured by mental health professionals that this word is politically correct. That is a relief because the clumsy suggested alternative *thought shower* is repellent.

2   There is a full description of this technique in Phil Hayes (2006) book.

3   There is a coaching and group work technique called Constellations which has a faint resemblance to what I describe here and which arose out of a particular approach to family therapy. I am not a believer in Constellation theory, which claims that just 'representing' The System (always written with initial caps) somehow has magical powers to change it. 'Systems' in Constellation theory supposedly also have mystical memories going back many generations, even without anyone in the current System knowing anything about it. Amazing, rapid resolutions are allegedly possible. You will find words and phrases such as *ancestor worship*, *phenomenological*, *The Knowing Field*, *existential* and *morphic resonance* used to describe what supposedly happens. Some people for whom I have considerable respect believe in this theory. The more I investigated it, the more it sounded like a load of old

hogwash to me, but then I may be too much of a rationalist and a sceptic for my own good. If you google Constellations Theory you will find plenty of websites offering training. For a more sceptical view go to www.skepdic/ hellinger.html.

4   Career coaching is an expanding area and one obvious way that coaches can add value. To get yourself fully briefed on interview skills, you might read my book, *Job Interview Success: Be Your Own Coach* (2011).

9 Practising professionally

Coaching is a new profession. Many of us have come to it from allied disciplines such as management development, organizational consulting or therapy. In this chapter I look at what issues the professional coach needs to take into account and how some of the potential problems might be resolved.

Ethics

Coaching may present you with a number of dilemmas, none with easy, obvious solutions. There are few, if any, absolutes.

What alerts you to the presence of a dilemma? First, there could be a gut feeling that something, somewhere, is making you uneasy. Or there could be the knowledge that if whatever it was appeared in a newspaper, it would at the very least be embarrassing and hard to defend. Another symptom could be discomfort at the thought of having to endorse it to a person whose moral judgement you respect and whose good opinion you prize. There may be the knowledge that a proposed action is against the law or a realization that you may be infringing a stated (or implicit) value for you or your firm.

Dilemmas may concern priorities. Some possible ones might be: 'truth' versus 'sensitivity'; individual versus organizational need; organization versus community; business versus environment; short-term versus long-term impact; financial versus client need.

Dilemmas in action

These are real examples.

- You are giving individual coaching to a management team of six people, excluding the boss. You make the usual promise of confidentiality. As the coaching progresses, it seems clear to you that there are some important systems issues emerging about the way the *total* team operates with its customers.
- The chief executive of a company with whom you want to build business has set up a coaching programme for one of his team. He accepts that you will not be able to give any feedback direct to him.

However, he asks you to let him know if the person terminates the coaching or fails to turn up for a session.

- A client confesses to something illegal or to private knowledge of a crime.
- A client threatens harm to him- or herself or others.
- You are working with two people from the same management team. Their relationship is a hostile one. Both trust you and have a good relationship with you. Both tell you a large number of things about their own position, attitudes, hopes and fears, including how they feel about their colleague.
- You are coaching a client and gathering 360-degree feedback on him through focused, structured interviews from 10 people nominated by him. You discover that all his colleagues appear to hold extremely negative opinions about him. The more you probe for some positive features and behaviour, the more detail pours out about the poor esteem in which his colleagues hold him.
- You are working with a number of board-level individuals in an organization. You are approached by the board of their most significant competitor to undertake a similar programme.
- You are asked to coach two candidates for the same job, both of them clients in different organizations and in different organizations again from the one with the vacancy.

There are no easy answers to most of these dilemmas and it is perfectly possible that different coaches would respond in different but equally acceptable ways. For instance, some coaches will refuse to coach more than one member of the same team on the grounds that while the coach may be well able to keep the issues separate, the team members may not believe that this is so. In my own case, I will not now work as facilitator to a coaching client's team, though I used to do so. Now I will recommend a colleague on the grounds that the client's team will inevitably see me as biased towards the client, thus reducing my perceived value as an objective resource. Where I used to be willing to coach several members of the same team, I now avoid doing so on the grounds that such clients may find it difficult to talk openly about each other to the same coach.

Where organizations ask me for progress reports on a client as a condition of the work, I will refuse the work. I believe that such a progress report will be valueless because the real evidence of change is in the daily way the client actually does their work. As coaches we do not witness this, so how can we judge our clients' performance? Equally importantly, I know how impossible it would be to create trust if the client believed that the coaching was about *assessment* – a completely different process. Even where the client's boss has made the apparently bland request for me to confirm the client's attendance,

I refuse because, in its mild way, this amounts to coercion. I suggest that client and boss agree between themselves how to satisfy the boss's perfectly understandable need to know what is going on.

I will not work with direct competitor organizations simultaneously because it is inevitable that commercially sensitive information will be part of the coaching. I know that I can keep such secrets, but the client may still be concerned in spite of my assurances.

If you could not be a coach to two competing football teams simultaneously, it is difficult to see how you could coach two candidates for the same job. When unexpectedly faced with this dilemma recently, I consulted both clients, without of course telling them the name of their rival. One candidate told me he was 'perfectly relaxed about it and may the best man [sic] win'. The other told me, a trifle unconvincingly, that she would live with whatever I decided. My decision was to recommend a colleague for the candidate with whom I had been in a previous coaching relationship, not at that point live, and to go with the woman candidate with whom I had a very active relationship. In discussing it later, she confessed that she would have felt 'very hurt but concealed it' if I had chosen to coach both of them.

Where you have personally collected feedback for a client and this feedback unequivocally shows how much the client is disliked by colleagues, you have a duty to convey it to the client. It is patronizing to assume that the client will be unable to handle such feedback. The art is to write and then debrief it in a way that the client can hear without warping the essential truth of the messages.

There are shades of grey in the ethics of coaching as there must be in any profession. 'Multiculturalism' may bring you up hard against what you have assumed to be shared values with a client, exposing rifts that cannot be concealed. We may not always realize, for instance, that coaching is essentially based on the values of western democracies and it is obvious that many parts of the world do not share our assumptions here. A pleasant Nigerian acquaintance recently asked me for informal coaching where his problem was how to tell a gay colleague that he would go to Hell if he continued to be in homosexual relationships. A woman coach whom I was supervising brought me the dilemma of how to react when a Muslim client wanted to discuss how he could persuade his British wife to go with him to an Arab country where he had been offered a job. This client had described having become radicalized by a certain fundamentalist imam. Taking his wife with him implied her leading a highly restricted life. For instance, she would not be able to drive because if she had done so, and the car had broken down, this would involve being alone with a man. This coach said wryly, 'It did not seem to have occurred to him that as a devout Muslim he was alone in a room with a woman – me!' A client who asked me for interview coaching said that the job, as a senior bankruptcy specialist for a hedge fund, could potentially involve enforcing the assets of a whole (probably very poor) country. A client originally from mainland China, but now working for a US company, told me that he wanted help on how to subvert the directive from bosses to consult his staff on an important issue regarding their future.

Are we being Euro-centric or racist or unduly self-righteous and pompous to hesitate over such challenges? Are we being guilty of narrow-minded thinking? Should we work with clients on issues like these if we profoundly disagree with the moral basis of the dilemma? My own answer to these questions is 'no': refusing and respectfully explaining why seems the only option. You may want to consider where you would draw the line yourself on such issues and your conclusions may be different from mine.

At the beginning of the coaching I explain to clients that confidentiality is not a blank cheque. In the unlikely event of clients confessing to something illegal or dangerous to themselves or others, I forewarn them that confidentiality rules would not apply. My protocol here is that I would always try to persuade clients to take appropriate action themselves but if they refused I would do whatever I thought to be right, alerting the appropriate people or authorities while also doing everything I could to preserve the dignity of the client. Fortunately, I have never had to put this principle to the test. Common sense should override any exaggerated concerns about confidentiality.

For instance, in 2007, an employment tribunal ruled against the Citizens Advice Bureau (CAB) which had sacked a staff member for having called a doctor when a client described having taken a potentially fatal overdose. This saved the client's life. It is hard to see how such action could be 'wrong' or 'unethical'. CAB policy dictated that the proper course of action was to refer to a senior manager who would then consult a committee. CAB justified the sacking on the grounds that the staff member has made an 'irrational emotional error'. The tribunal had no difficulty in deciding that this judgement was 'ridiculous'.

Ethical guidelines

Ethical guidelines are essential because they are helpful. They make explicit what may be assumed and therefore misleading. I base mine on an amalgam of guidelines suggested by the European Mentoring and Coaching Council (EMCC) and other professional coaching bodies. The aim is to keep guidelines as simple as possible, without underestimating the complexity of the issues.

1 You act at all times to protect the public reputation of the coaching profession.
2 You clearly describe your levels of competence and will never overstate your qualifications or expertise.

3　As a coach, you believe in the resourcefulness of each and every client with a matching recognition of the fact that all clients make themselves vulnerable in the coaching relationship. You recognize and protect this vulnerability.

4　Clients must be volunteers. If there is any element of coercion you decline the work.

5　You clearly set out the terms of the coaching contract at the beginning of the relationship and confirm it in writing: times, fees, cancellation policy and limits, if any, on telephone and email contact between meetings.

6　You will protect clients from exploitation of any kind: sexual, financial, emotional. The purpose of the coaching is the client's wellbeing and development; as a coach you demonstrate this in all your dealings with the client.

7　You make every effort to protect the client's confidentiality and this will be fully discussed at the beginning of the coaching contract and will be raised with the client whenever it could be an issue. The coaching relationship is not privileged under law and clients need to be told that this is so. You will encourage clients to take appropriate action themselves, without the intervention of the coach. In the extremely rare cases where the client discloses something dangerous or illegal, you may be obliged to inform the relevant authorities with or without the client's permission.

8　Confidentiality involves preserving the names of clients unless they have given active assent to disclosing them. The confidentiality rule applies to third parties who are funding the coaching: recipients of the coaching can decide what they disclose, for instance to a funding sponsor, but the coach will not do so without the explicit consent of the client.

9　The data that you collect for a client belongs to that client: they have a right to hear it, however uncomfortable it might be for you or the client.

10　Where there is the possibility of a conflict of interest, for instance over boundaries or roles, you and the client will discuss it and look for a fair resolution. You will always look for a way to preserve the client's best interests. If there is any conflict of interest which could damage the coaching relationship you should consider withdrawing, explaining why to the client in a way that protects the client's dignity.

11　Where you have a business relationship with a third party concerning referrals or advice, you will disclose it.

12　Where you feel that the coaching is not appropriate for the client or is not working effectively for some reason, you are obliged to discuss it sensitively with the client. Where the solution involves referral to another professional, you will make every effort to handle the referral respectfully.

13 You manage your own issues in a way which means that they do not intrude into the coaching relationship.

14 Where there is some fundamental clash for you involving moral values between you and the client, you respectfully discuss it with the client before deciding how to proceed. This could involve referring the client to another coach.

15 You have regular sessions with a supervisor, peer or mentor to review and reflect on your practice. 'Difficult' sessions or clients should be discussed as soon as possible with another coach or supervisor. You commit to regular training and updating.

Supervision

Coaches need supervisors. But what is supervision for?

What a strange word *supervision* is, when used in the context of professional development. A supervisor in the managerial world is someone who has direct line management responsibility for your work. This is the very thing that a coaching supervisor does not and cannot have. The need for it most probably arose in the therapeutic world from a realization that most practitioners were working solo and therefore were unlikely to have managerial restraints on their activity. There is also a distinction between a coach having *coaching* – a place where the client-coach can discuss any and every issue – and *supervision*, where only professional issues are on the agenda.

What is supervision?

In her book on supervision, Julie Hay (2007) defines three levels, equating roughly to your levels of experience.

1 *Normative* supervision applies to the beginner level and here the supervisor is in effect extending the training of the coach by providing benchmark standards. The supervisor may also be an assessor and the supervision sessions may have an openly directive flavour.

2 *Formative* supervision may be appropriate when your experience is more extensive, but here again a more experienced coach/ supervisor may offer advice and direct feedback. The aim is greater self-awareness and greater understanding of the psychological patterns that may play out in the coaching as well as offering unconditional support.

3 *Supportive* supervision has more of a peer–peer flavour and is suitable for more senior and experienced coaches. The role here is to exchange reflections, for the supervisor to spot patterns that the coach may be missing, and possibly also to provide a place where the coach can discuss how any personal issues may be getting in the way of delivering excellent coaching.

How frequent should supervision be? Supervision is useful at more frequent intervals when you are in training or a relatively new coach than it is when you are more experienced. However, there is also a good case for supervision when you are very experienced indeed. The long-serving coach may need supervision to guard against potential jadedness or the complacency of burnout. For instance, a coach who becomes invested in being a *clever* coach may urgently require challenge and refreshment.

Watch out for signs of either burnout or 'rustout', both in yourself and in fellow coaches with whom you work on a regular basis and deal with them quickly. Clients notice these differences, possibly before you will. Any incongruity between what we claim and how a client actually experiences us is immediately apparent. Such signs might include:

- feeling messianic – you can save your clients from their own failings;
- feeling wonderfully insightful all of the time;
- boasting about your expertise as a coach;
- failing to experience at least a quiver of apprehension before meeting a new client;
- believing that you know exactly what clients are going to say long before they open their mouths;
- claiming that you have acquired special powers of problem-solving simply through people being in your presence;
- noticing a high degree of irritation and distraction with your clients – reverting to Level 1 listening a lot of the time;
- knowing that you are seeking new gizmos, 'tricks' and 'techniques' to jazz up your coaching to keep boredom at bay;
- realizing that a higher than usual percentage of your clients are opting for fewer sessions than originally booked, matched by a smaller percentage than usual of people who are extending their programmes.

These dangers can be overcome by applying some realism and common sense and discussing them openly with a supervisor. It is also invaluable to have an experienced practitioner with whom to discuss difficulties and triumphs. It is not a guarantee of perfect practice, but it may make poor practice a lot less likely.

Getting best value from a supervision session

Choose your supervisor carefully. Liking and mutual respect are important. It takes about 1000 hours of practice to become experienced enough to handle the range of everyday coaching situations and about 3000 hours to be equipped to work with virtually any client. Regardless of the actual amount of experience, it probably takes at least a chronological year to become reasonably adept as a coach and another three or four years to operate at a high level with any client most of the time. This is the level at which you would be acceptable as a supervisor with another coach because 3000 hours of coaching and several years of practice imply a successful coach with a high level of repeat business based on word-of-mouth recommendations. Even this may underestimate how much experience you actually need to become a master practitioner: for most professions it is around 10,000 hours and it is unlikely that coaching is any different. Training and qualifications to become a supervisor are now emerging in the UK, but again, as with coaching itself, there is little regulation or standardizing and most providers are their own judges on the quality of their work.

Notice your own reactions to the supervision sessions. It is highly probable that you will be feeling apprehension combined with excitement, pleasurable anticipation and interest. This is useful – it reminds us that our clients make themselves vulnerable in their work with us. Similarly, in order to get value out of a supervision session, we also make ourselves vulnerable by being willing to own up to doubts and mistakes and to receive feedback.

Concentrate on you and your coaching style, not on yet another intellectual analysis of your clients' issues. There is only you and your supervisor – you are the raw material, not your clients. The questions should be, 'My dilemma with this client is x', not 'this client's problem is y'.

Good questions for supervision sessions include:

> Which clients am I finding it most enjoyable to work with? What does that say about me?
>
> What is the best/worst coaching moment that has occurred since we last met?
>
> What ethical issues am I troubled about?
>
> What dilemmas am I facing (with particular clients, or in general)?
>
> What issues do I find recurring with my clients? What might this suggest I am noticing or ignoring? What does that say about me and my practice?

Which skills and techniques do I find easy?

Which skills and techniques am I avoiding because I find them difficult?

What feedback have I had from my clients? How should I be addressing the themes that come out of this feedback?

How am I developing as a coach?

What else is going on in my life that could shed light on the above issues?

Alternatives to a paid supervisor can work well. These will include a co-coaching arrangement with another coach or a group meeting where coaches will take it in turns to explore their issues, coaching-style. Some groups also usefully do live coaching with each other for review and feedback. This is another invaluable way to benchmark your practice and to get skilled and thoughtful feedback from people in the same business.

Being realistic about supervision

What can supervision actually do, compared with the claims that are often made for it? In the UK, many of the professional therapeutic bodies insist on a high ratio of therapy-giving hours to supervision hours, sometimes as high as 8:1. Similarly, I have seen some coach-accrediting organizations suggest a ratio of 25:1 for coaches. That also seems high. In my own case, since on average I give 18 hours of coaching in a week of part-time working, I would need to be employing a supervisor every two weeks – but of course I do not.

In practice, inflated claims are sometimes made for supervision, confusing it with *audit*, a different process which involves the measurement of one professional's results against an objective benchmark, or with *quality control*, where, among other methods, feedback is collected from customers, or with *governance*, where ethical standards are monitored – with sanctions for miscreants. Supervision cannot do any of these things and is a softer option than all of them. Excluding psychotherapy, other professions do not demand such a high level of supervision, and many professions which also involve 'emotional labour' do not have it at all, so what makes coaching so special? I am troubled by the exaggerated claims sometimes made for supervision as a process. We need to remember that most supervision is just two people in a room talking about the work one has done when the other was not present. If supervision had not already been invented for therapists, would we necessarily believe it an essential process for coaches? If the real question is, 'How can we ensure that we do good work for our clients', is supervision the best method? How can we be sure, for instance, that supervision is superior to continued training? I know of no research showing that coaches who have supervisors do better coaching than coaches who do not, partly because there are no agreed definitions of what constitutes good coaching and even fewer of what constitutes good supervision.

I cannot see how supervision *guarantees* either the quality of the coaching process or protection for the client. Much of the quoted proof that it does so comes from providers of coaching supervision or from people offering training for supervisors, so they would say that wouldn't they? In the social work profession, there is an elaborate and careful system of supervision which has been in operation for at least 40 years, yet the dreary and predictable round of child protection and probation service failures continues. Whether supervision works depends at least partially on the honesty and self-awareness of the supervisee. A dishonest or un-self-aware supervisee could, in theory, fool a credulous supervisor.

A supervisor is also assumed to have access to greater wisdom and experience, but there is no certainty that this is the case. I know of one provider of supervision training who is prepared to take on coaches with as little as 40 hours of experience and I find it hard to see how such a coach could conceivably offer much more than well-meant listening to anyone they were supervising. In some parts of the therapeutic world, there seems sometimes to be almost as much supervision as there is therapy – an ever-reflecting series of supervisor–supervisee mirrors, including supervision for the supervisor. All this adds to the costs that have to be borne by the client.

I have worked with six different supervisors in my coaching career. All have contributed something different to my own development but what they have in common is that they improved my capacity for self-reflection and increased my feelings of *prudent confidence*. I have heard many other coaches describe the same thing and have heard it at first hand from my own supervisees. But does a more reflective and prudently confident coach do better work? We assume that this is so, but it is hard to prove. For instance, I was faced recently with giving a coaching session to one of the most challenging clients of my entire coaching career, a person profoundly damaged by the tragedy of her history, given to shouting and other kinds of hysterical behaviour in the sessions and openly acknowledging that she needed therapy as well as coaching. I was quailing inside at the prospect of working with her and actively considering terminating the relationship. Luckily, I had a supervision session with Julia Vaughan Smith immediately prior to the session with my client. Julia listened quietly, steadied me down, reminded me of what it was probably possible and not possible to do with this client. In this way I entered the session calmly grounded and with a lot more focus than would have been likely without it. But did it mean I did better coaching and if so, how much better? I really don't know and I think it would be impossible to prove one way or the other.

The pious preaching and the reality are probably rather different where supervision is concerned. I observe that independent coaches, as opposed to those working as internal coaches (where supervision may be provided for them at no personal cost) are remarkably reluctant to spend their hard earned fees on supervision. This may tell us more about the perceived value of supervision in practice than any of the rhetoric. In general, I see supervision as one part, an important one when done rigorously, of the continuing professional development to which all of us need to commit. We may need it in different ways and at differing levels of frequency at different stages of our coaching careers. We also need to seek out other forms of development such as training to update our skills and qualifications, attending seminars and conferences, reading and vigorous networking with other coaches.

Evidence

In coaching itself, we know that the value of the process is immeasurably increased when it is based on observation and external data rather than just on storytelling from the client. The same principle applies to your own development as a coach. There are a number of ways you can seek such evidence. For instance, you can ask a client straightforwardly, and without any cringing apologies, for permission to record a session, using it as the basis for your own reflection and for a supervision session. Reassure the client that the purpose is your own professional development and the recording will only be heard by your supervisor, perhaps offering the client the recording after your supervision session is over. It would be rare for clients to refuse this permission. This enables a supervisor to get first-hand evidence of your coaching practice rather than just relying on your account of it.

You might also try asking a willing client to write a reflective diary after each session, matching it with one of your own. Topics could include: highlights and lowlights of each session; useful and less useful coach behaviours; thoughts and feelings that it was difficult to express in the session itself; and so on, exchanging the diaries towards the end of the coaching programme. This is a humbling and challenging experience for any coach, usually revealing a wide discrepancy between what the coach and client believe has happened.

It is good practice to invite a third party to run a simple emailed questionnaire for you with clients who have completed their coaching. Ask them for feedback on how useful the coaching has been, what changes they have made in their lives as a result of the coaching and any suggestions they have about what you might do to improve your effectiveness. For some ideas on how to do this, see my book, *Developing a Coaching Business* (2006). The reason for asking a third party to perform this service is that you will get more truthful answers that go beyond conventional politeness. It is now easy to set up such questionnaires on the internet, for instance using Survey Monkey. Where you work for a coaching firm, it is essential to conduct such client surveys from time to time. If you work independently, you may be able to offer a mutual exchange service with another coach.

Reflective practice

As part of their progress towards the Diploma in Coaching, candidates are asked to keep reflective diaries on a selection of coaching sessions. Many find it so useful that they continue the practice on an occasional basis, sometimes using it as preparation for group or individual supervision, but sometimes just for their own benefit, thus creating a fascinating log of their own learning. The headings are simple:

- a summary of the client's issues;
- what worked and didn't work during the session;
- what the challenges were for you;
- which techniques and approaches you drew on, with some reflections on why you chose them rather than alternatives;
- your feelings as the session went on;
- how you managed to stay centred – or not, as the case may be;
- what you learnt about coaching as a result of the session;
- what the client's feedback was;
- what you need to bear in mind for the future.

Keeping notes

As a coach you absolutely must keep and file notes on each client. This is a different process from the reflective diary I describe above. The focus is on the client, not on you. As your practice grows, you will begin to forget details of what your clients have said at their earlier sessions. Similarly, you may forget how many sessions a client has had and paid for, or there may be confusions between you about this. A professional coach spends time before a session reviewing notes from the earlier sessions as a way of getting in the right frame of mind to work with a client. Finally, if by any unfortunate chance your notes were subpoenaed by a court, you would want them to be immaculate.

New coaches often want to know whether you should write notes during the session. My own practice is that I rarely do, but I respect other coaches who make the choice to write at the time. It is a matter of personal preference.

These are the various arguments for and against.

Taking notes during the session

For	**Against**
It is a reliable way of remembering what the client has said and of recording details accurately.	You may find you have jotted down the inessentials, or have written notes that are too full to be read quickly next time.
It looks as if you are taking the client seriously.	The client may wonder what you are writing.
You don't have to spend time later reconstructing the conversation.	You have to break eye contact with the client in order to write; the notebook forms a barrier between you.

Making notes after the session

For	**Against**
You can concentrate wholly on the client.	You may forget some of what has been said or remember it inaccurately.
There is no barrier between you.	Not taking notes can worry the client who may think you are likely to forget vital details.
Writing the notes later makes it easy to edit down to the essentials.	You have to spend time after the client has left writing up the notes.
It sharpens your listening skills when you know you are going to have to write up your notes later.	Your listening skills may not be as good as you think they are.

If you coach using the telephone, you may be able to have the best of both worlds, though be aware that there is a danger of distracting yourself with the note-taking and a temptation to write down a jumble of everything the client says, which may or may not make sense later.

Basic principles

Keep notes short and simple: a page and a half of bullet points is usually more than enough. Keep judgements out of your notes – limit them to the factual and descriptive and always write notes in a way that would not embarrass you if they were seen by clients – which clients have the legal right to do. Store the notes in a secure, locked cupboard or filing cabinet but tell a trusted colleague how to gain access to the notes if for any reason you are unable to run a session or need to get access to your notes when you are not in your office. It is best practice to keep the client's contact details separate from the actual notes of each session. This enables a PA or admin assistant to contact a client without having to risk breaking confidentiality by accessing session notes.

Use the notes to record:

- client's name, date, session number and time taken at each session (e.g. *Jane Smith, session #3, 14.1.08., 1 hour 45 minutes – client 15 minutes late*);
- how much time has been invoiced, or when an invoice is due;
- presenting issues for the session;
- what was discussed;
- outcomes of any forms or tools you used – e.g. psychometric questionnaires;
- any handouts you gave the client or reading suggestions;
- agreed action points and accountabilities;
- next steps/any items agreed for discussion at the next session.

Some coaches prepare simple forms to help create order with their notes. Feel free to do this if it will help you.

Client   Chris Scott Invoice submitted March 21

Session   #2 of 6

DATE   24 APRIL

ISSUES

Review of action points since last session

Experimented with new type of departmental meeting – i.e. with 'show and tell'/fun elements; project reviews; etc. as agreed. 'Went brilliantly' – lots new energy in team. High approval rating. Will do now as routine.

Had conversation as agreed, with Nigel (boss). Tried offering him feedback – 'semi worked'.

Goals for this session

1 Improve ability to say no to inappropriate demands.

Offered saying no protocol. Practised with me asking for quick-fire series of ludicrous things. 'I find this so hard – hear my mother saying got to be good girl.' Self-limiting beliefs territory – reminder – she agreed. Got better with more practice. Offered feedback on where she comes across as determined, where still tentative. Confirmed that did NOT seem 'rude'.

---

2 Tackle B – poor performer in team.

Discussed evidence of B's performance. B 'gets away with it because believes organization won't ever sack anyone'. Brief discussion organizational culture. My challenge: 'What are you doing to sustain this?' Answer: 'Ducking it!' Explained feedback principles. Did initial practice. NB: return to this again next time with tougher scenarios.

3 Feedback on FIRO-B.

Fed back her scores with interpretation.

	Inclusion	Control	Affection
Expressed	5	2	5
Wanted	2	6	7

Discussed light this shed on assertiveness and leadership feedback she's already had.

ACTION

- Return to Nigel and reopen discussion; get assent to study leave.
- Find one opportunity a day to say 'no' using techniques practised today.
- Practise giving *positive* feedback using feedback principles to praise min. one person per day between now and next session.

Sending notes to clients

Some coaches follow up a session by sending a long letter or email to clients with their notes from the session. I don't recommend this. First, it will inevitably be your slant, not the client's, and who should say whether yours is the 'truth'? If the client disagrees with your version, then you could be involved in wearisome exchanges about who is right. Second, it will take time, so will you charge for this time? I believe this practice may reflect the origins of therapy in medicine and has percolated into coaching from this route. I know one orthopaedic consultant who not only sends follow-up letters to his patients with a summary of his findings but actually dictates them in the patient's presence. This is good practice for doctors because it overcomes the potential confusion we patients can experience when, in the heightened emotion of the consultation, we cannot absorb everything that our doctors tell us, but it is only necessary where there is an expert to non-expert relationship, which is not what coaching is.

To me it seems pointless to send notes to the client about the session. It is the client's job to make their own notes and I encourage them to do this. I notice that many have special notebooks in which they record our joint work.

Where they have the luxury of a PA, the PA may be commanded to start a coaching file which is produced for each occasion and includes the client's retrospective and preparation notes.

Training and development for coaches

Training can make a substantial difference to your effectiveness as a coach. It can offer you a framework for understanding and assessing what you are doing, feedback on how you are doing it and the chance to swap bright ideas with other participants. Furthermore, with the coaching market saturated with coaches, all claiming equal expertise, corporate clients are now insisting on qualifications.

More and more providers are entering the coach-training field, many of them of dubious merit. For instance, some widely advertised so-called training courses are really pyramid-selling schemes where a relatively small initial sum buys you a set of workbooks and DVDs with the promise of 'sales leads to coaching clients of your own'. These turn out to be other people who have responded to similar advertisements in the national press, and your task is then to sell the same scheme to them through 'coaching'. Some providers do not actually coach at all – they just train coaches – so it is hard to see how they are keeping their own practice up to date or on what basis they think they can advise beginners.

There are many ways in which training can now be delivered: by open/distance learning, by electronic means and through teleclasses where there could be many dozens of learners on the line with one tutor. These methods are a great deal cheaper than doing the same thing face to face. Where pre-prepared materials are concerned, once the development money has been recovered, there is far less cost to the training provider than there is with face-to-face training. They have the great advantage of being flexible – with open learning materials, for instance, you can work at your own time and pace. As with any kind of learning delivered at a distance, everything depends on the quality of the materials. Some of this is deplorable, some excellent. Technology now makes it possible to see examples of actual coaching and right/wrong ways of coping with common problems, and this can bring theoretical concepts to life in interesting ways. Chat rooms, blogs and specialist discussion groups can offer learner support. I am a supporter of blended learning in the right place and for the right purpose. However, my own belief is that face-to-face training is easily the most effective way of learning how to coach. This is because coaching is a complex and subtle skill. It is difficult to acquire from watching a video or reading a book. You can read descriptions of coaching and watch others do it, but until you actually do it yourself and are observed and given feedback, you may have no idea what your actual standard is.

Delivering face-to-face training is expensive for both provider and student. In general the principle of 'buy cheap, buy twice' prevails, though note that buying at the upper end of the market does not necessarily guarantee higher quality training.

The most effective training for coaches is often about challenging ingrained poor practice as well as finessing an already sound style. Without that instant individual feedback from a practice partner or experienced tutor, bad habits can become chronic handicaps, simply because they are never challenged. Some of the most common mistakes we see trainee coaches make, for instance, arise from lack of awareness. This includes: not realizing how intrusively long a coach's typical question is; failing to set goals; unawareness about asking advice-in-disguise questions, wrongly believing them to be innocent, open questions; the coach talks too much or far too little; failing to notice how often rapport is broken when the coach's anxiety subtly changes the dynamic, and so on. This is the kind of thing that would be hard to spot when you are one of 30 people on a telephone line, viewing a DVD, or just reading a few pages on a website.

In choosing a training provider, these guidelines may help you reject the charlatans and identify the quality providers.

- Look for realism and modesty in what providers say about their training. Anyone promising the full, once-and-for-all authoritative guarantee that they can turn you into a fully-fledged coach within a few short days will be misleading you. A training course starts, rather than ends, the process of growing as a coach. Beware particularly of that exclamatory text which offers amazing discounts if you buy NOW!
- 'Free' workshops often turn out to involve paying several hundred pounds for essential workbooks plus accommodation, so investigate before booking.
- Look for a low ratio of participants to tutors: 1:10 is about the maximum that can be guaranteed to provide enough individual attention.
- Five days of face-to-face training is the minimum for serious initial acquisition of coaching skills.
- Look for providers who are also successful practising coaches with a demonstrable track record in the field in which you intend to practise. Some training companies save money by employing recent graduates of their own courses, thus most probably perpetuating the Chinese whisper effect of poor-quality training. Ask how many years of successful practice as coaches the actual course tutors have.
- Beware of coaching based principally on any one theory or school of thought. Coaching works best as an eclectic and pragmatic art.

- Look for a high ratio of practice to lecturing.
- Look for an emphasis on personal feedback.
- Ask about links to accreditation and who will be doing any accrediting. The accreditation should fit within a national and ideally an international framework – be suspicious of any that do not.
- Press for information on how strictly the verification process is handled. Many accrediting bodies have only the most notional part in maintaining quality.

Accreditation

Assessment of your actual coaching through observation or recordings should be at the heart of any accreditation process rather than writing essays or asking your clients to fill in a questionnaire about you, useful though these processes can also be as back-up to the main question: 'How good a coach are you?' This coaching should be based on your work with a proper client, not just another participant on your course and who therefore knows all the 'rules'. Some training providers accredit students solely on the basis of a 'dissertation'. Interesting and challenging though this no doubt is, it does not prove anything about their likely quality as coaches. You could write a brilliant essay about coaching and be a terrible coach or be a brilliant coach and be unable to write an essay about it.

As a new profession, the whole question of accreditation is a concern. When I began my own coaching career there was no training, there were no qualifications and clients never once asked me whether I was trained and qualified. Now they do. They look for qualifications as a sign that a coach is serious and not just another well-meaning dabbler or someone casually thinking that they can augment their pension with a little bit of coaching.

Comparisons

The greater the potential for danger to life, limb, soul and pocket, the more important this issue becomes. The issue is accountability. Thus the professions where there is tightly-administered accountability include medicine and its allied professions, the law, religion, architecture, accountancy and flying. So, for instance, you cannot pilot a plane solo, practise medicine, call yourself a nurse, be a priest in the Anglican Church, or practise as a lawyer unless you have passed examinations controlled by a professional body. In these cases, *licensing*, which can include active re-registration and continuous retraining (now compulsory in many professions), controls access to the profession.

The situation in coaching

The current situation is improving all the time. The European Mentoring and Coaching Council (EMCC) is the lead body in the UK and has done sterling work towards assessing training courses and now offers accreditation to individuals at several levels. Other bodies include the Association of Professional Executive Coaches and Supervisors (APECS) and the International Coach Federation (ICF).

However, to have real control over quality there would need to be a national or international body – say the equivalent of the various institutes in financial services (chartered accountants, secretaries, etc). To be effective, these bodies need the power to control entry to the profession, backed up by statute as well as money to set and test standards. Crucially they would also need consensus on what constitutes a good outcome of a professional intervention plus a complaints mechanism and accountability procedure with teeth – to discipline and if necessary expel miscreants. Along with this they would need public support and agreement that the profession is important enough to be worth controlling – that is, it has the potential to do significant harm as well as good – the support of all practitioners and staff to administer all the above.

There is no national or international coaching body in the UK which can deliver all of this at the moment. The existing accrediting mechanisms do not and cannot control access to the coaching profession. Anyone can call themselves a coach regardless of whether they have been trained or hold a coaching qualification. It is impossible to identify misdemeanours because there is no widely agreed analysis of what constitutes success in coaching, let alone what constitutes failure. There is no effective means of disciplining a coach who has been accredited but who is guilty of a professional misdemeanour, because there is no way to prevent a poor coach from continuing to practise.

The actual *knowledge* content specific to coaching is growing but is still relatively small, though there are substantial sister-fields in therapy, sports training, management development and organizational development. This is the opposite situation from, say, the knowledge of tax law needed by an accountant. An excellent coach has *wisdom* and *skill*. Real success as a coach is the result of a great many hours of practice with real clients and commitment to continuing professional development rather than the accumulation of factual knowledge which can be tested straightforwardly through an exam, though knowledge of underpinning theory is also vital and will deepen your awareness of the origins, benefits and limitations of many of the ideas on which coaching is built.

Parallels with other professions

The nearest parallel is with psychotherapy. There are many university accredited courses leading to qualifications in psychotherapy. However, there are a number of rival psychotherapeutic bodies in the UK and there is no universally agreed approach. Indeed, there is sometimes a high level of unseemly squabbling, reminiscent of the bickering between religious sects about who has access to the true faith. You can call yourself a therapist and practise as a counsellor or a therapist without licensing or training, though this is becoming increasingly difficult. The existence of training and of professional controls does not prevent corrupt therapists having sexual relationships with their clients nor other kinds of inappropriate behaviour. This suggests that controls are weak.

Even in professions such as medicine with the tightest controls, it can be notoriously difficult to expel a poor performer. For instance, constant rudeness and arrogance are not normally bad enough behaviours *on their own* to justify being struck off the medical register, however many patients complain. By contrast, a coach who is rude and arrogant would not stay in business very long.

Return on investment

Many coaches have an anxiety they will only express quietly and in private: does coaching really work? And if it does, how will we know? I contrast coaching with the occasional work I do as a mediator. There may be several days of intensive preparation followed by a full-on day of mediation. Most cases reach settlement: an agreement is reached and if it is a formal mediation, a legally-binding document will be prepared and signed. I go home from such days knowing I have made a real difference. The parties can measure the cost of my fee against the hugely greater cost of going to court or of letting the dispute maunder on with legal fees mounting on both sides. Coaching is different. The client's aims are vaguer and the outcomes are far, far harder to measure.

With coaching now becoming a familiar part of management development, the question of whether it delivers a good return on investment becomes ever more pressing. It is common for commissioning clients to ask: 'How do we know it will work? What can you tell us about how you assess success?' This is a tricky question. If we fail to take any of the credit for the apparent successes of our clients, we do not honour the coaching process. If we take it all, we do not honour our clients. It is an infrequently discussed danger of coaching that we can be over-keen to see our clients 'succeed' as a way of proving to ourselves and others that we add value. For instance, if I coach a client for a job interview, how much of the credit can I claim if that client gets the job? A client who wanted interview coaching once asked me straight out as a condition of hiring me what percentage of my interview coachees did actually get the jobs they applied for. If the percentage is at the level of chance, then what does that say about my coaching? But if it is high, then that may say more about the poor quality of the selection process than about anything I do in the coaching room.

Coaching is, or certainly should be, a voluntary process. So any clients who seek coaching could be different in some way from clients who do not – for instance, they may already be more self-aware and probably therefore already more successful. This makes it difficult to compare a coaching cohort with a control group unless there is also a large waiting-list group. Knowledge and skill may also leak from individuals getting coaching in an organization to individuals who are not – in fact we have to hope that it does. Very few organizations conduct any kind of evaluation before a coaching programme begins so it is usually impossible to assess how much change there has been in an individual let alone in the organization.

Asking clients after the event can be difficult because memories fade, even where the coaching has been successful – the lessons are internalized to such a high extent that the client forgets their origin. Then, too, success in work or in life is never down to any one factor. There are usually far too many variables to be able to say for certain that it was the coaching that made the difference. For instance, in any large-scale coaching project, there are not only many clients, but many different coaches. It may be impossible to establish how much of the success or failure of the coaching was because of the strengths and weaknesses of any individual coach. Coaches vary in their style even when they come from the same firm and have been trained using the same methodology. It can be difficult to separate out the impact of the individual coach from the value of the coaching process generally.

Clients themselves may be no better able to assess this than supposedly objective researchers. It is common, for instance, for clients to say, 'I did it myself, and I do know I couldn't have done it without you – but I don't really know how or why.' Then, too, enjoyment of the coaching does not necessarily correlate with behaviour change. It is relatively easy to assess the immediate impact of the coaching by asking the client for feedback on each session/ coach. This is valuable for the coach but not necessarily for the organization. For instance, the client can have enjoyed the sessions but may fail to make any changes in behaviour. Alternatively, the client may not have enjoyed the sessions but may make significant changes in what they do as a result.

Concern with measurement may also lead to attempts to measure the only things that can be measured. Dismayingly often, these are the most trivial things. For instance, you can easily measure how many sessions any individual client attended, but how far does this tell you whether or not that client had value from the process?

It helps to be clear what commissioning clients actually want because a number of separate processes may be wrapped up in a request for proof that coaching works:

Research could be a separate process, involving looking at long-term outcomes, coaching style, and assessing the value of different theoretical and practical techniques.

Audit may involve benchmarking costs and outcomes with those obtained in other ways or in other organizations.

Evaluation may try to measure what tangible and intangible benefits have been obtained by the individual and the organization. Few robust studies have been carried out here, though those that have do suggest both tangible and intangible benefits to both individual and organization. One example is the study carried out by Merrill Anderson in 2002 with 43 participants on a leadership development programme in the United States and Mexico. This study looked at evaluation from a four-level framework. First, what did individuals feel about the coaching, second, how were they applying the learning? The third level asked for third-party validation – how others had seen this learning applied. Finally, clients were asked for causal connections between the coaching and measurable changes in the performance of their units. Even when results were adjusted to exclude relatively 'easy' measures such as staff turnover, 77 per cent of the participants cited coaching as having had significant impact on bottom-line results. Altogether, the return on investment was calculated at a staggering 700 per cent (Anderson 2003). Other studies have suggested that coaching has improved managerial performance in areas such as leadership, teambuilding and developing staff.

One neat way of calculating return on investment has been developed by the Ohio-based company Sherpa Coaching. This still involves an element of inspired guesswork but you might like to try it with the help of a willing client.

Step 1	Estimate the total value of resolving an issue – or the costs involved in *not* resolving it.
	Example: client retained two of his most talented staff, both of whom had been in danger of leaving. Coaching had concentrated on how to re-motivate them through redesigning their jobs and managing them in a different way.
	Avoided recruitment costs and disruption to business.
	Benefit: £110,000

Step 2	Multiply the sum you arrived at in Step 1 by the percentage you and the client attribute to the coaching. Let's say this is 50% =
	£55,000 (half of £110,000)
Step 3	How confident are you both in the accuracy of Steps 1 and 2?
	Let's say the answer is that you are 80% confident.
	Adjusted total benefit: £44,000 (80% of £55,000)
Step 4	Subtract the cost of coaching (£6,000).
	Net benefit: £38,000 (£44,000 – £6,000)
Step 5	To calculate return on investment, divide the net benefit by the cost of coaching and turn into a percentage. In this case:
	£44,000/£6,000 × 100 = 633%
	Return on investment = 633%

In other words, this was a substantial return on investment.

As a coach, there are a number of actions you can take to ensure that there are answers to the legitimate concerns of the commissioning organization about how its money is being spent:

- Ensure that the goal-setting process gets enough time at both the outset of the coaching and in every session (see Chapter 6).
- Make your goals measurable as far as possible and involve the boss in the goal-setting.
- Link business results with the relationship and skills issues.
- Ask for feedback all the time on how the client is progressing towards achieving these results. Ask what and how the coaching is contributing.
- Where you are involved in a large-scale project, look for ways to build evaluation in from the start.

Coaching still has a long way to go as a profession. The word *coach* may be on its way to becoming a laughably vague term much like its close cousin *consultant*, a word that often conceals a temporarily stalled career. While in practice – and longer term – the market decides who is an excellent coach and who is a fraud, this may not be immediately apparent to those doing the hiring. Making what contribution we can to continued professionalism is a duty we all share.

10 The heart of coaching: the coach–client relationship

I see you
I am here
(West African greeting – and reply)

What actually goes on between coach and client? Why does coaching work? What makes the difference between an averagely acceptable coach and a brilliant one? How far is coaching actually the partnership of equals that so many of us say we create? Where are the limits to coaching? I look at these issues in this chapter as well as at some further and possibly more advanced approaches to coaching which need experience, courage and confidence.

Recently I have realized that I am often working with 'coaching divorcees'. These are executive coaching clients who have already had one coaching relationship that has not worked out. All of the coaches concerned in these cases had already been through an initial selection protocol, either by a tendering process or as part of a framework agreement. I know from talking to some of the disillusioned HR people who had hired them that their CVs had appeared impressive. If they had been required to describe what they could do at a 'beauty parade' in front of potential buyers they had talked it up well.

There's a pattern in these failed coaching assignments and it's this: all the coaches involved were over-reliant on 'techniques'.

> *Coach A* held her sessions in a branch of a busy sandwich chain, so bad marks already for total lack of privacy. She then insisted on beginning the process with two minutes of deep breathing, asking the client to close her eyes. This must have been entertaining for the other customers, even if it was acutely embarrassing for the client.

> *Coach B* had got himself hooked on neurolinguistic progamming (NLP) techniques and seemed to believe that visualizing was the solution to every problem. He asked the client, and this was in the first 10 minutes of the first session, to imagine himself standing under a waterfall where 'all your past mistakes and confusions will be washed away'. This coach obviously missed his vocation as an

evangelical preacher. Later on in the same session he asked the client to imagine his future life spread out in front of him and to take a step into it. The client's comment: 'I didn't really know what he was talking about and I couldn't do it – felt stupid.'

Coach C ignored his client's account of how unconfident and exposed she felt in her male-dominated organization and suggested that she rehearse a challenging presentation by pretending that she was a man. 'I couldn't be vulnerable with him,' said this client, with remarkable restraint.

Coach D spent the two sessions she conducted with the client giving him mini-lectures, for instance on 'Listening' (pity she didn't do more of it herself).

From the direct accounts given soberly and in a generous spirit mostly of puzzlement by these and other clients it is clear that this sort of coach believes that 'techniques' will solve every client problem. When the techniques don't work, they have no underpinning psychological knowledge or insight and therefore nowhere else to go.

This is the paradox: you have to learn technique in order to bypass it – also true of learning to act, to play a sport or a musical instrument. In acting you have to acquire and then go past methods to get to the meaning of the text. To inspire the orchestra, a conductor has to be an accomplished musicologist before going beyond what is simply written in the score. A jazz musician must acquire a thorough grasp of musical technique before being able to improvise successfully.

It is the same with coaching. You have to learn the techniques in order to discover where they fit into the true learning that comes about through coaching. This learning can only happen in the crucible of the coach–client relationship. This is because the coaching client is not an *object* to be worked on but a *subject* to be worked with by another human being. The Viennese philosopher and writer Martin Buber, whose ideas have had considerable impact on Gestalt therapy, wrote astutely:

> The deciding reality is the therapist, not the methods. Without methods one is dilettante. I am for methods, but just in order to use them not to believe in them. Although no doctor can do without a typology, he knows that at a certain moment the incomparable person of the patient stands before the incomparable person of the doctor; he throws away as much of his typology as he can and accepts this unforeseeable thing that goes on between therapist and patient.
>
> (Hycner and Jacobs 1995: 17)

A colleague and I were assessing would-be coaches in order to fulfil a contract we had won. We set up a process where we observed the candidates through a session with willing guinea-pig clients. One would-be coach intruded grossly into her client's physical space, at one point almost sitting in her lap she was so close; she continually pressed her pet solution onto the client; she talked too much.

And yet ... and yet her client, correctly identifying that we would probably not be offering this coach a job because of this behaviour, said wistfully, 'In spite of all that, I really liked her and it was actually useful. I will do some of the things she suggested because I knew how much she wanted to help me.' I am not advocating this artlessly naïve and unskilled coaching, as I am certain that this coach would soon have floundered helplessly with many of the demanding clients we had in the pipeline. However, the intention to help in this session was so strongly conveyed that some decent coaching did actually take place.

I have come to see that this wish, when accompanied by strongly-conveyed emotional authenticity, can demolish many of the barriers seemingly imposed by lack of technique. In his enjoyable book *Provocative Therapy* (Farrelly and Brandsma 1974), Frank Farrelly recounts something similar where a student therapist was able to break through the casually callous assumptions of more experienced colleagues that a chronic mentally ill patient could be abandoned 'because he could never get better'. Recounting this, furiously and with angry tears, to the patient, the man was amazed that someone could care so much. He comforted the student, ran away from the hospital and got a job, never to return. As Frank comments, '[this] reinforced my idea that even though you had no business being *right* or effective, you could be' (Farrelly and Brandsma 1974: 9).

Power in the coaching relationship: the outer signs

Talking about coaching as a relationship of equals has become a mantra in the coaching world. It is one of my own basic principles and values (see page 9). Working in partnership is what gives coaching its power. How far can this pious hope be true in practice?

When you contrast coaching with other professions, there are some startling differences. Where many of the traditional professions are concerned – accountancy, law, medicine – most people would much prefer not to have to consult them. Almost all are associated with an actual or a potential crisis. Coaching clients are always facing change, but they may see this as bracing rather than threatening. Once they get into the swing of it, clients may look forward to coaching sessions rather than approaching them with the dread that a visit to a lawyer or doctor could invoke.

THE HEART OF COACHING: THE COACH–CLIENT RELATIONSHIP

The traditional professions are selling the superior knowledge that their specialism gives them. Sadly, this has often led to conveying an attitude of superiority. The more obviously service-based and possibly more overcrowded professions (think of financial advisers, architects, interior designers) have always had to take a more client-centred approach. Most coaches will go to considerable lengths to *live* equality in the relationship as well as talking about it. This contrasts with the way many people from the traditional professions treat their clients. So, for instance, I have never once been on mutually first name terms with any doctor to whom I was a patient, indeed most commonly have been talked at as an anonymous 'you' or addressed, uninvited, by my first name while the practitioner expects to be addressed as 'Dr'. By contrast, I work with many doctor-clients, use their first names from the start and expect them to address me likewise. I always offer tea, coffee or water, thus introducing the social nuance of guest and host – also a relationship of equals.

There are some ways in which the relationship favours the coach. Many coaches insist that the client comes to them: mostly this is what I do. When the client comes to us we have already disturbed the balance of power. The client is on our territory and, a bit like being a guest in our house, knows that he or she is expected to play to our rules. We set the method for the coaching, including the method that says the agenda is the client's. We set the time frame for the length of each session. We set the fees.

Against this, we may offset a number of factors that play to the client's power. The client can and often does negotiate fees downwards, depending on the state of the coach's order-book. The client may take a far more active role than the coach in deciding the appropriate number of sessions. Apart from the initial session, where most coaches will have a well-rehearsed protocol, the agenda for the sessions is entirely in the client's hands. And, as in any overcrowded profession, all clients know that there are many other coaches out there eager for business.

In his devastating critique of psychoanalysis, Jeffrey Masson (1990) suggested that even the best therapists cannot avoid creating an exploitative and controlling climate because it is so ingrained in the profession. The critical difference with coaching is that our clients are mentally healthy, and where they are not, their 'symptoms' are normally the ones of familiar minor dysfunction.

Also, certainly where executive coaching is concerned, we are dealing with robustly successful, senior and well-paid people used to having their own way and dealing with suppliers of all sorts as part of their daily lives. For many coaches in the most obviously elevated end of the market, their clients could be earning 10 times or more the income of the coach. Many are also well-known public figures. This makes a difference – the coach will usually approach the client with at least some vestige of the world's respect and may even be unconsciously basking in power borrowed from the client.

There are other, more subtle, ways in which the coach–client relationship is not one of equals. For the most part, as a coach, you set aside a great many of your opinions during the course of the conversation. The client is allowed to express opinions. The coach is willingly more restrained. It is the coach's responsibility to reach out to the client, not the client's to reach out to the coach. The coach is responsible for setting the climate of the conversation – not the client. The client is invested in his or her own learning – not the coach's. The coach has to affirm the client, but the client has no such responsibility towards the coach.

Unconscious processes

Throughout the coaching process, there may be some unconscious processes going on which may explain phenomena which are otherwise inexplicable. For instance, why do you instinctively like some clients more than others (or they like or dislike you)? Why do some clients seem to bring odd expectations to the coaching relationship? Some ideas from therapy may help explain at least some of what is happening.

Projection

As a coach you remain non-judgemental and unattached to your own ideas about what might be good for the client. This is why self-awareness about the phenomenon known as projection can be so useful. Essentially the assumption is that we all have dark sides which we may not acknowledge about ourselves. We say to ourselves, in effect, 'I don't like this about myself. I'll project it onto someone else and that way I can criticize it because then it's nothing to do with me.' Or there can be positive projection where we fantasize an ideal set of characteristics, the ones we might like to have ourselves, onto another person. The phenomenon of projection may take a number of forms:

- At its simplest, we may project an emotion we are feeling onto someone else. This is because we cannot or will not own the feeling in ourselves. So, for instance, I might say to a friend, 'You seem worried' when actually it is I who am worried, but don't want to face my worry.
- As coaches, we might start thinking, 'This client is hostile to me' when in fact you are feeling hostility towards him or her.
- We may see others as the cause of our problems, especially those closest to us.

- We imagine that another person possesses the ideals and qualities we fail to incorporate into ourselves and our lives.
- We may create cycles of unrealistic infatuation which then turn to bitter disappointment in jobs and relationships, leading to cynicism and resentment. You can see this most weeks in newspapers where an idolized celebrity, previously the subject of flattering and wholly unrealistic reporting, is unmasked as being a mere human being after all.

When we criticize other people, what we criticize may be the very thing we most fear could be true about ourselves. Where you find yourself having these judgemental thoughts, it can be a useful discipline to stop and ask yourself, 'Are these feelings or behaviours that are actually true for me?'

Perhaps the most powerful single idea relating to projection is that how we speak about others always says a great deal about how we see ourselves.

Transference and counter-transference

Again, these are concepts from psychodynamic therapy and you should note that they are roundly rejected by psychotherapists from some other schools. I find them useful. The idea of transference is that clients unconsciously project onto you and the coaching relationship patterns and assumptions from earlier relationships in their lives. These projections will be distortions – they are preventing the other person from seeing you as you think you really are. Most usually, they may transfer to you feelings they have had or still have about significant figures from their past. So a client who constantly rebelled against an authoritarian father may see male figures such as a coach in the same light as he saw his father, even though the coach concerned is a mild and pleasant person who is totally unlike the father. Older women may create expectations of being *mother* or *teacher* to a client and this could trigger both rebellious adolescent behaviour and expectations of being nurtured.

Counter-transference may also be going on – that is when you as coach do the same to the client. So a challenge from a client may painfully reawaken ghosts from an early relationship. For that moment, the client is standing in for the ghost and you respond as you might have to him or her in the past.

The more transparent you are in your working with the client, the less likely these phenomena are to derail the process. For instance, Glenda is a client who appears to be resisting delivery on the actions she and her coach have agreed. Her coach takes up the story.

CASE STUDY

Glenda

Glenda told me that she just hadn't had time to do her 'homework'. This was our fourth session and in each of the last three the same thing had happened. I said, very calmly, 'Glenda, I'm really puzzled and intrigued. I'm also feeling a bit stuck and wondering if you're not doing this stuff because I'm not coaching you properly or in a way you can relate to. This is the fourth session where you've said you haven't had time to do the follow up. I'm wondering what's going on here for you ...' Glenda looked sheepish and then annoyed: 'You aren't my headmistress you know!'

Coach: No, I'm not. But I'm wondering now if I remind you of one you used to know! (there was a pause and Glenda's face changed colour)

Glenda: Well, yes. You're about her age when I knew her and I was constantly in trouble for not doing my homework and when I left I swore I'd never let anyone boss me about again.

Coach: How else do I seem to remind you of her?

Glenda: You don't – except that you seem very confident and together.

Coach: What else?

Glenda: Can't think of anything else!

Coach: What would you like to say to that headmistress if she were here?

Glenda: Please respect me. Don't come down on me like that – it wasn't fair, though I know I was a right little pest.

Coach: In what ways am I different?

Glenda: Far, far more – in fact you're not like her at all really!

We then had a candid discussion about our relationship and what needed to happen to make it work. I, for my part, was of course quite unable to promise that I would be anything other than myself, including not being like her headteacher. Glenda was able to look at all her troubled relationships with authority in this light. The frankness and intimacy it created were the turning point in the coaching.

Paralleling

Closely linked with the idea of transference and counter-transference is the idea of parallel processes. This can seem like a strange phenomenon: the client reproduces the same behaviour and feelings in their session as they did in whatever incident they are describing. This creates a parallel emotion in the coach. An example might be that a client is describing overwhelming stress in her job. She says it shows itself in impatience and irritation with her direct reports. As the coach you begin to experience the same feeling in relation to your client: irritation and impatience. Here is Carly, a relative newcomer to coaching, describing how both paralleling and projection occurred in a session with her client. Carly had been introduced to the concept of paralleling through a session with her supervisor.

CASE STUDY

Carly

My client is a 28-year-old woman of Asian origin, the only girl in a large family. The family had arranged her marriage but the marriage is not happy, and she is thinking of leaving, knowing how badly this will play in the culture of which she is a part. She has successfully avoided having a child despite strong family pressure to do so. She had already talked to me about the dominance of her father in the family and her resentment about how being a girl had meant that she was expected to do household chores which her brothers had been and still were spared. The presenting issue for coaching was her lack of progress in her career. I also come from an immigrant family and had a dominant dad, though I have successfully wriggled free. My client began to complain about her boss, saying that he either ignored or bullied her. After the session when I reflected on it, I realized that I had taken part in a perfect example of paralleling, probably with projection and counter-transference thrown in! As my client went on with her story I began to feel that she was whining and complaining. I felt annoyed. I found myself thinking, 'For goodness sake, just ask for what you want! You deserve to be overlooked! Don't be such a wimp.' Although I of course did not actually utter those dreadful words, I know that an edge of impatience crept into my voice. Unusually, I ended the session 10 minutes early. I probably came across as much more curt than I normally am. Now my challenge is to spot this stuff and manage it better!

Why does this happen? One cause is that the coach is over-identifying with the client, inwardly looking for similarities as an unconscious way of tapping into the client's issues. An alternative, or additional, explanation is that the client, again at an unconscious level, wants to recreate the drama and intensity of the issue in order to force the coach into finding a resolution. In practice I believe that while both these forces may be at work, the most likely immediate trigger is the coach's uncertainty and panic about how to respond to the intensity of the client's emotion. In terms of managing these parallel processes, the key is awareness. Notice that it is happening. Physically make a change – for instance, in how you are sitting. Break the trance-like state which has most likely taken hold of both of you. Consciously mismatch the client. Suggest a stretch or another drink. Ask yourself if you are getting so hooked up in the client's issues that you have lost sight of the essentials: that it is the client who has to find the solution, not you. Useful interventions when you notice paralleling happening are questions which will enable you to position yourself consciously outside the client's issues, for instance by saying:

> So, to summarize, the issues are a, b, c. Which of these do you feel is the most important?

> Or

> I'm finding myself a bit overwhelmed in the issue here, can we just take stock of where we are with it?

Being real

In any relationship where helping is involved, there is always a strong possibility of both sides tapping into the deepest roots of human longing. Psychology as a subject has its roots in philosophy, medicine and religion. Magic, superstition, spiritualism and mysticism are lurking just around the corner. When something is wrong, we can crave some magic, whether it is a wonder-crystal with the power to ward off danger, faith healing to save us from death, ley lines which will explain puzzling events, or an exorcism which will banish evil spirits. The power of belief in this respect can be overwhelming.

It is only 150 years or so ago that mental illness was widely believed to be possession by the devil, and there are some religious faiths where people still believe that. The idea that there are people with special powers seems to be something we can all find potentially appealing. It is comforting, if also a little scary, to think of giving yourself up to someone who can reassure through their links to the Divine, or through their special insight . . . sliding smoothly into *second-sight* and *psychic*.

Beware of letting your coaching become contaminated with the same ideas. It is easy, believe me. I have occasionally heard clients introduce me to colleagues at a social event as a 'witch', or slightly less alarmingly as a 'white witch'. In the light of this I go to some pains to demystify the coaching process. You cannot work as an equal with someone who believes that you are some kind of secular priest or shaman. Clients may not always welcome this at first – it might be more comforting to believe in the wizardry. But long term this cannot be right.

Several studies have shown that in some cases placebos (pills that contain no drugs) and placebo procedures (for instance opening a patient's chest and sewing it up again without any other surgery having taken place) can have almost as much positive benefit as conventional drug or surgical treatment. Placebos have sometimes proved many times more effective as treatment for depression than the commonly prescribed drugs and also seem to be powerful in pain control. An intriguing US study carried out by the American Council on Exercise showed that runners who thought they were getting a boost from 'super-oxygenated water' (in fact ordinary tap water) ran three 5km time trials on average 86 seconds faster than a control group. Where alternative medicine is concerned, defenders of homoeopathy, for instance, will maintain that it works despite the intrinsic implausibility of the theory that even though no trace of the homoeopathic element can be found in the 'medicine', the water retains a 'memory' of it. We may speculate that what does work is that the homoeopathic doctor him- or herself believes fervently in the remedy and conveys this to patients who are also willing to suspend their disbelief. This belief on both sides that the 'cure' will work is what may give it its power.

If we take the lesson from placebo research it is possible to see that when both coach and client believe in the power of the coaching process, we are likely to elevate its effectiveness many times over. If as the coach you are sceptical about whether it 'works' then you will convey this to the client. A client who is sceptical about coaching will immediately limit the chances that it will be useful for him or her. There is power in coaching and I want my clients to believe in that power. However, the power is invested in the relationship itself and in the coaching process, not in the supposed supernatural abilities of the coach.

Research into therapy, including, so-called meta-research (research into the research), for instance by David Elkins (2007), shows clearly that success in therapy has nothing to do with the intellectual cleverness of the practitioner or their theoretical orientation. Instead, the common factors seem to be:

1   The ability of the practitioner to create a climate of warmth, acceptance and rapport.
2   The nature of the 'therapeutic alliance' – how the practitioner and client work; the transparency and clarity of the goals.
3   The context in which the client seeks help and whether or not they have supportive people in their lives who are prepared to help them make positive changes.

4 Client and practitioner believing equally in the plausibility of any approaches that are used, including many that are intrinsically implausible, and in their mutual expectation that a positive outcome is possible – in other words what we might call a placebo effect.
5 The kinds of techniques used.

Of these five factors, the least important seems to be the last, with some researchers estimating that as little as 8–15 per cent of the eventual successful outcome had anything to do with particular techniques. We have yet to see whether coaching-specific research will throw up similar results, but my guess is that it will. Trust and warmth are the essential cornerstones in coaching, as in therapy.

Permission to be yourself

When I was relatively new to coaching I acted on an unstated belief that I had to remain in some kind of positively neutral gear throughout the conversation. The client could get upset but I couldn't. The client could be boring but I had to simulate interest. The client could give me feedback at the end of the session but I had to be restrained.

I see now how wrong that was.

In fulfilling a contract for coaching with one organization, there was a 'meet the coach' preliminary event at which, unlike three colleagues, I could not be present. I joined the group the next day for the first of their coaching sessions, held within the timetable of a five-day course. One of the managers in the group who had selected me 'blind' to be his coach told me that he had done so precisely because I had not been present the previous day. His reason, he explained, was that he wanted me to be a 'totally neutral coaching machine' and the less he knew about me the better. In my early days as a coach I would have accepted that, but not now. So in discussing this wish for neutrality, it quickly became apparent that this client felt that the more he knew about me, the more he dreaded that I would judge him. I found the idea of being a 'neutral coaching machine' highly distasteful and I also know that this is not how coaching works. In my refusal to stay at the level of personal invisibility, I was able to show him that he could explore his issues with a real person and be accepted for who he was.

The real catalyst for change is in the coaching relationship itself. What the client does with you, he or she will be doing everywhere else. Therefore the most important data you have about that client is how he or she is in the moment with you. This is the data that many if not most coaches pretend to ignore and it may also be known but constantly avoided by most others around the client. Does this client create feelings of fear in you? That is what she will be doing at work. Does this client lose you in his rambling descriptions of what is happening with his team? Ten to one he will be a poor communicator with others. Is the client over-deferential with you? Does the client speak with such extreme slowness that you find yourself becoming bored and impatient? Others will be responding in the same way. Does a client try to exert inappropriate control in the conversation with you? That's what others will experience too.

This data is every bit as important as what the client tells you about events and people outside the room. It is pricelessly valuable. Ignore it at your peril. It is far more significant than either you or the client speculating about inner motivation, intellectualizing or analysing. *How are they affecting you now this minute?*

Giving feedback

You have to become an expert in the art of giving feedback. This is probably the single most striking way in which a coaching conversation differs from any other conversation our clients are likely to have. Unlike the client's line manager, we have no power to hire and fire. Unlike the client's partner, we have no wish to create or destroy love. Unlike the client's friends, we need not feel we could be putting the friendship at risk if we speak candidly. Coaching is one of the few occasions where anyone is permitted, even encouraged, to comment on the immediate behaviour of the other person. Being able to do this with the honest intent to help the other person learn and with no wish for self-aggrandizement endows the act of giving feedback with enormous power.

Just to be clear, *feedback* is not the same as *criticism*.

Being on the receiving end of criticism is devastating:

> Made me feel like a naughty child . . .

> Felt really frightened – wondered whether my career was on the line . . .

> It was so unfair! I was obsessed by the unfairness – couldn't hear what lay behind it . . .

Criticism attacks the person by making generalized judgements. Criticism is an opinion: *you are* [usually something unpleasant]. This brings out all the defensive and aggressive reactions described above because it contains hurtful generalizations: 'you are a poor communicator'; 'you are sloppy'; 'everyone thinks . . .' Criticism is tough on the person and is most unlikely to be heard or acted upon because it alerts the amygdala to danger (see page 31), so thinking processes become less effective. By contrast, feedback is tough on the issues and is given for one reason only: to help the person learn, and at a point where the feedback-giver judges the other person can hear it. Feedback is also about the things that we can change – it would be pointless, for instance, to give someone feedback about their height, their racial origins or their gait. Criticism looks to hurt and is usually a way for the criticizer to unload their anger.

In giving feedback:

- Ask permission every time: 'may I offer you some feedback here?'
- Stick to factual descriptions of what you have seen, using phrases like 'I noticed . . .', 'I saw . . .', 'I observed . . .', 'I heard . . .'

> I noticed that when you were talking about x, you seemed really alive and animated. You leant forward and thumped your papers.
>
> I heard you giving x a really straightforward explanation of what she needed to do – and I noticed how her face relaxed immediately.

- Don't interpret. Describe what you have seen without attributing a motive. So avoid saying something like

> So I knew you were angry with x . . .
>
> I saw that you wanted to leave the room straight away.

Instead, ask a question, using phrases like 'I'm curious about . . .' This asks the client for his or her motivation rather than you making a guess at it, so say something like: 'I wondered what was going on for you at that moment?'

- Describe the impact on you:

> When you leant forward like that I felt alarmed just for a second. I wondered if you were angry with me.
>
> You started your presentation with a story and I was completely absorbed in it – I wanted to know what happened next!
>
> You touched your face a lot while you were talking and that had the effect on me of wondering whether you were really confident about what you were saying.

- Link it to the client's goal by using a phrase like 'I'm wondering how this links with . . .'

- Ask for the client's view of what you have said.
- Agree how you will work on the material that this incident generates.
- Look for opportunities to offer more positive than negative feedback, especially where a client can show you how vastly improved some skill or behaviour has become.
- Choose your words carefully. It is better to say something like 'I ended up feeling a bit alarmed about what you might do next' rather than 'you were intimidating'. There is a fine line between feeding back how the client has had an impact on you and seeming to have taken it personally. The whole point about your feedback is that you are not taking it personally even while you are describing the personal impact of the client on you.

Here is an example.

CASE STUDY

Candice

Candice was proud of her track record in production management, had an MBA from the London Business School, and was pleased to have won her job against stiff competition. But soon her boss was regretting the appointment, complaining that Candice was unable to speak or write without recourse to jargon and was generally unaware of her impact on others. Candice was both annoyed and hurt by this accusation, believing that the fault lay with others for not being clever enough to understand her.

Both Candice and her coach understood that Candice's job was on the line. Candice's coach negotiated an agreement that the coaching room was one place where she could expect real objectivity. When Candice began to use convoluted sentences with her coach, the coach found himself as baffled as her colleagues. Instead of glossing it over and pretending to understand, the coach stopped her every time.

> 'Candice, can I stop you here? I notice how many very long words and sentences you are using. Just now you described *production flexibility analysis* and *Kanaban* with *JIT systems* and *economic value added*, and a lot of other stuff that followed with more long words and technical phrases and I had no idea what

you meant. Instead of concentrating on what you went on to say I was still puzzling about those sentences. Then I began to feel stupid and that I somehow should be understanding you and it was my fault for not being able to. I wonder if this is an example of the effect you have on colleagues?'

After several more examples along the same lines, Candice began to realize that her coach was no different from her non-specialist colleagues, and that stepping back to ask 'What does a non-specialist really need to understand here in very simple terms?' would significantly change her impact on colleagues. Because no one else had felt able to take this intrusively detailed and high-risk approach, Candice had resorted to the all-too-human defence of denial. To Candice, being an expert mattered to her above all else and this is what had led to her exaggerated reliance on technical jargon. The over-investment she had made in being an expert also became part of the agenda for the coaching.

To use this approach you have to:

- intend to look – at everything: how clients greet you, how they come into the room, what they say in the first few moments, how they treat you, the language they use, the feelings they arouse in you throughout the session;
- recognize the data when you experience it and know the difference between how much of this data is generated by you and how much is being created by the client.

Knowing when *not* to give feedback or even to raise an issue is every bit as important as knowing when you must. I still wonder if I was just too timid to offer feedback to a woman client who had startled me on first meeting with her exceptionally high, girlish voice and lisp. The reason it mattered was that this client was constantly getting on shortlists for jobs and failing at the interview. My guess was that interviewers who were meeting her for the first time would feel exactly as I did, and that the distraction this created ensured that she never got the job. Rightly or wrongly, I felt that I was on risky territory: can such a voice be changed? Possibly, but only with enormous effort. I remained silent on the question of her voice.

Provocation and humour

I am utterly against the idea of the coaching room being some kind of place of worship where a holy hush prevails. In the early years of Person Centred Therapy, for instance, it always seems to me that clients were encouraged to ramble on for hours while the therapist stifled boredom, anger, pity, irritation, laughter, incredulity and all the other responses which the rest of the world might offer. (I am aware that this might not be a totally fair description of what actually happened.)

When I first started using humour and provocation in my coaching, I thought I was probably a bit eccentric. Other coaches might disapprove and maybe I needed to keep quiet about it. When I read Farrelly and Brandsma's book *Provocative Therapy* (1974) I realized that what I was doing was relatively mild by comparison but seemed to work for similar reasons. Frank Farrelly offers funny, teasing, intrusive, sexually provocative and impertinent comments to the client, often using street language; takes the client's fears and exaggerates them to the point where the client, often spluttering with laughter, has to defend him- or herself; offers surreal, outrageous and whacky 'interpretations' of the client's behaviour, but does all of this with care and warmth for the client as the cornerstone and with remarkably positive results. As Graham Dawes comments on the provocative therapy website (provocativetherapy. com):

> The shibboleths of psychotherapy shatter. Farrelly's mouth opens (often before he's even given the client a chance to explain the problem) and what comes out is everything you've been told never to say to a client. He even encourages the client in their craziness, throwing out all sorts of advantages their crazy behavior will bring to the client (albeit the advantages are crazier than the client's behavior), providing the client with a wealth of justifications for their behavior (albeit the justifications are more spurious than any the client has come up with), exhorting them to continue with the behaviors they say they want to stop (albeit cheerfully confirming that the consequences of continuing will be those the client is most anxious to avoid).

I don't go this far. But I do sometimes use approaches that are recognizably in the same genre. The underpinning hypotheses are these.

1   If you provoke the client, *using their own internal frame of reference*, with humour and perceptiveness, the client will tend to move in the opposite direction. In fact this is the typical response to advice-giving twisted and turned back to the coach's and client's advantage.

2   If you urge the client to continue doing their evidently self-defeating behaviour, the client will tend to move towards a healthier alternative.

The overt tone is teasing, joyfulness, lightness, bounce, chutzpah and challenge.

Example 1

Gloomy chief executive client, sinking ever lower in chair, avers that a slight blip in performance could mean the end of his career. I have worked with him on and off for some years, and I know the internal dialogue he will be creating:

Coach: Hmm, yes I agree, (copying and grossly exaggerating the client's slump) your life is over. I can see it now, Kim [wife] is getting up at five to go and scrub floors in that beer-stinking local pub. Your kids are standing at the door crying and saying that they hate their bogstandard comprehensive school and you're lurking upstairs feeling like crap because it's all your fault.

Client: (sitting up in chair, trying not to laugh) That is SO cheeky. Of course it wouldn't be as bad as that. (now actually laughing) At the very least Kim could be getting up at seven and making me a cup of tea while I loll in bed before she goes off to scrub floors at an office!

Result: exaggeration has forced the client to self-correct. Gloom has vanished and never reappears in the session.

Example 2

Senior foreign and commonwealth once diplomat fears delegating and doesn't know how to do it. Result: life clotted by 16-hour days, creates bottlenecks for his frustrated staff, wife furious because she sees him so little. Client has offered all the familiar excuses to his coach about why delegation is 'impossible' thus revealing his inner frame of reference.

Coach: (exaggerated righteousness) Absolutely. These staff are hopeless. Whoever appointed them? (jabbing finger at client) You could lose control here. It's correct that you should do all their work as well as your own. (loudly) You're a saint for sacrificing yourself like this! To risk your health and marriage is so noble! Only you can do all this work to your own high standards. The organization will thank you – in fact you'll probably get a knighthood in the next Birthday Honours . . . or maybe even the Royal Victorian Order as well, the Queen will personally . . .

Client: (interrupting, looking confused and startled but beginning to smile) I think you're going a bit barmy here – are you serious?

Coach: (over-solemn face) Of course I'm serious. I think the Foreign Secretary will single you out for your exceptional devotion, and why stop at that, the Prime Minister will personally thank you . . .

Client: (snorting with laughter, in spite of himself) OK, OK, I get the picture. The Office never will thank me. I won't get the knighthood. And if I did my wife may have divorced me by then. I assume you think there's hope for me. If so please tell me what I should be doing and stop sending me up!

Result: prolonged laughter. Coaching resumes with focus on how delegation could happen without losing sight of quality standards. Client comments later that he hadn't known that coaching would involve 'surrealistic comedy with myself as the straight-man'.

It is even possible that Sigmund Freud himself was also an exponent of provocative therapy. It is clear that he considered himself exempt from the strictly-no-reactions rule he suggested for others. Dr Roy Grinker, an analysand of Freud in 1932, is reported as describing the great man's practice of allowing his Chow dog, Yofi, to stay in the room. When the dog scratched to go out, Freud said, 'You see, even the damned dog is bored with you.' When the dog scratched again to return, Freud said, 'Well Yofi has decided to give you a second chance so maybe I should too.'

Being open to influence: receiving feedback

The feedback process in coaching is two-way. It's not just you pronouncing on the client. You will also be inviting the client to pronounce on you. Again, this is unusual in virtually all professional relationships except perhaps coaching's close cousin, training. In asking for feedback you will again be modelling how sincerely you believe in the two-way nature of the relationship. You can ask about the content and style of your coaching as well as about the relationship:

How have you found this session?

What worked especially well for you?

What worked less well?

How are we getting on together – you and me?

When people offer you feedback, they may be uncertain how you will receive it, or they may just not know how to do it properly. So the feedback may take any of these forms:

> Apparent attack (criticism) – 'You asked a lot of questions but I didn't get any of the advice I need.'
>
> Apparent compliment – 'You're brilliant at seeing beneath the surface.'
>
> Vague hints – 'You're a bit hard to understand at times.'

Don't simper at compliments; don't get angry, defensive, self-justifying or confess 'guilt' if the client has criticisms. Instead, repeat and summarize the feedback and ask the client to tell you more. You may get some pleasant surprises as well as getting vital information about how to improve your practice.

Tough speaking

Giving feedback is a form of confrontation and most coaching will involve some use of confrontation from time to time. If you never confront clients, then you need to ask whether you are colluding – going along with their view that everyone else is at fault but them or that it is impossible for their situation to improve.

Confronting needs to be done with extreme care: you can destroy the client's trust in a few seconds if it is done clumsily. Even if done well, it may dismay the client. Confrontation may also lead to denial, making the resistance more extreme than it was in the first place.

Reasons for confronting

Usually there are three types of situation that you and your client could explore:

1   Discrepancies between espoused values and values in action. This is where the client says one thing but does another. An example might be a client who says she believes in equal opportunities but actually recruits and selects people on the basis of stereotype or old boy/girl networks.
2   The client agrees that a change needs to take place, but postpones the moment when it will happen. For instance, the client may say they are fed up with the current role and want to leave but make no actual attempt to seek another job.

3   You have serious doubts about whether the client's proposed course of action is actually wise or desirable. For instance, the client may be overwhelmed with anger about a boss's behaviour and be prepared to storm into the boss's office the next day. You feel certain that this will not get him the outcome he says he wants.

For confrontation to be successful your own motivation has to be a sincere wish to help. If there is even a smidgen of feeling that you want to get at the client, or teach them a lesson, don't do it. You must also have reliable data to back you up. Rumour, gossip and scuttlebutt do not amount to reliable data. Ideally you need to have experienced whatever you are talking about at first hand. There must be a relationship of trust and liking between you and the client, so confrontation is not usually a technique to be used in the early stages of the process. You must have a high level of skill in giving feedback, including the ability to create real rapport and to manage any fallout from the conversation.

How to confront

Introduce the subject straightforwardly and make the link to the stated results that the client wants, alerting the client to the possibility that you are going to say something which could be difficult to hear but stressing how much you value and want to support the client. Base what you say on data; keep it descriptive and non-judgemental; talk about 'what is', not 'what should be', then ask how the client sees it. And explore the implications. Ask what will happen if the situation does not change and brainstorm solutions, including offering any bright ideas of your own about alternatives. Make it clear that it is the client's choice whether or not to make the changes.

Humility

I was working with a client who was in long-term remission from cancer. In talking calmly and optimistically about his treatment, he remarked that the single most therapeutic part of his many visits to the hospital were the conversations he had with his oncologist. This woman had acknowledged the limits of her knowledge as well as stressing her confidence in what did work. She adopted the position of treating patients as fellow adults, mixing judicious optimism with honesty about her own and her profession's limitations. This is a hard act to carry off. Do it too much or in the wrong circumstances and you destroy your client's confidence in you. But act all-seeing and all-knowing and you will be too invested in protecting your image. Coaching is full of paradoxes and this is one of the most profound: we have to be powerful and powerless simultaneously.

The critical test is: is this in my client's interest? If yes, then:

When you are puzzled, say so:	I'm feeling puzzled about the connection between what you've said about x and what you've said about y: what's your take on that?
When you feel confused about where the conversation or session is going, raise it:	I notice we've spent nearly an hour on what you've done since we last met; we still haven't set any goals for this one! How do you feel about that?
If you feel caught in a dilemma, describe it:	I'm in two minds here about what to do. Or I'm caught between a number of different ways of responding here.
When you have made a mistake, acknowledge it and apologize:	When we met for our last session I feel I pressed you too hard on x issue. I did notice that you seemed uncomfortable but I still carried on didn't I? I'm sorry. That was a mistake.
When you feel out of your depth, declare it:	I'm not sure I know what to do here.

Owning up to apparent weakness or uncertainty may have more impact than you realize. As a coach you need a high degree of self-management. You must be centred, self-aware and with a high degree of all the many intelligences that the role requires: analytical, emotional, spiritual and systems intelligence. Yet at the same time you are human; there are things you don't know and areas where you are uncertain. Conveying these to clients whose lives have often been lived in dread of such 'weakness' may have only beneficial effect.

Acknowledging

We are often the only witnesses to enormous acts of courage and learning. What may seem like small steps to others are often huge leaps for a client. So a client who has overcome her genuine phobia and fear of HIV infection to have much-needed electrolysis may only have you to tell. A client who has given up what to him was the scaldingly shameful and lifelong habit of biting his nails may only feel able to glory in his achievement with you. You may be the sole recipient of an email from an apparently confident senior executive who wants to tell you joyfully about having overcome her fear of giving a presentation to her board. A client who has experienced the death of a profoundly disabled child may not feel able to tell anyone else that although this death was a sad event, it was also welcome, received with relief, and was not the tragedy that the rest of the world assumes.

Acknowledging is yet another way in which coaching is different from a 'normal' conversation. In *acknowledging*, the coach recognizes an important aspect of who the client is rather than noticing what the client has *achieved*. The coach is acknowledging the being self, not the doing self.

CASE STUDY

Peter

Peter is a client who has struggled with an enormous amount of personal and professional change. He has had to start a new job, recruit a new team and get to know a new boss at the same time as coping with three bereavements.

Peter: These last few months have been the toughest I can remember.
Coach: Yes, I'd like to acknowledge your courage and resolution in keeping going.
Peter: (surprised and pleased) Oh, thanks. Gosh. I feel great!

In *acknowledging*, the coach notices and mentions positive qualities in the client: humour, energy, clarity, courage, doggedness, willingness to learn, humility, and so on. Note that, in acknowledging, we are not giving empty compliments. Lack of authenticity will be immediately obvious to the client.

When the client cries

We can cry with laughter – or with sadness. We can laugh with anger or with joy. Crying is just at one end of the spectrum of human emotion and since we are dealing with the whole person in the coaching room it is inevitable that we will see tears from time to time.

Trainee coaches often express understandable anxiety about what to do when a client cries. It is unusual for a relative stranger to break down in front of you. Also, adults may feel that crying is childish or shows that you are out of control or incompetent and can't cope. It certainly exposes the vulnerability of the person who is crying and some clients may find it humiliating.

However, in my experience, the person who is most likely to be worried about the crying client is the coach. The reasons may be a mixture of embarrassment at seeing an apparently well-adjusted person break down, or a fear that the client may discomfit themselves then or later by their tears, regretting having shown apparent weakness. Some coaches describe a dread that they may join in.

As coaches we may also worry that we have in some way caused the tears through clumsy coaching. The language here is often telling: 'I made him cry', implying that it is our responsibility. My own view is that crying is one of the multitude of choices that clients make during their work with us. Coaches cannot *make* clients cry – any more than they can make them laugh, or bored, or command them to feel any other emotion. The client chooses, unconsciously perhaps, but chooses nonetheless. Often the coach's worry about whether the client can cope is just a way of projecting their own worry – 'Will I be able to cope with a client who cries?'

The biggest trap for a coach with a weeping client is to imagine that your role is to fix the tears. Ask yourself what message it would give your client to do anything at all which implied that their tears are not legitimate. Through their tears the client is giving you a privileged opportunity to understand more about them. Platitudinous there-thereing does not help, nor does any of the range of mumbled clichés about time healing, or 'a good cry does you good'. The second biggest trap is to join in. There is a place for your own emotional reaction, but if you are crying as helplessly as your client you will be in no position to help.

Your most appropriate response depends on that split-second moment of judgement that only you can make:

> You're looking upset – do you want to go on?
>
> Of course you can cry – this is one place where you can.
>
> If it would help to cry, that's absolutely fine.
>
> You've been through a horrible experience, so of course you feel upset.
>
> These feelings are so strong – of course they will produce tears.
>
> Silence: sometimes you can best convey empathy and acceptance simply by saying nothing.

Clients who prefer to contain their tears will stop at this point. Clients who do not, may let go and cry. It is always a good idea to invite clients to manage the moment with you. A possible response here is: 'Take as long as you like – tell me when you're ready to go on.'

Far from feeling that tears are an embarrassing intrusion into the coaching, to be swept out of sight as soon as possible with both coach and client conspiring in the illusion that nothing happened, the skilled coach realizes that tears are wonderfully useful material for the work. When I meet clients some time after the coaching has finished, many of them will tell me that these moments are the ones that stick in their memories as among the most helpful in the entire process.

CASE STUDY
Martyn

Martyn and I worked together on and off for a number of years through a variety of jobs and roles. He remembers the moment when he wept for the first and only time during one of our sessions.

> I'd suddenly fallen out of love with my job. I'd been dreading bringing it up because I felt that it was important for you to see me as always on top of things. You encouraged me to name the anxiety and I took the risk of letting my emotion show. I trusted you with that and realized it was OK to fail sometimes because you accepted that it was, and you accepted me in spite of my seeing myself as a potential failure.
>
> Our discussion later of why I felt that, and your response that it would in no way affect your view of me, was one of the best moments in our work together – a real moment of learning because I realized I did not have to be a brilliant performer or totally optimistic all the time. We had looked together into what felt like an abyss at the time. In a weird way, crying released the anxiety and straightaway afterwards I'd got it into more perspective.

What this story shows is that by accepting the intensity of the moment and the legitimacy of the emotion, you show that you accept the legitimacy of the person.

Traumatized, bereaved or stressed clients

To live our lives with reasonable confidence we have to assume that the world is a safe, predictable place. Essentially we believe in our own value and right to exist. All of this is overturned in psychological trauma. I would define trauma as an event or series of events where the client experiences feeling out of control and chronically unsafe. Their assumptions about justice, personal safety, health or cause and effect are often replaced by the confusion of betrayal and bewilderment. They may feel exhausted, powerless and needy. Feelings of being essentially a good person may be replaced by feelings of being essentially a bad person because 'bad things only happen to bad people'. In effect their psychological contract with the world around them is experienced as breached.

Enter this area only if you are confident, experienced and know the boundaries of your own skill. In fact you may be thinking that this is exactly the sort of territory in which any coach should think twice. Of course the immediate response may be to feel alarmed and frightened by the extent of the client's distress: *this is too much, I'm out of my depth.* When, on mature reflection, you trust that feeling, you must strongly encourage the client to consult a specialist in this area. In fact, see your task as coaching the client around the issue of finding specialist help. Be suspicious, equally, of over-eagerness to get involved because you are enjoying the drama of it all without necessarily having the skills and awareness that you need.

It is obviously true that there are many potential snares. You may be deluding yourself about your levels of skill. You may meddle with techniques which you only quarter understand. The client may endow you with skills and knowledge which you do not in fact have. You may make a mess of it.

The case for not backing away in terror is that when all the following conditions are in place, you may want to go ahead.

- The client has previously been stable and functioning well.
- The trauma is not overwhelming the client – this may be the case even when it has been precipitated by real tragedy.
- The client chooses you as the person who can help them.
- The client believes that there is no other obvious source of help (note that this is probably not true and one of your roles could be to refer them to specialized helpers).
- You can work comfortably and openly alongside other professionals with whom your client is in touch.
- The client makes this choice because you have probably worked with them over a long period of time, maybe several years through a number of different jobs and roles.

- There is a high level of trust and liking between you.
- The traumatic incident occurs while you are in the middle of a coaching programme.
- You know enough and have had sufficient training to deal with what the client brings.

Over a long coaching career, all of this may happen more often than you expect. Examples from my own practice include a diplomat unexpectedly caught up in offering consular services to British survivors of a major natural disaster which had happened while he was on holiday in the same country, a senior partner whose stress levels got well out of control when his accountancy firm was formally investigated in the aftermath of a political scandal, and a medical director whose personal reputation was seriously compromised by crisis events in his hospital – and too many clients to list who suddenly lost their jobs in the aftermath of a merger or downsizing programme. The examples I have described here are those of obvious crisis and trauma, but you will meet much milder versions of the same phenomena on a more frequent basis: the abrupt discovery of a major health problem, a partner who suddenly leaves, a son or daughter who develops a drug problem, a career-threatening episode, and so on.

These are the symptoms to look out for:

- *Flashbacks*: reliving an event as if it is happening all over again, often triggered by an innocent reminder from someone else or from seeing a single word in a newspaper.
- *Nightmares and poor sleep*: for instance, waking early and finding it impossible to get back to sleep.
- *Numbing and avoidance*: a client who had been attacked by a mugger a few metres from her own home talked of feeling 'hollowed out'. Another client described being separated from the experience, as if he was in a film where he was somehow outside the whole traumatic event in which he had been involved. Seeing himself on the television news added to this feeling.
- *Intrusive negative thoughts*: imagining catastrophe; ruminating about the worst possibilities. For instance, the medical director client imagined scenes of public disgrace where he was summarily ejected from his hospital with his belongings in a bin bag, struck off the medical register, his pension denied him and a hostile article about him in every newspaper.
- *Survivor guilt*: Where the client has survived an incident in which others have lost their jobs, been injured or killed, after an initial period of euphoria, there can be feelings of unworthiness and guilt. *Why me? Could I have done more? Was I selfish? Am I a coward?*

- *Preoccupation with 'if onlys' and 'what ifs'*: The client whose reputation was at risk repeatedly went over the events leading up to the crisis, asking himself what would have happened if only he had not done or said particular things.
- *High levels of arousal*: jumpiness, irritability, hyper-vigilance, rapid heartbeat, sweating.

These are difficult phenomena to deal with. At their most extreme, they are properly described as post-traumatic stress disorder (PTSD). It's not surprising that clients will report anxiety and depression along with loss of appetite. Using alcohol, tobacco or drugs as a way of seeking to anaesthetize yourself against the distress is also common.

I like the guidance given by the psychological trauma specialists, the Centre for Crisis Psychology, as published in the classic book, *Coping With Catastrophe*, by Peter Hodgkinson and Michael Stewart (1998). Essentially this is that an empathetic but directive and structured approach sustained over a period of time is what will work. The directive approach is justified by the helplessness that such clients report. Temporarily, they are not in the resourceful state in which coaching will work. There will be an educative element to it where you will be in the role of teacher with a client. Tell the client that this is what they will experience and ask for their consent to it. Tactics that I have used successfully with such clients include:

- Normalizing the client's reactions: for instance through explaining the change cycle (see page 157).
- Encouraging them to read self-help material on PTSD such as the pamphlet by Martina Mueller of the Oxford Cognitive Therapy Centre (2007).
- Reconstructing the whole story with them, concentrating on its factual aspects first and creating the environment where the strong feelings that this will create can be accepted and contained: be wary of assuring the client that you 'understand'. You don't and can't 'understand' because you have not been through the experience, though what you can say with truth is how their story is affecting you. When my accountancy client was describing his dread of what the investigators would find and his fear of humiliating collapse during the process of being interviewed, I said something like, 'This sounds so difficult and I can see the hurt and stress it's causing you. Just listening to your story, I'm feeling some of that tension and anxiety.'
- Facing the fears created by avoidance and consciously filling in any missing factual elements: for instance, the client who had been mugged had somehow got to the point where she believed that her

assailant had followed her for weeks, marking her down for attack. Discovering, through reading court accounts, that it had actually been a random and opportunistic crime was an important part of her recovery.

- Teaching de-arousal techniques such as steady diaphragmatic breathing and classic muscular relaxation.
- Teaching techniques which show the client how to interrupt negative ruminating, for instance through physical or mental distraction.
- Respectfully and firmly questioning flawed logic: so for instance, a client whose son had drowned had come to believe that 'anyone close to me could be in danger'. From this, he had rapidly moved to 'it will be bad luck to be near me so I'd better keep away from everyone'. Challenging the grossly faulty generalizations here was enormously helpful to this client's adjustment (for more on spotting these patterns, see page 172).
- Creating, with the client's help, a programme of simple physical activity to be followed every day.
- Strongly encouraging the client to consult their GP and to consider a short-term recourse to medication as a way of managing the worst symptoms.
- Recommending trauma specialists who can deploy techniques such as progressive desensitization, helping people to re-enter situations where they have developed phobic responses (uktrauma.org.uk has a list of such specialists).
- Giving the client a relaxation recording to play before going to sleep.
- Suggesting the value of keeping a daily journal of the positive aspects of whatever is happening – for instance, the levels of support and sympathy they are receiving from others in their lives.

These are not one-off interventions. If you find yourself in this position, consider being prepared to offer telephone and email support on a no-limits basis and to follow up through a structured process over as many weeks as are needed, agreed with your client, but only if, again, you are experienced and confident of your skills.

Knowing when too far is too far

The coaching relationship is delicate. Too much pressure on the client and it will fracture. Too little and the coaching will feel inert, suggesting that it will not lead to the changes the client wants to make in his or her life. Knowing when to press and when to hold back is a matter of the finest and most split-second judgement.

CASE STUDY

Robert

Robert was a miner's son, left school at 16 and began teaching himself some of the principles of para-legal work while he worked in a solicitor's office. At the age of 40, by now an experienced solicitor himself, he had done brilliantly well and had become head of legal services for a local authority. His starting issues for the coaching we embarked on together were to bring more finesse into his managerial style – a nice, safe topic.

Soon, however, it became clear that the underlying issues were his profound lack of self-confidence and his acute social isolation. He had no friends at work and no social life. He had married his childhood sweetheart at 19 and his wife had opted to stay at home, even though they had no children. The relationship was one of mutual dependency but at the point where Robert started the coaching, he was expressing a strong wish to break out of the stifling pattern he and his wife had created: 'I want to get out at weekends, go to football, meet more people, but if I do she will feel it's a threat. She just wants me there so that we can do the garden, watch a video, just the two of us together.'

As his coach, I felt we had reached a crossroads.

JR: What do you really want?
Robert: I do want to have a better social life and one that's outside this charmed circle of just me and her.

Robert described how this would look, sound and feel in response to the question, 'If you could have this ideal life what would be happening?'

JR: So what are the blocks to setting about this?

There was a long pause – perhaps 12 seconds. Robert looked at me, looked tense, wrung his hands slightly and looked at his feet. Very slowly he said: 'I can't move on it. If I discuss it with her, she'll panic. It will raise the whole question of the relationship and I can't do that to her.'

What does a coach do in these circumstances with a client who has described what he wants so vividly yet also describes a total block to action? Challenge? Suggest a tiny first step? Withdraw? After a few moments more of silence, I asked how Robert felt about staying with the idea of doing nothing: 'Fine – for now' was his reply.

Later I pondered this exchange, wondering whether I might have pressed him harder, discussed it with my supervisor and concluded in the end that it had been right to hold back. Eight weeks later, Robert called me, devastated, to tell me that with no warning or previous threats, his wife had killed herself, swallowing a lethal dose of paracetamol. He discovered that she believed she had terminal cancer (she hadn't). Robert's judgement about his wife's fragile mental state was totally correct, including a diagnosis of agoraphobia, which he had not shared with me. What he had not anticipated was how violently her feelings would implode. His weighing up of what he could cope with if he had confronted his wife was also correct. And my judgement about what would have been *too far* was correct, though I did not have anything like all the relevant data at the time.

Subsequently, in training new coaches, I have seen how easily the coach's eagerness to help can stray into too much intimacy too soon, ignoring the warning signs from the client which say 'keep off'. When this happens, the client's energy goes into repelling what he or she perceives as an attack, rather than into learning and change.

Handling these moments

- When the client tells you straightforwardly that they want you to stop, stop.
- Be alert to the evidence from the client – small frowns, a tapping foot, looking away.
- You can't go on with a task-based agenda when this happens – the pause or the resistance becomes the agenda.
- Name it: 'I notice we seem to have hit a pause here. What's going on for you?'
- Agree jointly how to handle it.

Talking about yourself

Coaching is a unique kind of conversation. It differs from other close, intimate kinds of exchange. In a conversation with a friend, we often aim to demonstrate our kinship with the other person by emphasizing that we, too, have had a similar experience. For instance, here is a sample conversation you might have with a friend:

Friend: I'm really worried about my scan results. Perhaps I've got cancer.
You: Oh, don't worry too much about that. I had a similar thing a few months ago and it was nothing to be concerned about. Yours is probably just the same.
Friend: Oh, that's a comfort, perhaps mine will be all right too!

A coaching conversation would be different:

> Client: I'm really worried about my scan results. Perhaps I've got cancer.
> Coach: Yes, I can understand that concern. Say more about the worry . . .?

New coaches often ask how appropriate it is to talk about your own experience. The urge to do so can be strong. It could help create empathy. It could show that we, too, have our vulnerable side and it could help discharge the emotion that a distressed client can create in the coach.

Coaching is about the client's issues, not the coach's. Talking about yourself will readily distract the client into discussing your experiences and concerns – or even trying to coach *you*. Your experience could trigger a powerful emotional reaction in your client, and not always a helpful one. For instance, the client may, at that stage in the coaching, feel that he or she needs to see you as someone above the hurly-burly of human emotion.

A client once told me towards the end of our coaching programme that the reason she had selected me rather than the other two coaches she had considered was that I had appeared 'very calm and therefore probably a whole person, not a fragmented mess like me'. This client's starting-out issues concerned managing the turbulent emotions she experienced in her workplace. If I had appeared to burden her with any of my emotion then it could have implied that there was no hope for her either. Sometimes, the wish to share a client's pain can seem overwhelming, particularly where the client is describing a loss or trauma that you feel is akin to something you have experienced yourself. There are two related points to make here. The first is that you will be making assumptions that your experience is actually a close parallel to the client's – never the case, however similar it might seem. The second is that you may appear to be making a bid to usurp the client's experience – 'my tragedy is worse than yours'. Alternatively, the client may interpret your comment as 'Well I've coped with my difficulty, so you can jolly well cope with yours – forget it – move on!' It will also be harder to re-establish coaching conventions – the conversation may veer towards a nice friendly chat.

In the initial 'Hello-and-how-are-you?' part of the session, a client will virtually always politely ask you how you are. Ninety-nine per cent of the time a conventional 'fine' or 'very well' is the appropriate answer. Exceptions could be when you know the client well enough to share a major triumph or upset in your life and feel that the client has the right to know that he or she may observe tiny changes in your usual demeanour. Without hearing your explanation for such changes, the client might well misinterpret your behaviour as being some reflection on him or her. Equally, giving yourself brief permission to talk about it will, paradoxically, help you manage its impact on you.

With experience, you may feel that, as in these very rare cases, the benefits of talking about your own issues and experience could outweigh the disadvantages and benefit the client. However, *when you are still building your experience, don't risk it.*

When there is *profound challenge* in your life, it must be right to share at least some of it with your clients. In dealing with two bereavements, the death of a beloved young god-daughter in the middle 1990s and the death of my dear husband in 2010, I found my clients responded with delicacy, tact and fellow-feeling. None recoiled in embarrassment – as far as I was aware – and of course I might not have been aware of any embarrassment they did feel. I believe I did good enough work during these times. It took hugely more effort to do virtually everything in the way of essential preparation or record-keeping. But once I was with my client, I gave myself up wholeheartedly to being there. Contrary to the view that only by remaining detached can you be helpful, I confirmed my belief that the opposite was true. I took the risk of disclosing some of the rawness of my emotion and asked for some modest support back: empathy, understanding, tolerance. As a result, I increased the amount of empathy, understanding and tolerance I could offer those clients: take some, give some.

Client relationships in coaching are delicate. 'I'm paying you to be nice to me,' said one client sternly, 'but I do think you mean it.' They are not purely 'professional' in the sense that I do what one former mentor advocated and forget them the moment they are gone; nor are they friendships. They grow somewhere in that shadowy territory between the two. Turning to clients, however briefly, for a moment of trustful comfort and understanding felt entirely right.

As coach with a client, my basic belief is that we are all in this together. I don't want to be an omnipotent, detached coach. I want to be there in the middle of the human struggle along with my clients.

Managing boundaries

One of the reasons that therapy has acquired a bad name in some quarters is that it has become clear that there are some therapists who have inappropriate sexual relationships with their clients. The current evidence is that those who do so are a very small number but that they are serial abusers – that is, they do it often. All the regulatory bodies for psychotherapists explicitly warn against it. As with doctor–patient sexual relationships, it is grounds for being struck off. This is because where the relationship is one of healer–afflicted there is a power differential, and to cross the boundary from healer to lover is thus rightly regarded as abusive. Virtually all of the abusers are male. They justify their behaviour as acts of altruism. The relationships take place, they say, out of pity for the client, usually when the female client believes she is unattractive. As with all abusive relationships, the core of the abuse is in the exploited vulnerability of the abused person.

Remember, too, that power has aphrodisiac qualities and if our clients attribute power to us or we to them, then this dynamic may be at work – see any scandal in which a famous politician's bedroom secrets are revealed. When the press ponders aloud, 'How did someone as physically unattractive as x draw a beautiful woman like y?' the answer is usually his fame and assumed power.

Although I believe it would be rare indeed for anything similar to happen in coaching, it is still possible. As in therapy, clients may reveal matters to us that they have told no one else. Several clients have told me that I know more about them than anyone else except their partners, and sometimes they have shared secrets with me that they have not shared even with a partner. Where this is linked through the coaching with permanent and positive change, it is perfectly natural for the client to have feelings of gratitude and warmth towards the coach and for the coach to delight in being on the receiving end of such feelings.

The intensity of the one-to-one relationship in these circumstances may often have some erotic undertones. When you take a whole-life perspective, you will inevitably get to know something about the client's personal life, and this may include his or her sexual relationships. Talking about it puts it on the agenda. So where coach and client get on well, that powerful instinctive drive to love and be loved may well be in the air, especially if one or both of the parties has some sexual dissatisfaction in their lives.

Examples might be a coach and client of the same age and background finding that there is some sexual chemistry between them at a time when both have unhappy marriages. Another example might be an older male client who may not often have the experience of being listened to intently by an attractive younger woman – and in this case she happens to be his coach. An older female client may enjoy being coached by a younger man for the same reasons. There is the same potential for disaster lurking here as there is in therapeutic relationships. Being listened to with unconditional acceptance is a rare event for most people: it is gratifying. Just as in therapy, a woman client whose self-confidence is at a temporarily low ebb, or who has been abused in the past, may believe that sex is her only gift or that a sexual exchange is a reliable way to find affection. An older male coach could in theory be as tempted to 'rescue' a vulnerable young woman client with sexual reassurance as his misguided therapist counterpart could do. Some clients undoubtedly do use seductive behaviour and this can be destabilizing, especially at times of upheaval in your own personal life. Beware especially of wanting to seem attractive to your clients in the absence of feeling attractive to your own partner, friends or family. If you find strong sexual feelings intruding into your coaching, it is time to end the relationship.

In any professional relationship, there may be other possibilities for the exploitation of trust. So there are doctors, solicitors and accountants who steal from their clients or who exploit a lonely client's need for friendship by persuading them to make bequests, and so on. Where the professional concerned has acted out of veniality, they are rightly punished. All of this is less likely in coaching where the relationships are more commonly short and finite.

Note that a client may also abuse a coach. This is even rarer than a coach abusing a client. However, it is possible. Just occasionally my colleagues and I encounter clients whose distress is overpowering and where the coach becomes the target. One colleague describes such a client.

CASE STUDY

Anna

Anna arrived for her session with the stated aim of getting coaching on finding a new job. She spent most of the first hour crying, telling me that her life was a mess and that she was sure I couldn't help her. As she warmed to her theme of how I couldn't help her she became angry and agitated, shouting at me, telling me that my fees were outrageous, her employer was mad to pay them, that I was enjoying the spectacle of seeing her cry just as everyone else in her life had done. I assured her that I was not enjoying it, suggested we stop the session if she was finding it distressing but also offering to carry on once the initial storm had passed. I realized afterwards that I was receiving the displaced vengeance from years of disappointment and sadness. I was probably the first ever target of her rage who just sat still without retaliating.

An American contact once described to me the ultimate horror: being stalked. The client in this case, through her own well-thought-through decision in work with her coach, had ended her partner relationship. The rejected partner had stalked the coach, blaming her for the decision. Ultimately this man plea-bargained his way to five years on probation and supervised medication but only after subjecting the coach to over a year of terrifying threats. Clear breaches of the law should always be reported to the police.

The saving grace in coaching, and the reason abuse is bound to be so much rarer, is that the power is so much more evenly balanced. Our clients do not come to us for healing and are therefore less likely to regard us with the awe that could lead to abuse on the part of the coach.

Can we do harm?

If we believe in the power of the coaching relationship then it may follow that we may be able to harm our clients. A lot of coaches worry about this. I have doubts about how far we can truly hurt a client. We may waste a client's time. We may bore clients. We may annoy them. We may do embarrassingly poor coaching, but serious, lasting injury? Some of the muddled thinking on this topic has probably come from comparing coaching with psychotherapy and from comparing psychotherapy with medicine, dentistry or nursing. Unlike a doctor, we do not prescribe drugs with the risks of getting the dose or the drug wrong; unlike a surgeon we are not doing operations which can be bungled. The danger of iatrogenic (clinician-caused) harm is very real. What is the equivalent in coaching? It can only be the belief that our clients are too immature or fragile to manage their own responses to our behaviour. My own view is that the psychological fragility of clients, whether for therapy or for coaching, is greatly exaggerated. Indeed, it may also be exaggerated by clients. If part of your way of staying stuck is to erect a mighty wall around yourself labelled, 'keep off – fragile', then this may be an extremely skilled way of manipulating the world around you to ensure that your self-protective delusions and fantasies remain intact. In fact, the client may be tougher than the coach. If you give in to such apparent fragility, you may in effect be handing control of the session entirely to the client. But the ultimate protection for clients is that in coaching we avoid advice-giving and interpreting; we treat the client as an equal at all times and protect the client's dignity. Our aim is always that the client makes their own well-based decisions.

It is easy to believe so profoundly in the power of coaching that we overestimate both its power to do good and to do harm. We can only ever work within the limits of the material that clients are willing to give us. Similarly, we work with clients at their own unique stages of their life journeys and with whatever skills we have at that particular time.

Can a client become a friend?

Just occasionally a client may become a friend. Clients are often drawn to us and we to them because there is some essential like-mindedness. With coaching becoming increasingly specialized, this will be even more likely. As coaches we operate most successfully, in the business sense, in the worlds we understand from our own past experience. This is where our networks, contacts and expertise are rooted and this is what gives us credibility with our clients. All of this makes it more probable that some of our clients will be drawn to us because they have a lot in common with us psychologically and by history.

Signs that a client might become a friend could include events that encompass any two or three of the following on either side where the motivation is to spend social time with the person because you like them for themselves, not because it might enhance the business relationship:

- playing sociable games like squash, golf or tennis;
- sending or receiving a birthday, Christmas or condolence card;
- sharing gossipy emails which have nothing to do with the coaching;
- socializing on home territory;
- going to major sporting, cultural or other events purely for fun, not because it is 'corporate entertaining';
- attending Christmas or leaving parties and weddings.

I have done all of the above with some clients, and enjoyed it. But when this becomes the dominant pattern, you cannot be coach to that person. They have crossed the line from client to friend. Friendship is a coach-free zone, just as family is. Coaching is about outcomes, learning and change. The client pays for the empathetic objectivity that the coach provides. None of this is true of friendship. When I am with friends I am off duty as a coach – it's what I do all day; I don't want to do it in my leisure time and I hope my friends do not expect it of me. However, rules are sometimes difficult to follow and I bend them frequently. As I write this, I have just entered a date in my diary to see a former client, now friend, who has persuaded me to agree to a one-off session. This woman has generously acted as advocate for me over the years we have known each other, referring dozens of her colleagues to me. In saying yes, I have already reminded her of all of the above, have told her that we will have the session at my apartment and end with a nice glass of wine. She has made it clear that she expects to pay the going rate, but I will not, of course, be charging her for the session, though I may demand a pleasant dinner somewhere that we might both enjoy as my 'payment'.

In general, coaches are less fretful and more relaxed about these boundary issues than therapists. However, we are in grey territory here. As coaching continues, sometimes over several years and through a variety of jobs, you and your client will get to know each other well. Bear in mind that you will probably know the client a lot better than he or she knows you and in fact one sign that it has passed into a friendship is the point where you find yourself disclosing personal feelings and circumstances to a client. But even where this is not the case, real spark, real liking, playfulness, grace, trust . . . all these are likely to grow. There will be a closeness which is unlike the relationship you had at the outset. This was forcibly brought home to me with a distinguished woman client with whom I had worked on and off for five years. I had been well acquainted during this time with her struggles to survive her cancer long enough to properly enjoy her personal life and to get her organization back on track. The news of her sudden death was shocking, though thoughtfully conveyed to me by her deputy before I could be taken by surprise through reading of it in the next morning's papers. At her memorial event I felt overwhelmed with sadness during the skilfully put-together video tribute made by her colleagues. I still think of her often with a pang of loss and feel privileged to have known such a remarkable woman.

When it is unequivocally clear that a client has become a friend, it is best to draw attention to what has happened and to explain why the coaching relationship cannot continue, rounding it off gracefully. In practice it is unlikely that the client-friend will want to continue and a bigger danger is that the coaching will just peter out. If there is still a need for coaching, you might want to make a recommendation about another coach, but of course the decision rests with the client. Be chivalrous about your replacement. Don't ask about the coaching and do control any irrational twinges of jealousy you may feel about your successor.

Dependency

I hear a lot of worrying about 'dependency' from the coaches I train. Maybe they have been affected by tales of clients who develop unhealthy reliance on their therapists: how often this actually happens I have no idea, maybe as rarely as it does in coaching. Possibly, as with so many themes in therapy, this concern goes back to the early days of psychoanalysis where patients were expected to attend hour-long sessions several times a week. In 21 years of practice with clients of wide-ranging ages, types and professions, I have yet to encounter a client who appears dependent on me. Supposing for a moment that this is possible, what would the signs of dependency be? You would probably see any of the following: constant pressing for advice, referring every decision big or small to the coach, exaggerated deference to the coach's view, pushing boundaries by trying to convert the coach to becoming a friend, wanting extra sessions when there is no apparent agenda. All of this is extremely unlikely in coaching. Coaching is not about *curing* or *fixing*. It is overtly a non-hierarchical relationship. It is expensive and most clients will have to justify how this expenditure adds value, even if only to a sceptical spouse. I have sometimes suspected that it may be more likely for the coach to be dependent on the client than the client on the coach.

In practice, I would turn this concern on its head by saying that there is everything to be said for healthily close relationships between coaches and clients because this roots the coaching in emotional connection, the only way real change is likely to happen (see Chapter 2). I positively encourage contact between sessions by email, text and phone to keep the momentum going. Doing this makes the work so much more productive and enjoyable. So for instance, my clients A and B, both in their late forties, and in different organizations, lost their jobs in the same month as a result of brutally abrupt cuts. They both knew they needed coaching to recover their self-confidence and to find new jobs. A, whose finances I knew to be in a somewhat perilous state, funded herself and paid me for 10 hours of coaching at the bottom of my fee range. B, an existing client, negotiated a generous leaving package which included a year's worth of coaching from me – as and when he needed it. A carefully spaced her sessions but at the end of them, despite skilled networking and coming close to a number of jobs, was still unemployed. I made it clear to her that she could keep in touch with me for as long as it was useful and we exchanged emails, texts or brief phone calls on a weekly basis over the following six months. I also gave her a pro-bono session of last-minute coaching for the interview which eventually landed her an excellent job. I had made it clear to A that this was 90 per cent altruism and 10 per cent self-interest, telling her that I hoped she would continue to work with me as her coach when she eventually found a job. B scheduled fortnightly and then monthly two-hour sessions with me during his first five months of job-searching. After six months of unemployment, he was headhunted for his ideal job. During the extensive period of courtship between himself and the potential employer, we met three times and at the final stages were texting, emailing or on the phone most days. When the job was in the bag, I took him for a celebratory glass or two of champagne.

Was any of this *wrong* or showing a need for dependency on either side? I don't think so. I have never taken an egg-timer approach to my work. On the contrary, I have assumed that for every client who gets time they have not paid for, there will be one who pays for time they never use. I expect clients to play their part in managing our relationship and by and large they do.

Endings

Coaching is expensive and most coaching programmes will be limited by what the organization or individual can afford, often no more than six two-hour sessions and sometimes fewer than that. How should a coaching programme end? Some coaches find that the client does not take up their full quota of pre-paid sessions. When this happens, coaches can feel both guilty and rejected. Where the coach wishes to end the coaching but the client wants to carry on, the client may feel cast aside and hurt. Clients may also feel uncomfortable: they do not really need or wish to carry on, but do so out of fear that they may hurt the coach's feelings. Sometimes both coach and client may continue to meet when both would really like to stop – so, in this way, both end up doing what neither really wants.

Where you sense that you have reached a full stop, always raise it. The client may or may not be prepared to be honest with you.

CASE STUDY

Roger

Roger claimed to be a highly self-aware person, but he had received what he saw as a crushing disappointment in his career. He had already worked with two other coaches and a therapist. He told me mournfully that he was not a rich man and although he had found the therapy helpful, he had not been able to afford to continue paying his therapist for the weekly sessions. (Our programme was being funded by his organization.) In fact this history should have alerted me to the unlikelihood of success with me, and with the benefit of hindsight I should have taken a lot more time than I did to explore his previous experience of both coaching and therapy. After four sessions of frustration and a strong feeling of no progress, I eventually challenged him and said: 'Roger, I've reached the end of what I think I can do. We keep coming back to the same point where you seem to be trying to rewrite your history. I think we ought to stop.'

'Funny you should say that,' said Roger, and then in a moment of real candour, 'I got to exactly the same stage with Lucy [his therapist] and she told me that unless I was prepared to stop "sitting in my own shit", as she put it, she couldn't go on with me.' I asked him: 'So are you prepared to stop sitting in your own shit?' He replied: 'Yes, yes, and I'm finding these sessions really helpful.'

I felt dubious, but we made another date. Roger failed to show for this date. When I called his office he was apologetic: 'I'm terribly sorry, I completely forgot it.' I told him to call me again when he was ready.

He never did.

Another client whose presenting issues were around how to develop as a leader in his financial services company set a date with me but cancelled it at extremely short notice, then agreed another which was also cancelled. Then there was silence. My two or three enquiring emails and voicemails were stoutly ignored. It nagged at me. It was unsatisfactory: was it me? Had something major happened in his life, but if so what? Discreet enquiries among his colleagues led to a dead end. After a while I forgot him. Three years later, I had a call from a senior HR person in his firm based in the US where he was now working. The question was, could I recommend another coach for this man? I took the opportunity to ask if she knew why he had given up on me. 'Ah yes,' she said, 'you raised the question of what he might want to do as an alternative to his career with us and he simply couldn't cope with it. He freaked. He'd always assumed till that moment that it was a career for life.' I could never have guessed that what to me was such an innocent question could have had this major effect and clearly I had not built sufficient trust with this client for him to be honest with me. I wondered how I might have spotted the problem and dealt with it more effectively. For instance, did I take my own advice about probing for feedback at the end of the session in question?

One useful tactic may be to agree an initial set of sessions with a review point halfway through, matched by an invoice point. The review point will include the mutual opportunity to assess:

> How far are you toward reaching your goals?
>
> What tangible evidence is there that there is change in your life?
>
> How are you and I doing in our coaching relationship?
>
> How much more coaching do you feel you would find useful?

I rarely regard a coaching relationship as truly over. Clients frequently return when they have new jobs or challenges, or email me with their news sometimes years after the formal coaching has finished. However, I do like to mark the final session of any one stage with a review. In this review I will ask clients to think back to the issues they initially presented and to look at what has changed, including any feedback that they have solicited from colleagues. I will also ask for their feedback on the coaching process and on me, always asking:

> What were the real high spots for you?
>
> What encapsulates the learning?
>
> What would you advise me to go on doing, adapt and change in my coaching?

Where the coaching has begun with a three-cornered process involving the line manager, repeating the process is another useful way to round it off (see pages 136–139 for more on this). After that session I will normally email clients with a friendly note, expressing the hope that they will keep in touch. In general, managing and marking the ending is a lot better for both sides than letting it peter out.

Finally

The place of insight

It matters as a coach to have psychological insight. Feeling that you have useful insight into others is probably one of the main reasons that people become coaches. Insight is closely linked to curiosity about people, another important qualification for being a coach.

However, it is also important to keep the question of insight in proportion. Mind-reading is an inexact art. There are two principles here. First, the best and most valuable insight to have is into yourself. Second, it is far more important for the client to have insight into themselves than for you to do so. This quote from Carl Jung's book *Modern Man in Search of a Soul* ([1933] 2001) says it all:

> Nothing is more unbearable for the patient than to be always understood. It is relatively unimportant whether the psychotherapist understands or not, but everything hangs on the patient doing so.

Also, while you are searching for insights, you will be distracted from your main task of listening at Levels 2 and 3 to your client. You will be worrying about yourself and how to ask *clever* questions. The point about coaching is to ask *wise*, not clever, questions and to keep out of the client's way.

This means that you do not have to labour to make connections for the client. Instead, say, 'What connections do you see between x and y?' You do not have to read a client's motivation. Instead, say, 'What was your motivation then?' You do not have to grasp all the content of the client's issues – effort spent on trying to discern all the nuances will tend to pull the client's effort into helping you understand what they already understand. This will pull you away from *experiencing* what the client is telling you – a more useful emphasis. You do not have to offer insights to the client. Instead, say 'What insight do you have now into that incident?' Or you can ask, 'What learning did you gain from that?' – another way of asking the same question.

This does not prevent you from having insights – sometimes a coach will experience an intuitive moment when an insight appears which is potentially useful to the client. My rule here is that I try never to present it to the client as a profound truth. Instead, I might say something like, 'Can I offer you a potential insight here? It may or may not be right, but it's occurred to me that . . .' – and then I describe my insight and ask, 'How does that seem to you?' If you are wrong, the client can then tell you so. If you are right, then the client has the benefit of your ideas.

Often, insights that seem inspired and brilliant to the coach are about the coach's gratification and rarely have meaning to the client. What seems clever to the coach is often blindingly simple to the client, whereas the insights and connections that clients make for themselves are part of what coaching is all about.

Going beyond technique

In general, as a coach, your best instrument is yourself. You will need all the tools and techniques and many others described in this book, but if you cannot use your authentic self you will be consistently disappointed in the work you do.

As with so much else in coaching, this is the central paradox. You have to be fully present, yet not intrude too much. You have to bring the full force of your personality into the coaching room, yet it must never overwhelm the client. You have to know all the techniques, yet restrain yourself from using them except when they are totally appropriate. You have to be able to form a relationship of intimacy with the client, yet it must never cross the boundary into a friendship while the coaching is continuing. You have to be vigilant about yourself and your own interventions while simultaneously maintaining a high level of alertness to everything the client says and does. You have to keep a degree of control over the overall process, yet allow the client to take control as well. Coaching is about feeling and acting in a more powerful way, yet, to work, both coach and client have to stay together in powerlessness. One way to think about it is to accept that if you see yourself as *doing coaching*, it will be far harder than just *being a coach*. Doing coaching is intrinsically stressful because you are trying so hard, whereas being a coach is easy and fluid because you trust the process.

Letting go of the need to be right or to find solutions for the client

The heart of this approach to coaching is to let go of the need to be right and to let go equally of the need to find solutions for the client, and then to knit those beliefs into your every interaction with them. Time and again I see beginner coaches dutifully mouth the words about partnership or about not giving advice to their clients but then getting overwhelmed with anxiety when they see the client struggling or not apparently making what the coach considers to be 'progress'. The inevitable result is that the coach slowly but surely begins to do most of the work in the session and the client's energy drains away. An even more exaggerated version of the same phenomenon is where, in their need to feel useful, the coach begins to lecture or in some cases hector the client. You don't need to be right. The client does not need to leave every session with a neatly packaged action plan. Sometimes clients choose confusion, inactivity and procrastination. The client is the one who will live with or without the solution and that is always their choice.

Being centred

As a coach, you need to be as centred as possible. This means that your own concerns and anxieties have to be banished during a coaching session. This is difficult, but it is a state to strive for. If you are not centred, you will find intrusive worries affecting your behaviour and therefore your effectiveness with your client. These might be thoughts and feelings such as:

Am I good enough? Am I asking clever enough questions?

I don't like this client.

I'm afraid of this client.

I'm too important to be working with a junior/young/not very bright client like this.

I need to take control to prove who's in charge here

and so on.

One way of putting this is that there is a spectrum of possible places to be mentally during coaching. At one end is the anxious, defended, protected ego, described by Thomas Crane in his book, *The Heart of Coaching* (1998), as 'Fortress Me'; at the other is the centred person who can stay relaxed and alert. Fortress Me is self-conscious rather than self-aware, critical and judgemental rather than accepting and discerning, arrogant rather than self-confident, spiteful rather than inquisitive and controlling rather than adaptable. Fortress Me tries to be perfect. The centred coach will accept good enough as the norm but with the aim of keeping on learning. The paradox is that you cannot really have the aim of *doing* brilliant coaching without a self-serving element creeping into your work, though you can have the aim of *being* an excellent coach.

Becoming, and staying, centred

There is no one right way. Each coach has to find their path. Experienced coaches find that any or all of these help: meditation, prayer, yoga, listening to music, moderate physical exercise such as walking, cycling, jogging or swimming, when the mind can be suspended.

Most of the world's great religions are about releasing the grip of the ego on the personality. You do not need to subscribe to any of them to find your own path, but as a coach you do need to be able to detach yourself from the needs of your ego, to set your own needs aside and to listen deeply and non-judgementally.

We meet ourselves time and again in a thousand disguises on the path of life.

Carl Jung

In the West African greeting I quoted at the beginning of this chapter, there is a wonderful acknowledgement of the importance of two people meeting and seeing – really seeing each other; being present – and being fully present. That is what the best coaching is all about.

Bibliography

Anderson, M. (2003) *Bottom Line Organizational Development*. Oxford: Butterworth-Heinemann.

Ariely, D. (2008) *Predictably Irrational*. London: HarperCollins.

Bandler, R. and Grinder, J. (1979) *Frogs into Princes*. Moab, UT: Real People Press.

Bandler, R. and Grinder, J. (1982) *Reframing*. Moab, UT: Real People Press.

Bandura, A. (1997) *Self-efficacy: The Exercise of Control*. New York: Freeman.

Bentall, R.B. (2010) *Doctoring the Mind: Why Psychiatric Treatments Fail*. London: Penguin.

Berglas, S. (2002) The very real dangers of executive coaching, *Harvard Business Review*, June.

Berne, E. (1964) *Games People Play*. London: Penguin.

Berne, E. (1975) *What Do You Do After You Say Hello?* London: Corgi.

Bevan, J. (2002) *The Rise and Fall of Marks & Spencer*. London: Profile Books.

Block, P. (1981) *Flawless Consulting*. San Diego, CA: Pfeiffer.

Bluckert, P. (2006) *Psychological Dimensions of Executive Coaching*. Maidenhead: Open University Press.

Bridges, W. (1991) *Managing Transitions*. Reading, MA: Addison-Wesley.

Briggs Myers, I. with Myers, P. (1980) *Gifts Differing*. Palo Alto, CA: Consulting Psychologists Press.

Brockbank, A. and McGill, I. (2006) *Facilitating Reflective Learning through Mentoring & Coaching*. London: Kogan Page.

Bryce, L. (2002) *The Coach*. London: Judy Piatkus Publishers.

Carson, R. (1987) *Taming Your Gremlin: A Guide to Enjoying Yourself*. London: Harper & Row.

Casement, P. (1985) *On Learning from the Patient*. London: Tavistock Publications.

Clarkson, P. (1995) *The Therapeutic Relationship*. London: Whurr.

Cockman, P., Evans, B. and Reynolds, P. (1999) *Consulting for Real People*. Maidenhead: McGraw-Hill.

Covey, S.R. (1992) *The Seven Habits of Highly Effective People*. London: Simon & Schuster.

Crane, T. (1998) *The Heart of Coaching*. San Diego, CA: FTA Press.

Csikszentmihalyi, M. (1990) *The Psychology of Optimal Experience*. New York: Harper & Row.

Csikszentmihalyi, M. (2003) *Good Business: Flow, Leadership and the Making of Meaning*. New York: Viking.

Doidge, N. (2007) *The Brain That Changes Itself*. New York: Viking.

Egan, G. (1998) *The Skilled Helper*, 6th edn. New York: Brooks Cole.

Elkins, D. (2007) Empirically supported treatment: the deconstruction of a myth, *Journal of Humanistic Psychology*, 47(4): 474–500.

Farrelly, F. and Brandsma, J. (1974) *Provocative Therapy*. Capitola, CA: Meta Publications.

Farwagi, P.L. (1998) *The Life Balance Programme*. London: Orion Publishing Group.

Feltham, C. and Horton, I. (eds) (2000) *A Handbook of Counselling and Psychotherapy*. London: Sage.

Flaherty, J. (1999) *Coaching: Evoking Excellence in Others*. Oxford: Butterworth-Heinemann.

Frankl, V. (1959) *Man's Search for Meaning*. New York: Pocket Books.

Gallwey, T. (2000) *The Inner Game of Work*. London: Orion Publishing Group.

Griffin, J. and Tyrell, I. (2004) *Human Givens*. Chalvington: HG Publishing.

Goleman, D., Boyatzis, R. and McKee, A. (2002) *The New Leaders*. London: Little, Brown.

Harris, T.A. (1973) *I'm OK – You're OK*. London: Pan.

Harvey, J. (1988) Eichmann in the organization, in *The Abilene Paradox*. Lexington, MA: Lexington Books.

Hay, J. (2007) *Reflective Practice and Supervision for Coaches*. Maidenhead: Open University Press.

Hayes, P. (2006) *NLP Coaching*. Maidenhead: Open University Press.

Hazler, R.J. and Barwick, N. (2001) *The Therapeutic Environment*. Buckingham: Open University Press.

Hemon, A. (2011) The aquarium, *The New Yorker*, 13 June.

Hodgkinson, P. and Stewart, M. (1998) *Coping With Catastrophe*. London: Routledge.

Hycner, R. and Jacobs, L. (1995) *The Healing Relationship in Gestalt Therapy*. Highland, NY: The Gestalt Journal Press.

Jackman, J. and Strober, M. (2003) Fear of feedback, *Harvard Business Review*, April.

Jung, C.G. (1923) *Psychological Types*. New York: Harcourt Brace.

Jung, C.G. (1963) *Memories, Dreams, Reflections*. London: Fontana.

Jung, C.G. ([1933] 2001) *Modern Man in Search of a Soul*. London: Routledge.

Kegan, R. and Lahey, L. (2009) *Immunity to Change*. Boston, MA: Harvard Business Press.

Kellaway, L. (2005) *Who Moved My Blackberry?* London: Penguin.

Kline, N. (1999) *Time to Think*. London: Ward Lock.

Kübler-Ross, E. (1997) *On Death and Dying*. New York: Touchstone.

Lewin, K. (1935) *A Dynamic Theory of Personality*. New York: McGraw-Hill.

Lewin, K. (1948) *Resolving Social Conflicts: Selected Papers on Group Dynamics*, edited by Gertrude Lewin. New York: Harper & Row.

Lewis, T., Amini, F. and Lannon, R. (2001) *A General Theory of Love*. New York: Vintage.

Locke, E.A. and Latham, G.P. (1990) *A Theory of Goal-setting and Task Performance*. Englewood Cliffs, NJ: Prentice Hall.

Luft, J. (1970) *Group Processes: An Introduction to Group Dynamics*. Palo Alto, CA: National Press Books.

McGilchrist, I. (2009) *The Master and His Emissary. The Divided Brain and the Making of the Western World*. New Haven, CT: Yale University Press.

McLelland, D.C. (1985) *Human Motivation*. Chicago, IL: Scott, Foresman.

Martel, Y. (2002) *Life of Pi*. Edinburgh: Canongate Books.

Masson, J. (1990) *Against Therapy*. London: Fontana.

Mearns, D. (2003) *Developing Person-centred Counselling*, 2nd edn. London: Sage Publications.

Mearns, D. and Thorne, B. (1999) *Person-centred Counselling in Action*. London: Sage Publications.

Mueller, M. (2007) *Recovering from PTSD*. Oxford: Oxford Cognitive Therapy Centre.

O'Neill, M.B. (2000) *Executive Coaching with Backbone and Heart*. San Franciso, CA: Jossey-Bass.

Orbach, S. (1999) *The Impossibility of Sex*. Harmondsworth: Penguin.

Palmer, H. and Brown, P. (1998) *The Enneagram Advantage: Putting the Nine Personality Types to Work in the Office*. New York: Harmony Books.

Perls, F. (1969) *Gestalt Therapy Verbatim*. LaFayette, CA: Real People Press.

Peters, S. (2012) *The Chimp Paradox: Confidence, Success, Happiness*. London: Vermillion.

Rock, D. (2008) SCARF: a brain-based model for collaborating with and influencing others, *NeuroLeadership Journal*, Issue 1: 1–9.

Rogers, C.R. (1951) *Client-centered Therapy: Its Current Practice, Implications and Theory*. Boston, MA: Houghton Mifflin.

Rogers, C.R. (1980) *A Way of Being*. Boston, MA: Houghton Mifflin.

Rogers, J. (2006) *Sixteen Personality Types at Work in Organizations*. London: Management Futures/Milton Keynes: ASK Europe.

Rogers, J. (2006) *Developing a Coaching Business*. Maidenhead: Open University Press.

Rogers, J. (2007) *Adults Learning*, 5th edn. Maidenhead: Open University Press.

Rogers, J. (2010) *Facilitating Groups*. Maidenhead: Open University Press.

Rogers, J. (2011) *Job Interview Success: Be Your Own Coach*. Maidenhead: McGraw-Hill.

Samuels, A. (1985) *Jung and the Post-Jungians*. London: Routledge.

Schein, E.H. (2006) *Career Anchors: Self Assessment*, 3rd edn. New York: Pfeiffer.

Schutz, W. (1984) *The Truth Option*. Berkeley, CA: Ten Speed Press.

Schutz, W. (1989) *Profound Simplicity*. San Diego, CA: WSA Bantam.

Schwartz, J. M. (1996) *Brain Lock*. New York: Regan Books.

Senge, P. (1994) *The Fifth Discipline Field Book*. London: Nicolas Brealy Publishing.

Siegel, D. (2010) *Mindsight*. Oxford: Oneworld.

Stacey, R.D. (1996) *Strategic Management and Organizational Dynamics*, 2nd edn. London: Pitman Publishing.

Stoltenberg, C.D. and Delworth, U. (1987) *Supervising Counselors and Therapists: A Developmental Approach*. San Francisco, CA: Jossey-Bass.

Sullivan, W. and Rees, J. (2008) *Clean Language: Revealing Metaphors and Opening Minds*. Carmarthen: Crown House Publishing.

Tolle, E. (2001) *The Power of Now*. London: Hodder & Stoughton.

Ward, P. (1997) *360-degree Feedback*. London: Institute of Personnel and Development.

Waterman, J. and Rogers, J. (1997) *An Introduction to the FIRO-B*. Oxford: Oxford Psychologists Press.

Whitmore, J. (1996) *Coaching for Performance*, 2nd edn. London: Nicholas Brealey Publishing.

Whitworth, L., Kimsey-House, H. and Sandahl, P. (1998) *Co-active Coaching*. Palo Alto, CA: Davies Black Publishing.

Wildflower, L. and Brennan, D. (eds) (2011) *The Handbook of Knowledge-Based Coaching: From Theory into Practice*. San Francisco: John Wiley & Sons.

Yalom, I.D. (1991) *Love's Executioner and Other Tales of Psychotherapy*. Harmondsworth: Penguin Books.

Yalom, I.D. (2002) *The Gift of Therapy*. London: Judy Piatkus Publishing.

Contact details

I like to hear from readers. My website is www.JennyRogersCoaching.com. If you have feedback, ideas and suggestions, email me at this address: Jenny@JennyRogersCoaching.com. For information on training courses or supervision, please consult the Management Futures Ltd website, www.managementfutures.co.uk.

Index